Religion in
the Public Schools

Religion in
the Public Schools:
An Introduction

Richard C. McMillan

MERCER

ISBN 0-86554-093-4

All books published by Mercer University Press
are produced on acid-free paper that exceeds
the minimum standards set by the National Historical
Publications and Records Commission.

Library of Congress Cataloging in Publication Data
McMillan, Richard C.
Religion in the public schools.
Bibliography: p. 275.
Includes index.
1. Religion in the public schools—Law and legislation—United
States.   I. Title.
KF4162.M4   1984   344.73'0796   84-9147
ISBN 0-86554-093-4 (alk. paper)   344.304796

TABLE OF CONTENTS

To
Mary
and my girls:
Bonnae, Debbie, and Kim

PREFACE

This book is addressed to the parish minister willing to seriously consider the proposition that an individual in a democratic society should be free to choose or reject religious faith without public pressure or governmental interference. The minister unwilling to consider this proposition will find little of interest in the pages that follow.

There are many frames of reference from which to approach the relationship of religion and government. I have intentionally selected the legal frame of reference because, in a pluralistic society, given the ideal of religious liberty to which the country is constitutionally dedicated, solutions that will protect the rights of all persons can be found only in a legal context. Adhering to the Constitution, the religion-government relationship must be viewed in terms of self-imposed legal parameters. It is for this reason that the reader will find extensive duplication of relevant decisions by the Supreme Court in chapter 5. From the educational perspective, those decisions are of great significance.

In the pages that follow, I shall develop the thesis that the constitutionally defined and appropriate relationship of religion to public education is attained only through studies about religion. As public institutions charged with responsibility for the intellectual growth of future citizens, public schools are an appropriate setting for academic study about religion, but, in a pluralistic society dedicated to religious freedom, governmentally sponsored and required acts of religious devotion have no place in public schools. Many opportunities exist in the daily life of a child for acts of religious devotion outside the public-school setting, but the education of a child in many important academic subjects is incomplete without some study of religion.

Moreover, religion studies may increase understanding of religion and decrease religious bigotry.

Having followed this controversy for years, I am frequently overwhelmed by its complexity and potential for emotional involvement. Although the discussion that follows is a sound interpretation of the relationship of religion to public education in the United States, it is not the final statement on the matter. Whatever your personal beliefs, I ask only your consideration of this increasingly volatile and complex area of public controversy.

Many persons have contributed directly and indirectly to this book. I will always remain indebted to Dr. W. Waldo Beach, Dr. William H. Cartwright, and the late Dr. Edward C. Bolmeier of Duke University, who encouraged my developing interest in the relationship of religion to public education during my graduate study. They have remained profound and compelling influences over the years. I owe a deep expression of gratitude to two gentlemen, Dr. Albert L. Meiburg and Dr. Morris Ashcraft, who, serving consecutively as Dean of the Faculty at Southeastern Baptist Theological Seminary, invited me to teach a course in religion and public education at that institution. Throughout that teaching experience, the friendship and support of Dr. Robert E. Poerschke, Professor of Christian Education, was deeply significant for me. Of course, I cannot forget the stimulating interaction I enjoyed with the students who endured my efforts throughout the years I taught at Southeastern. No teacher could ignore the contribution of his students to the development of his thought. Neither can I forget the encouragement and support of my colleagues at Averett College and the Mercer University School of Medicine. I also owe a deep expression of gratitude to Dean William P. Bristol of the Mercer University School of Medicine for his support of my efforts. The one person, however, who continues to make my every effort worthwhile is my wife, Mary.

CHAPTER 1

The First Amendment

In the history of human affairs, man's most enlightened and commendable decisions have typically involved both a positive and negative potential. Their positive potential is the enormously constructive influence such decisions protend for the quality of human life. The negative potential is seen in the unending struggle required to maintain their intent, a struggle which frequently involves a substantial measure of social ferment. This duality of potential has been apparent in the relatively brief history of the first two clauses of the First Amendment to the Constitution of the United States.

> Congress shall make no law respecting an establishment of religion, or prohibiting the free exercise thereof. . .

That statement is perhaps the most magnificent legal affirmation of religious freedom ever made. Notwithstanding its lofty potential, the years since its adoption in 1791 have borne witness to the difficulty of interpreting and implementing such a statement.

In the United States, the Supreme Court is the agency charged with responsibility for interpreting the Constitution.

The Court's role as arbiter of disputes places it at the center of perpetual controversy, controversy that frequently exceeds purely legal concern and boundary. While this highly visible and demanding position is appropriate in a representative republic, it also subjects the Court to public criticism, sometimes of an intense nature. Such criticism may be constructive, for one could anticipate significant political danger if citizens were indifferent to that division of national government that undertakes final interpretation of the Constitution. Honest and informed disagreement with the judgments of the Court represents a healthy state of affairs; criticism and dispute resulting from ignorance is destructive to the social fabric. This discussion focuses upon a topic in which, unfortunately, public controversy is more often marked by the latter than by the former.[1]

The Commission on Religion in the Public Schools succinctly described the nature of Supreme Court decisions: "The Constitution means what the Supreme Court says it means—it's as simple as that. This principle is a fundamental characteristic of government by law in our democratic society."[2] That this lofty evaluation of the authority of the Court is not the product of modern-day liberalism is illustrated in the reasoning of Chief Justice Marshall in a decision announced in 1803.

---

[1]Though access to the decisions of the Supreme Court is sometimes difficult, at least one of three sources for the decisions of the Court may be found in law libraries; often one of these sources may be found in collegiate or public libraries as well. The three sources are: the *United States Reports,* published by the United States Government Printing Office; the *Supreme Court Reporter*, published by West Publishing Company; and the *United States Supreme Court Reports, Lawyers' Edition*, published by the Lawyers Co-Operative Publishing Company. Furthermore, if sufficient information is available (name of the case, date of the decision, and the docket number if possible), a free copy of a decision may be obtained by writing: U.S. Supreme Court Information Office, One First St., N.E., Washington, D. C., 20543.

[2]Commission on Religion in the Public Schools. *Religion in the Public Schools* (Arlington VA: American Association of School Administrators, 1964) 7.

The Constitution vests the whole judicial power of the United States in one supreme court, and such inferior courts as congress shall, from time to time, ordain and establish.

It is, emphatically, the province and duty of the judicial department, to say what the law is. . . . If then, the courts are to regard the constitution, and the constitution is superior to any ordinary act of the legislature, the constitution, and not such ordinary act, must govern the case to which they both apply.

. . . a law repugnant to the constitution is void; and . . . courts, as well as other departments, are bound by that instrument.[3]

The Constitution is the supreme legal statement for the nation, and it is the responsibility of the judiciary, of which the highest court is the Supreme Court, to determine what the Constitution shall mean as it is applied. All legal enactments and all departments of government are subject to the Constitution and its interpretation by judicial review. This practice is fundamental to representative government. Society must be predicated upon some broadly applicable legal structure if it is to endure, and the final interpretation of that legal body cannot be vested in the individual citizen or in the many diverse segments or subgroups of society. Rather, there must be a specific court of appeal responsible for the final adjudication of legal disputes. As established by the Constitution, that final authority for judicial review rests with the Supreme Court of the United States.

It was, therefore, a stroke of political genius that led our Founding Fathers to provide the checks and balances for the American tripartite structure of national government, thereby removing the judiciary from direct control of either the executive or legislative branches. It was with equally remarkable foresight that they removed the Supreme Court from the vicissitudes and pressures of the political arena and popular election. The highest tribunal of the land, as conceived in our national structure, cannot be *directly* subject to the will of the people or of the other branches of government; it must be re-

---

[3]*Marbury v. Madison*, 5 U.S. at 173, 177-78, 180 (1803).

sponsible only to the highest laws of the land, a body of law that can be changed by the people through constitutional amendment.

But the Supreme Court faces two fundamental complications when it interprets the Constitution. First, although there are those who view the law in absolute terms, the existence of a judicial system is itself an admission that law, no matter how precisely formulated, must be interpreted in the context of its application. If law were a collection of absolute rules unaffected by the evolution of society and the peculiarities of each situation, the American legal system would surely not encumber itself with legal rights, trials by jury, and appeal processes. Hence, the Supreme Court is the constitutional jury, a jury charged with the weighty responsibility of interpreting the fundamental legal document of American government.

Second, this unenviable responsibility for constitutional interpretation is also complicated by the fact that it is extremely difficult, if not impossible, to determine the precise literal meaning intended by words used in historic documents like the Constitution. To comprehend the enormity of the task, think about how difficult it often is to understand precisely what is meant in immediate personal communication, and how difficult it is to understand precisely what is meant by statements written only yesterday. When one considers that almost 73,000 yesterdays have elapsed since the formulation of the First Amendment, the difficulty of ascertaining the precise intention of its writers is apparent. But, even if precise literal meaning could be determined, historical documents cannot be frozen in time if they are to be applicable to the changing experience of each new generation. Far too many changes have occurred in this society since the days just following the Revolution. Constant interpretation is required if the Constitution is to guide society in a changing milieu.

It is the constitutional affirmation of religious liberty and its interpretation by the Supreme Court that has generated the problem to be addressed: the relationship of religion to American public schools. The institutions, beliefs, and traditions of religion are woven into the fabric of American culture. The styles

of life that result from affirmations of religious belief are manifest throughout our society. But this religious presence is not
unified; our society is characterized by many different religious
institutions and expressions, and the First Amendment guarantees freedom from governmental control or interference to
each.

Public education has evolved as an important institution in
American society; an institution of the state, financed by public
funds, intended to sustain and enhance the common political
and social structure. Given the constitutional commitment of
our government to religious liberty, the religious pluralism of
our society, and the nature of public schools, what is the proper
relationship of religion to these public institutions? This is the
primary question to be answered in the pages that follow.

In order to lay a foundation for investigating this issue, one
must examine the nature of the religion clauses of the First
Amendment. This amendment directed Congress to refrain
from establishing any religion or inhibiting the free exercise of
religion. The constitutional intent, therefore, seems to have
been to place restrictions on the federal government's actions.
This technicality, however, apparently had little positive or
negative effect on the inexorable movement toward disestablishment that was under way, a movement evidenced in the
constitutions of the newly formed states immediately following
the Revolutionary War. When the Fourteenth Amendment finally made the First Amendment applicable to the laws of the
several states,[4] religious establishments were but a memory in

---

[4]*Cantwell v. State of Connecticut*, 310 U.S. 296 (1940), and *Murdock v.
Commonwealth of Pennsylvania*, 319 U.S. 105 (1943). [The reader should be
introduced to the notation system by which the decisions of the Supreme
Court of the United States are reported. Using the citation from *Cantwell*,
310 U.S. 296 indicates the volume and page of citation in the *United States
Reports*, e.g., volume 310, page 296. The citation for this decision in the *Supreme Court Reporter* would read 60 S. Ct. 900; for the *Lawyers' Edition*, 84
L.Ed. 1213. In all cases, the first numbers indicate the volume, the second
set of numbers refer to the page upon which the decision begins or from
which a quotation is taken.]

our national experience. Section 1 of Article Fourteen of the Amendments to the Constitution reads as follows:

> All persons born or naturalized in the United States, and subject to the jurisdiction thereof, are citizens of the United States and of the State wherein they reside. No State shall make or enforce any law which shall abridge the privileges or immunities of citizens of the United States; nor shall any State deprive any person of life, liberty, or property without due process of law, nor deny to any person within its jurisdiction the equal protection of the laws.

In keeping with this "due process" amendment, ratified in 1868, state governments are equally prohibited from either establishing a religion or prohibiting its free exercise.

The word *respecting* is significant in constitutional interpretation. The Supreme Court has consistently held that Congress, and the states by virtue of the Fourteenth Amendment, are not simply prohibited from establishing a religion; they are equally prohibited from legal enactments that move in that direction. Chief Justice Burger, speaking for the Court in *Lemon v. Kurtzman*, wrote:

> The language of the Religion Clauses of the First Amendment is at best opaque, particularly when compared with other portions of the Amendment. Its authors did not simply prohibit the establishment of a state church or a state religion. . . Instead they commanded that there should be "no law *respecting* an establishment of religion." . . . A given law might not *establish* a state religion but nevertheless be one "respecting" that end in the sense of being a step that could lead to such establishment and hence offend the First Amendment.[5]

It appears that establishment and its negative effect upon individual and social life was an experience that the Founding Fathers wanted this experiment in representative national government to avoid. In addition to the word *respecting*, two other words in the First Amendment are significant: *establishment* and *religion*. Chapter 2 will address the concept of establishment; and chapter 3, the problem of defining religion.

---

[5]*Lemon v. Kurtzman*, 403 U.S. 602, 612 (1971).

Not only are the individual words important in the First Amendment, its clauses are important as well. The religion section of the First Amendment is composed of two clauses. The first has been called the "establishment clause"; the second the "free exercise clause." As the following quotation illustrates, the establishment clause is general in nature, focusing on institutions and groups. The test of violation is straightforward: if legislation either advances or inhibits religion, such legislation exceeds governmental power. The free exercise clause, on the other hand, pertains to the individual. Violation is predicated simply upon coercion of individual religious belief by government. Justice Clark's comments provide an excellent overview of the Court's position.

The wholesome "neutrality" of which this Court's cases speak thus stems from a recognition of the teachings of history that powerful sects or groups might bring a fusion of governmental and religious functions or a concert or dependency of one upon the other to the end that official support of the State or Federal Government would be placed behind the tenets of one or of all orthodoxies. This the Establishment Clause prohibits. And a further reason for neutrality is found in the Free Exercise Clause, which recognizes the value of religious training, teaching and observance and, more particularly, the right of every person to freely choose his own course with reference thereto, free of any compulsion from the state. This the Free Exercise Clause guarantees. Thus, as we have seen, the two clauses may overlap. As we have indicated, the Establishment Clause has been directly considered by this Court eight times in the past score of years and, with only one Justice dissenting on the point, it has consistently held that the clause withdrew all legislative power respecting religious belief or the expression thereof. The test may be stated as follows: what are the purpose and the primary effect of the enactment? If either is the advancement or inhibition of religion then the enactment exceeds the scope of legislative power as circumscribed by the Constitution. That is to say that to withstand the strictures of the Establishment Clause there must be a secular legislative purpose and a primary effect that neither advances nor inhibits religion. . . . The Free Exercise Clause, likewise considered many times here, withdraws from legislative power, state and federal, the exertion of any restraint on the free exercise of religion. Its purpose is to secure religious liberty in the individual by prohibiting any invasion thereof by civil authority. Hence it is necessary in a free exercise case for one to show the coercive effect of the enactment as it operates against him in the practice of his religion. The distinction between the two clauses is apparent—a violation of the Free Exercise Clause is predicated on coercion while the Establishment Clause violation need not be so attended.[6]

There appears to be no more forthright summary of the Court's position respecting the meaning and implication of the two religion clauses of the First Amendment.[7] However, even such a comprehensive summary does not preclude the possibility of exceptions. As Chief Justice Warren admitted, it is often true that federal or state legislation may overlap, coincide, or harmonize with the tenets of some or all religions. For example, the fact that murder is illegal and that its prohibition coincides with the tenets of the Judeo-Christian tradition does not thereby establish that religion or that particular religious doctrine. On the contrary, the welfare of society demands such legislation, and social welfare is the overriding concern with respect to the legality of such statutes.[8]

Since Justice Clark's discussion in *Abington v. Schempp*, the Court has devised more precise tests for constitutional violation. Chief Justice Burger described four such tests in 1971. As he did not believe that the term *tests* was appropriate, the four should be seen as guidelines by which government-religion litigation may be evaluated.

> First, does the Act reflect a secular legislative purpose? Second, is the primary effect of the Act to advance or inhibit religion? Third, does the administration of the Act foster an excessive government entanglement with religion? Fourth, does the implementation of the Act inhibit the free exercise of religion?[9]

In that same term, the chief justice discussed a fifth guideline: the potential for political divisiveness inherent in legislation

---

[6]*Abington v. Schempp*, 374 U.S. 203, 222-23 (1963).

[7]For additional illustration of the Court's interpretation of the First Amendment, see appendix A.

[8]*McGowan v. State of Maryland*, 366 U.S. 420, 442 (1961).

[9]*Tilton v. Richardson*, 403 U.S. 672, 678 (1971).

which effects religion.[10] It is the stated intention of the Court to employ these guidelines in religion-government litigation. A recent example of their application may be found in the 1980 decision addressing the posting of copies of the Ten Commandments in public school classrooms.[11]

Two points must be remembered when reading this analysis of the First Amendment. First, freedom is never absolute, and the free exercise of religion must be so understood. The Court has frequently stated that behavior motivated by religious faith is not thereby exempt from the rule of law.[12] According to the Constitution, freedom of belief is as absolute a freedom as any guarantee to be found in political document or legal structure. Nevertheless, belief leads inevitably to action, and action is the point at which legal intervention may be required.[13] Despite the problems such a distinction may present for religious practice, it is a fundamental legal tenet that belief is beyond the control of law, but actions resulting from religious belief may be subject to regulation in order to preserve the welfare of society and the freedom of individuals. It is, therefore, in the public arena that religious freedom must undergo its most severe examination and possibly suffer limitation. However, even in sustaining this legal tenet, the Court has experienced difficulty. In delivering the opinion of the Court concerning a case in which Amish parents refused to allow their children to attend public secondary schools, Chief Justice Burger wrote:

> It is true that activities of individuals, even when religiously based, are often subject to regulation by the States in the exercise of their undoubted power to promote the health, safety, and general welfare, or

---

[10]*Lemon v. Kurtzman*, 403 U.S. at 622.

[11]*Stone v. Graham*, 101 S. Ct. 192 (1980).

[12]For examples, see *Reynolds v. United States*, 98 U.S. 145, 166 (1878); *Cantwell v. Connecticut*, 310 U.S. at 303-304 (1940); *Jones v. Opelika*, 316 U.S. 584, 618 (1943); and *West Virginia v. Barnette*, 319 U.S. 629, 643-44 (1943).

[13]For discussion of the distinction between freedom of belief and religiously motivated action, see chapter 3.

the Federal Government in the exercise of its delegated powers. . . . But
to agree that religiously grounded conduct must often be subject to the
broad police power of the State is not to deny that there are areas of
conduct protected by the Free Exercise Clause of the First Amendment
and thus beyond the power of the State to control, even under regulations of general applicability. . . . This case, therefore, does not become
easier because respondents were convicted for their "actions" in refusing to send their children to the public high school; in this context belief
and action cannot be neatly confined in logic-tight compartments.[14]

When considerations of the health, safety, or general welfare of
the public are at stake, religious action may be subject to the
police power of the state, but no "logic-tight" guidelines are possible in our society.

Secondly, absolute separation of religion and government in
our nation can no more exist than can absolute freedom for religiously motivated behavior. It is frequently argued that the
United States was founded upon Christian principles with the
intention that it be a Christian nation; ergo, separation of religion and government deviates from the intent of the Founding
Fathers. Although this assertion is of questionable historic validity, it is true that the Judeo-Christian tradition infused American culture and society from the beginning, as it has much of
the history and culture of the West for the better part of the last
two thousand years. Moreover, many Americans have a deep
commitment to religious faith expressed through a variety of
traditions and institutions. Because the Constitution prohibits
an establishment of religion, and a strict separation of religion
and government would violate our cultural heritage and the religious commitments of many in the nation, the Court has often
recommended a *neutrality* between religion and government.

The course of constitutional neutrality in this area cannot be an absolutely straight line; rigidity could well defeat the basic purpose of
those provisions, which is to insure that no religion be sponsored or favored, none commanded, and none inhibited. The general principle de-
ducible from the First Amendment and all that has been said by the
Court is this: that we will not tolerate either governmentally established

---

[14]*Wisconsin v. Yoder*, 406 U.S. 205, 220 (1972).

religion or governmental interference with religion. Short of those expressly proscribed governmental acts there is room for play in the joints
productive of a benevolent neutrality which will permit religious exercise to exist without sponsorship and without interference.

....

Adherents of particular faiths and individual churches frequently
take strong positions on public issues including, as this case reveals . . .
vigorous advocacy of legal or constitutional positions. Of course,
churches as much as secular bodies and private citizens have that right.
No perfect or absolute separation is really possible; the very existence
of the Religion Clauses is an involvement of sorts—one that seeks to
mark boundaries to avoid excessive entanglement.[15]

The struggle to actualize this "benevolent neutrality" taxes
even the most competent legal mind. To preserve the freedom
of the individual while providing the structures and associations
of society necessary for human fulfillment and social well-being
are goals which confound even the best of intentions. When the
preservation of freedom concerns the profoundly personal commitments associated with religious faith, the task becomes even
more complicated. Yet, though this is a task of unending difficulty, it is an integral feature of humanity's most magnificent
and worthy goals, and the blessing of citizenship in this nation.

Persons may not only believe what they wish—indeed their
personal commitments in any area remain beyond the limits of
governmental intervention—but, insofar as possible, expression of their beliefs will be protected because our government
is committed by solemn constitutional injunction to religious
freedom. Current world events illustrate the social distress and
personal trauma experienced when this commitment is absent
from national consciousness and legal structure. Furthermore,
as Chief Justice Burger argued in *Walz*, it is not only the individual whose rights of religious belief are protected; religious
institutions have the right to public advocacy of legal and constitutional interpretations and positions.

The Supreme Court, as the final arbiter of constitutional
questions, is dedicated to preserving these unique governmen-

---

[15]*Walz v. Tax Commission*, 397 U.S. 664, 669-70 (1970).

tal commitments. Religion has no greater ally or more valuable legal advocate than the highest court of this land.

The first sixteen words of the First Amendment to the Constitution lay the foundation for the most exciting and potentially rewarding experiment in religion-government relationship undertaken since the beginning of recorded history. Indeed, in a society as dynamic and pluralistic as ours, the durability of this relationship appears miraculous. Moreover, the durability of this relationship is the vital and necessary ingredient for continued social cohesiveness and development. We now turn to a discussion of the evolution of this remarkable relationship between religion and government.

CHAPTER 2

An Introduction to the Religion-Government Relationship

An investigation of the relationship of religion to public education in the United States must be prefaced by some consideration, however brief, of the development of the religion-government relationship in Western history. Though commonly referred to as the *church-state* relationship, the phrase *religion-government* is more appropriate. Analysis must focus upon religion in its most inclusive sense, not just upon the relationship of one religious institution, the Christian Church, to the state. The pages that follow will provide a brief and general survey of the evolution of the religion-government relationship in Western history, an analysis of the predominant outlook of modern Western man, and a potpourri of ideas that elaborate upon the unique religion-government relationship of our nation.

The Historical Development

The story of the evolution of the relationship of religion and government in the Western world is familiar, in its broad strokes, to any person with theological education; indeed, it is familiar to many school children as a result of their study of history and social studies. The history of the West is essentially the history of the Christian church for the period extending from around 500 A.D. to 1500 A.D. Considering the pervasive influence and extensive control the Church enjoyed at the end of the Middle Ages, it is difficult to comprehend its impotence during the latter stages of the Roman Empire. The Church's growth in influence during the first 1500 years A.D. is a remarkable story of success.

Accounts of the extensive and intense persecution of the early Christians by the Roman government are familiar to all and need not be reviewed. It was not until the Edict of Milan in 313 A.D. that the Christian church achieved any degree of governmental recognition by the Roman Empire, thereby bringing about an end to officially sanctioned persecution. In this agreement between Constantine, emperor of the West, and Licinius, ruler of sections of the Eastern Empire, the Christian church was recognized as one of the many officially sanctioned religions of the Empire. Although establishment of the Church was yet to come, the Empire's official recognition brought an enormous improvement in the status of the Church and paved the way for the Church's ascendence to a position of extensive influence during the final days of the Empire. During the two hundred years following the Edict of Milan, Christianity was to become "the professed faith of the overwhelming majority of the population of the Roman Empire."[1] The Church was well on its way to becoming the controlling force in Western culture and history.

As the Church gathered strength, a remarkable turn of events occurred. The once all-powerful Roman Empire crumbled into disarray, and the political vacuum created was filled, not by another political force, but by the theocratic power and structure of the Christian church. During this time of political disintegration, the monolithic structure and stability of the Church provided the only unifying force available for Western

---

[1]Kenneth Scott Latourette, *A History of Christianity* (New York: Harper and Brothers, Publishers, 1953) 97.

society and culture. As the result of invasion from without and decay from within, the failure of the political state to provide social cohesion opened the way for a unifying structure of a different nature, and the Christian church was, in large measure, established by default. As the most powerful institution in society, the Church was to set the tone and direction of the Western world for the next ten or more centuries. It was with excellent historical insight that Will Durant, in his epic study of the development of the Western world, called this millennium the "age of faith."[2]

In retrospect, one can appreciate the extraordinary nature of the service performed by the Church. Had the Church been incapable of providing some stability for Western society, one wonders what the final outcome of the fall of the Roman Empire might have been. While speculation is stimulating, it is certain that the history of West would have been markedly different. Yet, while the Church preserved the culture of the Western world and provided the only social stability available, it is clear that it was not able to sustain positive political leadership. It was not sufficiently devoted to the affairs of this world, and the period of its rule is one of the darker chapters of Western history.

With the demise of Roman political influence, the West entered a protracted period of stagnation that was known as the Middle Ages or, perhaps more accurately, as the Dark Ages. It seemed as though the fall of the Roman Empire had pulled the rug from under the zestful development of Western thought and culture characteristic of the Graeco-Roman era. At best, life during the Middle Ages was one of extreme difficulty and deprivation. Adhering to its theology, the Church promised a superior life after death for those who, despite the hardships of daily existence, kept the faith. In this way, the Church not only provided a modicum of social order and continuity, but also promised other-worldly solutions for the problems encountered

---

[2]Will Durant, *The Age of Faith*, part 4 of *The Story of Civilization* (New York: Simon and Schuster, 1950).

daily by those it governed. The power of the Church, in contrast to political powers, was concerned not only with temporal affairs, but with those eternal in nature and promise. As a result, it was substantially successful in diverting the attention of its subjects from this world to the world to come. People could endure the hardship of this world if they believed in the rewards of the world to come. Considering the squalor and deprivation of existence experienced by the Church's subjects, it is easy to understand the strength of ecclesiastical influence. The Church was established and was the single most cohesive and directional force in Western society.

A contemporary vantage point requires a caveat with respect to the fundamental nature of Christianity. Christianity was not and is not a religion that totally rejects this world. The New Testament narratives are filled with concern for the nature and quality of human life in this world. Moreover, the monastic movements of the Middle Ages attempted to bring some humane quality to worldly life, although they typically removed themselves from the mainstream of worldly life in their quest for this goal. Reformation and post-Reformation Christianity reflects a growing concern for the quality of human daily life. The fact nevertheless remains that the dominant and fundamental concern of the Church during the Middle Ages was the world to come. It was the world beyond this one that was to provide the meaning for an earthly existence.

The period of the established church—the Holy Roman Empire—apparently promoted a kind of cultural hibernation, a deep and prolonged winter in the development of Western thought and culture. A cultural springtime was sure to come and, with the Renaissance, the birth process of the modern world began. Disregarding historical nuances and technicalities, it may be said that the Renaissance signaled the beginning of the end of the age of faith, with its established monolithic church, and ushered in the beginning of the age of man, a world largely governed by reason and directed by human choice. The dawn of the "secular" world had broken and the nurturing rays of that sun would bring about the long overdue cultural springtime.

The Renaissance, however, should not be seen as a sudden burst of creative regeneration. Cultural change was, at first, only embryonic and manifested itself primarily in scholarly and artistic activity. As artists and sculptors dedicated their talents to the beautification of houses of worship, a revolutionary idea took shape: people could, prior to their entrance into the future world promised by the Church, beautify the world of everyday life and alleviate the harshness of earthly existence. While a world so rejuvenated by the artistic hand of man might not compare favorably with the splendor of paradise, it just might, nonetheless, ameliorate the dreary existence that people had become accustomed to during the Middle Ages. Before this creative thrust had been long in progress, musicians and actors began to make significant contributions to the enrichment of *this life in this world*. As a result of this artistic ferment, the notion that people could take charge of the quality of their earthly life began to emerge.

Scholarly efforts were less overtly dramatic in their inception, but their eventual impact was even more disruptive of the accepted order. During the beginning of the Renaissance, some scholars became enchanted with the classical literature of Greece and Rome, a literature largely ignored during the Middle Ages. Little creative thought was present at first; there was simply an attempt to recover and contemplate the classics of the past. Yet this revival of interest shifted attention from otherworldly priorities to the human potential portrayed in the ancient documents.

The dream of human development and social order expressed in the classics could not but overwhelm the attentive scholar when compared to the decay and despair into which humanity had drifted. As this scholarly study progressed, an interest in the study of human nature developed among those scholars we have called the humanists. This study of human nature through the medium of the classics was to bear significant fruit.

The more the men of the Renaissance exulted over the civilization of Greece and Rome, the more some of them fretted with irritation for their own. At odds with its antiworldiness, they took the field against what they disdained—its pettiness, its renunciations and restraints, the follies of its people, the vast flatulence of its learning. Nothing could stay their cultural sniping—not even Holy Church.[3]

As dissatisfaction with their present existence grew, people came to wonder why they could not take charge of and change it, why they could not recapture the dream that had inspired the artists and scholars of the classical world. As they studied the ancient civilizations, they began to ask why there was no such growth and effectiveness of cultural and social life in their world.

Thus, in this human awakening grew a strange new phenomenon—self-confidence.

The medieval man, with his feeling of personal insignificance, lack of self-confidence, "no sense of the past behind him, and no conception of the possibilities of the future before him," was rapidly giving way to the man possessed of the modern spirit—the man of self-confidence, conscious of his powers, enjoying life, feeling his connection with the historic past, and realizing the potentialities of accomplishment in the world here below.[4]

For good or for ill, the spirit of the Renaissance was this spirit of self-confidence. Emerging from a protracted period of stagnation for the human spirit, Renaissance man began to breathe fresh air, invigorating air filled with the intoxicating scent of confidence in the power of the human mind and spirit. Most would not deny that the world to come might have untold rewards and matchless blessings, but the application of human thought and effort could significantly improve this world. R. Freeman Butts interpreted this attitude as the spirit of secularism and argued that it was the key to understanding the Renaissance. Although latent in the Middle Ages, this secular

---

[3]Adolphe E. Meyer, *An Educational History of the Western World* (New York: McGraw-Hill Book Co., 1965) 159.

[4]Ellwood P. Cubberley, *The History of Education* (Boston: Houghton Mifflin Co., 1948) 243.

mentality began to permeate Renaissance culture, changing significantly humanity's view of itself and its world.[5]

Other compelling processes and events contributed to this changing view of life. The Church unintentionally advanced the spirit of the Renaissance by attempting to convert the heathen to Christianity or, failing that, dispatching them to their just reward. Beginning with the Crusades, geographic exploration considerably influenced cultural development. Through travel and exploration, the Western world discovered new cultures, moral codes, and modes of thought, and these new ways of life and thought undermined the narrow, fixed outlook that had dominated Europe. During this extended period, it became apparent that people outside Europe enjoyed fulfilling lives following codes of behavior and life-styles markedly different from those of the Western world. Western man encountered a disturbing problem: cultural relativity. A chink of imposing potential developed in the armor of the medieval synthesis.

Exploration beyond the geographic confines of Europe opened the way for commerical development. As the explorers returned with their wondrous goods, trade routes developed and trade centers became established at strategic locations. As the pace of commerce quickened, population density became a characteristic of these centers. The marketplace exercised increasing control over the economy as the Church lost its power to control the utilization of wealth. Moreover, the monopoly of wealth by the very few slowly eroded, giving way to a new, more equitable distribution of wealth with which to barter and accrue power. The social status associated with position and family heritage gave way to a social status derived from services rendered and goods bartered. As marketplaces became centers for business activity, merchants and craftsmen, because of their wealth, gained substantial influence in matters of society. Banding themselves together into guilds for common government and protection in this comparatively primitive setting,

---

[5]R. Freeman Butts, *A Cultural History of Western Education*, 2d ed. (New York: McGraw-Hill Book Co., 1955) 165.

the merchants and artisans influenced the emerging shape and direction of society. It was from these guilds that the middle class developed and, as it did, the feudal system with its few very rich social leaders and its masses of persons so poor that mere survival was a constant struggle, was broken down.[6]

The religious movement known as the Reformation also had significant impact upon the development of the modern outlook of Western society. The intricacies of this series of events and procession of influential thinkers is familiar,[7] and only those major outcomes of the Reformation that impinge directly upon our present concern will be discussed.

The first and most far-reaching result of the Reformation was that the Christian *church* became the Christian *churches*. Fundamentally, the events of the Reformation caused Christianity to become sectarian and Europe to become pluralistic. No longer was there a specific Christian point of view; no one religious authority; no unified institution to provide for human spiritual *and* political needs; no single theology or form of piety upon which people might rely; not even a single route to the salvation the Church had so long promised and the terms of which it had so long governed.

This splintering of the Church had enormous impact on society, but a second consequence of the Reformation was equally important in its effect on human thought. As a result of the Reformation, responsibility for religious faith and growth shifted for many from an institution to the individual. Many Christians, it is true, remained committed to the traditional expression of that faith (what we now know as the Roman Catholic Church); but Martin Luther had opened the religious door to the mood of the times. Even John Calvin's experiment in Protestant theocratic government, with its implications for controlling individ-

---

[6]Ralph L. Pounds, *The Development of Education in Western Culture* (New York: Appleton-Century-Crofts, 1968) 84ff.

[7]One of the best sources for a study of this period is Will Durant's *The Reformation*, vol. 6 of *The Story of Civilization* (New York: Simon and Schuster, 1957).

ual faith, proved unsuccessful. For many Europeans, the idea
that each individual was responsible for his or her own salvation
was a refreshing, liberating option; opening possibilities for religious growth that were not again to be completely surrendered
to external ecclesiastic control or government regulation. Even
the reforms undertaken by the Roman Catholic church could
not draw large numbers of dissenters back into its fold. The Bible would remain central, and theological and doctrinal systems
would be formulated that would give many of the diverse Protestant groups a lasting identity and a potential for limited spiritual control; but Western society was witnessing the birth of
personal, individual religion. It was a religious faith developing
directly from the religious experience of the individual, and the
individual would become the new priesthood in Protestant theology. No longer was salvation, at least in Protestant theory, to
be found beyond the personal response of the individual to
God. Of course, much of this individuality of religious faith was
shortly swallowed up by the institutionalization of the Protestant faiths. But, in its inception, Reformation theology placed
salvation directly in the hands of each believer, and the unified
authority of one Christian church and its dogma was to become
a memory for Western man.

A third significant outcome of the Reformation was the
breakdown of the unified governmental structure that the
church had provided. The development of nations with different religious establishments was a sign of the times. As the
church splintered and its power diminished, political structures
emerged, emphasis shifted, and people became citizens of this
world as well as of the world to come. The division of the one
church into the many churches allowed expression of the national and ethnic divisions of Europe that had been dormant.
With this change in political structure came a sense of national
identity, accompanied by a sense of dignity, worth, and pride.
With increasing impetus, nationalism surpassed religious identification as the controlling factor in the day-to-day lives of common citizens. Personal stability and success were now in large
measure determined by the success and stability of one's
earthly nation. Even when national rulers were said to rule by

divine right, a right supposedly bestowed by God and enforced by religious doctrine, national identity began to change the quality of life enjoyed by the individual. The shift from church control over all nations to a divided political authority brought variety to European life and changed the scope of human aspirations. Laws designed to preserve social stability and to achieve social progress primarily controlled the daily life of the individual while religious codes of behavior controlled a person's private life. The rule of law replaced the rule of doctrine in the political and social life of Europe. The medieval synthesis was bankrupt; Western society would not again cultivate the conditions of the Middle Ages.

Another development of enormous impact on the thought and outlook of Western man was the application of the methods of modern science to the world and its problems. A natural outgrowth of man's rediscovered ability to think for himself, the development of modern science added greatly to the belief that individuals could control the nature of their present life in this world and solve many of the problems that they had simply endured during the long, dark period after the fall of Rome. Stimulated by the humanist interest in classical thought, man utilized the vistas of modern science, turning his gaze first to the heavens and then to this world. Slowly but surely, the conviction grew that nothing was beyond the purview of this new and promising pathway to knowledge.

The essence of this embrace of science is best illustrated in the attitude that one should see reality as it is experienced rather than uncritically accepting the way it is said or expected to be. Human beings were urged to apply their reason and take their experience seriously rather than give in to their problems or rely upon external authority and ancient presuppositions for solutions as was typical during the Middle Ages. The example of modern science, therefore, clearly illustrates the shift of authority that occurred as the medieval world gave way to the modern world.[8] Rather than resorting to the Church for pro-

---

[8]This approach did not affect any other worlds that might await man "out there." The focus of modern science originally was on this world, the world of man's immediate experience.

nouncements concerning how things are or how they ought to be, man looked to himself, to his experience and his reason, for truth about this world.

In his work, Copernicus used this revived perception of reality. With his primitive telescope, he brought down the ancient and revered cosmologies that had dominated Western thought for centuries. The earth did not occupy the center of a fixed cosmic structure but was an insignificant speck in a vast solar system that rotated about the sun. Copernicus's thought was destined to revolutionize Western man's view of the world, the universe, and of himself. No longer was this world the center of an orderly and compact geocentric structure; human beings were now residents of a small planet on the fringe of infinite space. The retreat of ancient truth and religious dogma before the relentless march of modern thought was under way.

The investigations of modern science led to a new division of human experience. As scientists perfected their methodology, they focused their attention more and more on the objective world and on empirically verifiable data. Investigations of subjective experiences and processes proved generally fruitless from that perspective. As a result, a dichotomy developed between the objective and the subjective worlds of human experience. Included in the subjective world was the area of spiritual experience—the primary concern of the Church. Consequently, a distinction developed between the natural world with which science was concerned and the spiritual world with which the Church was concerned.

Thus, man grew increasingly confident in this rediscovered ability to think for himself, to exercise informed choice, and to solve problems that directly impinged upon the quality of life in this world. Unfortunately, the Church's reaction to these new developments lacked both grace and insight. Rather than responding positively and constructively, the Church felt threatened and became defensive in its attempt to protect ancient dogma. An ill-advised war with modern science resulted, a war in which the Church has yet to win a single significant battle. The world was thereby regrettably divided into sacred and secular, the realm of the spirit and the realm of commonly shared, objective experience.

The Modern Spirit

In this series of events, the Church lost political control of the West; it was disestablished. The result of Western civilization's movement beyond the Middle Ages has been called "secularization." Given the intrinsic nature of that movement coupled with the role the Church played in the Middle Ages, it was the only result that logically could have been anticipated. The stewardship of the Church during its time of establishment left much to be desired. The medieval synthesis—that union of religious thought and social structure that dominated the Middle Ages—was bankrupt as it related to human need in this life. Human experience made it obvious that people could no longer evade responsibility for the quality of their lives in this world if they were to improve society. Secularization was not a rejection of Christianity in particular or of religion in general, but was, in its inception, a rejection of the control of public life and social structure by any institution or set of values that preserved the bondage of humanity to ignorance and poverty.

It is, therefore, important to understand exactly what secularization means. According to D. L. Munby, a secular society (a society that has undergone secularization) is one that refuses to dedicate itself to any single view of the nature and meaning of the universe. Such a society is pluralistic; it allows, even encourages, diversity of belief and commitment. Hence, a secular society is tolerant. It attempts to define and maintain a distinction between belief and action. In such a society, freedom of belief approaches the status of an absolute, and action resulting from belief is controlled only when it infringes upon the rights of others or threatens the common good. A secular society attempts to distinguish between public and private morality. The institutions, structures, and aims of the society do not take precedence over the freedom of the individuals who make up that society. Thus, the secular society attempts to maximize individual freedom; the matter of ultimate commitment is totally the result of individual judgement. As a result of these characteristics, a secular society will have no official images, superimposed aims, or ideal types of behavior.[9]

This last characteristic should be useful in distinguishing between a secular society (as described by Munby) and a society in which the official sociopolitical religion is secularism. In a secular society, government may not impose positions respecting individual commitment, values, or belief upon the citizen. The rule of law is a basic necessity; but that law will provide for the protection of individual rights and the assurance of social stability and well-being. For a secular society, this body of law becomes the official public code of ethics, inasmuch as there can be such a public code.[10] By enlarging the freedom of the individual and providing a strong code of law to sustain the common good, the secular society nourishes itself by allowing the public expression of values and morals that may be religiously motivated. The secular society is devoted to the well-being of its total citizenry; there is no preferential treatment for any ideology, particular code of morals, life-style, or sub-group.

These remarks seem a fairly accurate description of American society and government.

> Constitutionalism plus religious pluralism forced the "secularization" of government—for "secularization" means the "desectarianization" of government; that is, the civil authority must become neutral where the particularistic claims of the sects are concerned. For government is for *all* men in society, and *all* men enter into the compact that forms it.[11]

---

[9]D. L. Munby, *The Idea of a Secular Society* (New York: Oxford University Press, 1963) 14-31.

[10]It is a mistake to completely equate law and morality in any setting, however benignly. Legal codes can never be sufficiently comprehensive to cover the moral issues of life. Law may coerce behavior, but morality must reflect a personal commitment rather than fear of legal retribution. An act may be morally wrong and legally correct; or legally wrong and morally sound. In the secular society, however, the fact remains that the law is the only official code of public right and wrong.

[11]Sidney E. Mead, "Religion, Constitutional Federalism, Rights and the Court," *Religion in Public Education*, ed. David E. Engel (Ramsey NJ: Paulist Press, 1974) 26.

The obvious similarity between a secular society as described and American society and government is not the result of some strange quirk of fate. The ideas and values that constitute the secular outlook, resulting from those changes in Western culture following the Middle Ages, are the ideas and values that coalesced to produce this nation; they are fundamental to democratic ideals.

Any government so dedicated must be careful to distinguish between a secular point of view and a religion of secularism. When a society enforces official value structures, beliefs, and commitments upon the individual citizen, secularism as a religion may be present and would represent an establishment of religion. According to Harvey Cox, secularization connotes a historical process, all but irreversible, in which societies are freed from the domination of closed metaphysical world views. A religion of secularism, on the other hand, is a new closed system with respect to social life.[12] It not only affirms that humanity and its world are significant and autonomous, but denies the meaning and significance of transcendent reality.[13] Secularism is a religious expression, emphasizing the present life of man and excluding belief in anything that cannot be empirically defined. It thus denies the relevance of transcendent reality or meaning.

It is frequently difficult to distinguish between "secular" and "secularism" because the deciding factor is not a difference in secular outlook, but the finality or ultimate status assigned to the outlook. A secular outlook focuses upon human beings in this world and attempts to improve human life, utilizing all appropriate resources (including traditional religion). Secularism shares this intention, but rejects transcendent values and commitments. The Judeo-Christian tradition illustrates the difficulty of making the distinction between "secular" and

---

[12]Harvey Cox, *The Secular City* (New York: Macmillan Co., 1965) 20-21.

[13]Schubert M. Ogden, *The Reality of God* (New York: Harper and Row, 1966) 12.

"secularism." It is possible, within the Judeo-Christian tradition, to make a case supporting humanity's attempt to better its condition in this present world—under God—as a supremely religious undertaking. However, that tradition would be violated if, in the process, this world became man's source of ultimate meaning and the object of his spiritual commitment.

The failure to properly distinguish between "secular" and "secularism" often leads to unfortunate results. For example, the following statement is fundamentally correct, but that fact is clouded by a failure to properly distinguish the secular from secularism.

> "Secular" means precisely the absence of any orientation to God; it claims that men can adequately live their lives without "outside interference." The secular point of view regards religion as one human interest among others, a kind of elective course for those who are interested in such things.[14]

In a context of social heterogeneity, all religions must be equally honored, and no particular religion may exercise control over the social structure. Religion is regarded, therefore, as one of the many significant commitments available to mankind. Religious faith is indeed an "elective,"[15] and a secular society is dedicated to preserving the freedom of the individual to elect that ultimate being or power to which he will devote his life. Such a society will be equally committed to the right of the individual

---

[14]John A. Hutchinson, *Faith, Reason, and Existence* (New York: Oxford University Press, 1956) 211-12.

[15]If religious faith were not an "elective" in a most fundamental sense, would not each child born into the world possess an inbuilt faith in some specific deity? Persons frequently react to words with such passion that they miss the concept intended. To view religion as an elective is immediately offensive to many churchmen, but if faith were not an elective, would the Christian church expend so much time, energy, and money on evangelism? Is not asking persons to *elect* the Christian faith one of the central missions to which the church has dedicated itself? A secular society will refuse to establish any faith, but it will be equally dedicated to the protection of man's right of election, of choice. Those who object to this position reveal their fundamental intention—the denial of human freedom of religious choice.

not to elect an ultimate. Moreover, that society will not interfere with, suppress, control or deny this right of election. A secular society, by guaranteeing liberty, will prove that it respects
and encourages this election; a society dedicated to secularism
will inhibit or deny this freedom of choice—as would a society
in which traditional religion is established. This distinction must
be drawn with great precision and maintained with deliberate
integrity for it represents the foundation of religious liberty.

The secular spirit as it developed during the Renaissance was
positive and constructive. It represented a shift from the devotion and attention lavished on other worlds to an equally intense dedication to this world and the present experience of
humanity. The denial of cosmic worlds was not intrinsic to the
Renaissance spirit. Viewed from the perspective of the Judeo-
Christian tradition, human beings as creatures of God, employed their God-given abilities to improve the world God had
given them and, according to the biblical accounts, pronounced
as "good." Thus, fundamentally, the secular outlook that
prompted humanity's pilgrimage from the Middle Ages into the
modern world was in keeping with God's apparent design as reported in the Judeo-Christian tradition. Considering the total
point of view expressed, can one read the Old and New Testa-
ments and believe that the conditions of the Middle Ages were
what God intended for his creatures in the world he had made
for them?

During the renewal of human self-confidence, which was
characteristic of post-Renaissance life, secularism emerged as
an ideology opposed to traditional religion. One reason for its
emergence is that the secular outlook provided a natural vehicle of expression for those who, for any number of reasons, rejected traditional religion. Rejection of formal, institutional
religion is not a new phenomenon in human thought, but the
secular celebration of this world and of human potential represented an avenue of considerable promise for antireligious
expression. The secular point of view is easily subverted.[16] An-

---

[16]In dealing with such expression, it is most valuable to determine precisely what is being rejected. The reality of the atheistic or antireligious po-

other reason for the antireligious position so often associated with the secular outlook is the unwillingness of the Christian church—as the dominant religion of the West—either to encourage human growth or to itself grow with humanity. The record of the Church's reaction to the human attempt to improve life during the Renaissance and Reformation is a sorry one indeed. Discouraging as it may be, many contemporary Christians appear to espouse the Church's negative attitude with respect to human growth and freedom. The unwillingness of much of Christianity to take this world seriously has significantly contributed to the rise of secularism.

Harvey Cox stated that a fundamental characteristic of the secular outlook is the distinction between this world and worlds beyond or above this one.[17] The rejection of an exclusive concern for cosmic worlds is clearly fundamental to the secular spirit. But, a more noteworthy dichotomy is also present—that between the present world and past worlds. The secular spirit not only refused to focus total attention on cosmic worlds or specific cosmic visions, that spirit also rejected a domination of man's present by past *human* worlds and the "answers" such worlds are said to provide. Cultural tradition may be employed in two ways: to restrict and direct human growth and social development or to assist humanity in attempting to improve its common life. The secular outlook will reject the former; it will affirm the latter. From this perspective, any truth, value, or lifestyle must contribute to the improvement of this present world or it will be viewed as irrelevant. However, the secular point of view will reject an element of tradition only on the basis of experienced irrelevancy.

As the Church, because of its intransigence and defensiveness, grew increasingly remote from Western society's attempt

---

sitions is not being denied. Nonetheless, one often senses in such positions the fundamental rejection of institutionalized or formal religion rather than a rejection of the spiritual dimensions of human experience.

[17]Harvey Cox, "Secularization and the Secular Mentality: A New Challenge to Christian Education," *Religious Education* 61 (March-April 1966): 83.

to make this life more positive and meaningful, many rejected traditional religion, considering it inhibiting and irrelevant. Secularism, a religious expression more in tune with this new mood, provided the alternative ideology. In this perspective, the finite was made infinite, the immanent was given transcendent status, and the secular merged with the sacred. Although secularism was an antireligious reaction, its concern with ultimate meaning and life-direction proved that it involved religious concerns.

The secular outlook does not surface only in contemporary religion, it is also required by our social commitments. When a sociopolitical structure refuses to place supreme value on, or affirm allegiance to, a specific religion—affirming, rather, the value and legitimacy of all expressions of religion—a secular commitment is required. Maintenance of religious freedom denies society or government the right to place an official imprimatur on any specific form of religious expression to the exclusion of others. Dedication to pluralism requires a secular position on the part of society and government, a position that denies official supremacy for any specific religious expression. Pluralism and freedom are, however, ill-served if that secularity assumes a posture hostile toward religion. When a secular position assumes final and closed qualities, freedom for individuals demands the disestablishment of religious secularism. Safeguarding individual freedom does not, however, require the overreactive establishment of some form of Christianity—a response some members of the Christian community strongly advocate.

Conceptual definitions, however, will not remove all the potential for conflict between the secular outlook and traditional religion.

> Our culture is perhaps the first completely secularized culture in human history. . . . The majority of us believe in God, take it for granted that God exists. The rest, who do not believe, take it for granted that God does not exist. Either way, God is taken for granted. . . . whether a man in our culture believes in God or not makes hardly any difference either from a psychological or from a truly religious standpoint.[18]

---

[18]Erich Fromm, *The Sane Society* (New York: Holt, Rinehart and Winston, 1955) 176.

In a secular society dedicated to religious freedom, the personal commitment of an individual to the god of a particular religious tradition should make no *official* difference, but such commitments are of enormous significance if the fulness of the human spirit is to be nurtured. Except for those obvious aberrations that wither as a result of their meaninglessness, or those that finally conflict with the law, religious commitments, while diverse in nature, typically are dedicated to improving the nature, quality, and direction of human life, both in its individual and social dimensions.

When the dogmatic posturing and special interests are set aside, the commitment to human existence under whatever god one elects is valuable in terms of the quality of life enjoyed in a society. The fundamental danger of a zealous secularity is that humanity's ultimate concerns (the foci of religion) will be trivialized and thereby will cease to nourish the meanings and commitments required to maximize human potential. While religious experience ranges from primitive superstition to highly sophisticated theological systems, all such experiences express the search for the *ultimate why* of human existence. Even in its "coming of age" (Bonhoeffer), humanity exhibits the need for transcendent reality (Frankl) and ultimate concern (Tillich). The honest and responsible search for the why of existence will influence positively human society as it molds the goals to which human beings commit themselves.

The decline of religious influence in society as compared with the growing influence of the secular outlook has been referred to as the "death of God." An examination of the literature shows this "death" to be subject to one of two interpretations, aside, that is, from the literal celebration of the demise of deity. One interpretation states that the traditional answers proposed by religion are no longer appropriate for the problems humanity encounters. The total experience of humanity is changing so rapidly that the rights and wrongs, the procedures and goals, the facts and truths of past generations and prior worlds, are no longer meaningful. And, regrettably, so much of this traditional insight was expressed with religious sanction, leading many to believe that the rejection of the old ideals required the rejection

of religion. The absence of certainty, the breakdown of continuity, the loss of meaning and control that results from this experience of irrelevance has been summarized in the phrase *the
death of God.* The certainty, stability, and meaning that life in
an earlier epoch was said to possess, largely based upon religious teachings, is now absent.

The second interpretation of this term is that the supernatural dimension is no longer required for human beings to acquire
knowledge or attain social progress. Human experience has
made the idea of the supernatural, in the traditional sense, appear increasingly untenable. It has been a common practice to
use "God" to explain those aspects of experience that man could
not otherwise explain. "God" was a concept used to fill the gaps
in human knowledge. As a result, when answers were found,
God was unnecessary. The more knowledge man amassed, the
less need there was for God. God, as a final source for answers
to the "how?" and "when?" questions, grew more irrelevant
with each major advance in human knowledge. For many persons, it has seemed more appropriate to tolerate the gaps in human knowledge while continuing to apply reason in the
conviction that appropriate information will be forthcoming.

> . . .as man has gained increasing mastery over nature through science
> and concomitant advances in technology, he gradually has lost his sense
> of helplessness and with it his need to believe in the supernatural. He
> has become more and more this-worldly and can say, quite readily,
> "This world is all that there is and it is enough."[19]

While frequently reflecting an atheistic commitment, both of
these interpretations reveal that the "death of God" reflects a
failure of institutional religion more than a celebration of the
death of deity. It results from the Church's continuing war with
the modern spirit and reflects a most unfortunate theological
view of this world. Although human thought will have no impact whatsoever on the life or death of God *qua* God, the belief
that the dominant religious tradition of the West is irrelevant

---

[19]Edward Cell, "The Question of Religion," *Religion and Contemporary
Western Culture*, ed. Edward Cell (Nashville TN: Abington Press, 1967) 14.

may have pernicious effects: Can humanity find an alternative that will provide the continuity and stability historically associated with religion? Can a religionless society sufficiently nurture the human spirit?

Despite these problems, secularization is not only healthy for mankind, it is equally promising for religion. In the total sweep of the Judeo-Christian tradition, there seems to be no significant evidence suggesting that God did not intend man to fulfill his positive potential as a human being. Neither does there seem to be any indication that ignorance and superstition should be maintained and that positive growth, for individuals and for society, should be discouraged. Secularization not only resulted from historical processes, it was, perhaps, absolutely necessary if human maturity under God is to be realized. It is, of course, important that the religious community continue to nourish human growth under God. The search, by the religious community, for ways to nourish such growth would evidence a maturity that would challenge man to attain full humanity under God—a position of spiritual leadership fully befitting the best of the religious tradition of Western society.

Rather, therefore, than waging an unending and debilitating war with secularization, religion might be advised to reconsider its raison d'être in the modern world. Some years ago, A. J. Heschel argued that religion has not declined because it has been proven wrong, but because it has been viewed as irrelevant. Faith has been replaced by creed, love by habit. Faith has become an heirloom of a bygone day rather than an experience of vital significance. Religion becomes meaningless when it begins to speak with authority rather than compassion. Religion is an answer to the ultimate concerns of humanity. When it is less, it is irrelevant. Institutional religion must, therefore, rediscover its reason for being.[20]

If institutional religion ignores this task of rediscovery, it will become increasingly irrelevant to the mainstream of modern

---

[20]Abraham J. Heschel, "The Religious Message," *Religion in America*, ed. John Cogley (Mountain View CA: World Publishing Co., 1958) 245.

Western life. If organized religion is unable to nurture the best in the human spirit, man will turn to philosophy, psychology, science, rationalism, cults, even to himself, in his search for ultimate meaning. So long as human perception and experience are involved, there will continue to be a variety of religious institutions, practices, and creeds. Despite this fact, humanity's religious quest has remained steadfast throughout history. Human beings will, by their nature, continue to experience ultimate concerns—to ask the ultimate "why?" about their lives, relationships, and world. They will be religious—even in the absence of a viable religion; but human religious needs will not be met either by the establishment of some form of traditional religion or by the official antireligious stance of secularism.

Not only must we avoid establishing traditional religion or religious secularism, we must likewise avoid a religion of Americanism—a religious nationalism. Recent literature has referred to this religious nationalism as "civil religion."[21] One of the foremost anthropologists of our time painted the following picture of the American creed—the basic tenets of this religion of American culture.

> The pattern of the implicit American creed seems to embrace the following recurrent elements: faith in the rational, a need for moralistic rationalization, an optimistic conviction that rational effort counts, romantic individualism and the cult of the common man, high valuation of change—which is ordinarily taken to mean "progress," the conscious quest for pleasure.
>
> Mysticism and supernaturalism have been very minor themes in American life. Our glorification of science and our faith in what can be accomplished through education are two striking aspects of our generalized conviction that secular, humanistic effort will improve the world

---

[21]For an introduction see: R. N. Bellah, *The Broken Covenant* (New York: Seabury Press, 1975); Michael Novak, "America as Religion," *Religious Education* 71 (May-June 1976): 260-67; S. E. Mead, *The Nation with the Soul of a Church* (New York: Harper and Row, 1975); E. M. West, "A Proposed Neutral Definition of Civil Religion," *Journal of Church and State* 22 (Winter 1980): 23-40.

in a series of changes, all or mainly for the better. We further tend to believe that morality and reason must coincide.[22]

Human beings are religious beings; they will continue to place their faith in, and commit their life to, something beyond themselves that appears to provide meaning and purpose for their lives. In their insatiable desire for meaning, human beings will continue to replace traditional religion with other creeds if traditional religion does not concern itself with their lives in a positive, constructive, loving manner. The religious experience will continue to nourish man's quest for the better life; consequently, traditional religions will survive, not through establishment, but to the degree those traditional religions intentionally nourish this religious quest.

The Separation of Government and Religion

Reformation theology's emphasis upon individual responsibility for faith and salvation was never understood, at least in mainstream Protestantism, to require an anti-institutional position. As the Protestant denominations developed theological and institutional identity, this identity was frequently interwoven with the emerging ethnic and nationalistic expressions of Europe. The control of European society by the monolithic Christian church gave way to control of the emerging nations by the Christian churches. A singular establishment was exchanged for many establishments, and the nations of Europe represented, in a variety of forms and to varying degrees, establishments of sectarian Christianity. It was against the backdrop of these diverse national establishments that this nation was born.

Scholars have identified several types of religion-government relationships that have been employed in Western history. Anson P. Stokes, in his classic study, presented eight models of

---

[22]Clyde Kluckhohn. *Mirror for Man* (New York: McGraw-Hill Book Co., 1949) 232.

this relationship.[23] These models, however, reduce to four fundamental types. Commonly referred to as a theocracy, the first relationship is one in which religion (a church) controls the state. The almost universal establishment of the Christian church during the Middle Ages is an example of this model. The origin of theocratic government is commonly traced to Pope Gregory the Great who ruled both church and state from 590 to 604 A.D.. A theocracy was also present in the Papal States of Italy, and to a substantial degree, in the Massachusetts Bay Colony.

The second type of relationship is one in which the state promotes a single religion or church—the state adopts one religion as the official religion of that state. In such an arrangement, public funds are used to support the established church, and public office is restricted to those who openly acknowledge affiliation with that church. The degree of freedom allowed other religious expressions depends upon the disposition of the government as that disposition is informed by the established religion. This relationship is frequently called Erastianism and was apparent in England and in the Colony of Virginia prior to the Revolution.

St. Augustine recommended the third type of relationship, that of the coexistence of religion and government. To a moderate degree, this relationship existed in the fifth and sixth centuries of European history during the transition from the Roman Empire to the Holy Roman Empire. Colonial Rhode Island followed this model, and it is the model specified by the Constitution of the United States.

The fourth form of relationship is present when the state assumes a posture hostile toward all religions. Religion is forced underground, and hostility is mutually expressed. This relationship was present in the regime of Nazi Germany and, to a lesser degree, in the policies of the Soviet Union. Of these four types of religion-government relationship, only the first two may be referred to as an establishment of religion.

---

[23]Anson P. Stokes, *Church and State in the United States*, 3 vols. (New York: Harper and Brothers, Publishers, 1950) 1:39-47.

The evils of establishment are obvious, even if one has no more than a cursory knowledge of Western history. Crusades, holy wars, inquisitions, religious restrictions for assuming public office, common taxation to support one religion, heresy trials, capital punishment for deviant belief, and the denial of freedom of religious expression are all illustrations of this evil.

> It was precisely because Eighteenth Century Americans were a religious people divided into many fighting sects that we were given the constitutional mandate to keep Church and State completely separate. Colonial history had already shown that, here as elsewhere, zealous sectarians entrusted with governmental power to further their causes would sometimes torture, maim, and kill those they branded "heretics," "atheists," or "agnostics." The First Amendment was therefore to insure that no one powerful sect or combinations of sects could use political or governmental power to punish dissenters whom they could not convert to their faith. Now as then, it is only by wholly isolating the state from the religious sphere and compelling it to be completely neutral, that the freedom of each and every denomination and of all nonbelievers can be maintained.[24]

The evils of establishment are unpleasant to recall, but recall them we must, for we are now two centuries removed from their oppressive effects in American experience and must remember those effects if we are to avoid working them into government again.

However, there were establishment results that were less devastating and visible but more insidious. A thorough summary of these results is found in a section of James Madison's *Memorial and Remonstrance Against Religious Assessments*.

> . . . experience witnesseth that ecclesiastical establishments, instead of maintaining the purity and efficacy of Religion, have had a contrary operation. During almost fifteen centuries, has the legal establishment of Christianity been on trial. What have been its fruits? More or less in all places, pride and indolence in the Clergy, ignorance and servility in the laity; in both, superstition, bigotry, and persecution. . . . What influence in fact have ecclesiastical establishments had on Civil Society? In some instances they have been seen to erect a spiritual tyranny on the ruins of Civil authority; in many instances they have been seen upholding the

---

[24]*Zorach v. Clauson*, 343 U. S. 306, 318-19 (1962).

thrones of political tyranny; in no instance have they been seen the guardians of the liberties of the people. Rulers who wished to subvert the public liberties, may have found an established clergy convenient auxiliaries. A just government, instituted to secure and perpetuate it, needs them not. Such a government will be best supported by protecting every citizen in the enjoyment of his Religion with the same equal hand which protects his person and his property; by neither invading the equal rights of any Sect, nor suffering any Sect to invade those of another.[25]

Aside from the profound inhumanity demonstrated during the history of Western establishment, Madison believed that neither government nor religion had been well-served by the more benign outcomes of establishment. Thus, the only persons who would favor the establishment of a religion would be those who sought the establishment of their own faith. History testifies, as do current events, that in the event of establishment, only those of the established religion benefit. It is disappointing to recall the frequency with which those who have fled religious persecution have, when sanctuary was found, established their own faith and persecuted those of alien religions. The oppression of religion undertaken in the Massachusetts Bay Colony is an excellent example. History appears to illustrate no redeeming factor for the establishment of religion and the denial of religious freedom that invariably results. Moreover, this is not a review of the results of the establishment of some other of the world's major religions or of some obscure sect or cult; but the review of the results of the establishment of the Christian church in Western history. One must, therefore, seriously question any steps respecting an establishment of religion in contemporary society.

Leo Pfeffer identified a number of factors contributing to separation of religion and government in the United States.[26]

---

[25]The text of *A Memorial and Remonstrance* may be found in *Everson v. Board of Education*, 330 U.S. 1, 63-72; it is originally cited in *The Papers of James Madison*, ed. William T. Hutchinson and William Rachal (Chicago: University of Chicago Press, 1962-) 8:298-304.

[26]Leo Pfeffer, *Church, State, and Freedom* (Boston: Beacon Press, 1953) 83-93.

First, the English Act of Toleration, adopted in 1689, provided a model for American colonial thought. This act accomplished precisely what its title implied—it granted limited legal status to sects and religions other than the Church of England. Such groups would no longer be persecuted; they would be tolerated by the government and the established church. The implication of toleration was a preliminary step toward religious freedom in England.

Another factor contributing to the separation between religion and government was the diversity of sects and denominations in the colonies. So many different beliefs prohibited the development of a powerful, single religious position that often breeds establishment. One source listed some thirty different Christian sects and denominations present in colonial America,[27] and none were able to generate an influence sufficiently widespread to allow establishment.

Also, Christianity lacked sufficient unity or adequate power to effect an establishment. Records indicate that the number of those colonists unaffiliated with a church approached ninety-five percent of the population. This fact does not mean that the colonists were typically irreligious or indifferent to the Christian faith. Rather, it reflects the effect of frontier conditions on organized religion. In such conditions, it was difficult for the Christian denominations and sects to provide an institutional identity. In a stable social setting, ministers, houses of worship, organized religious programs, and denominational or sectarian identity could be provided; in the frontier settlement it was frequently difficult to provide even a minister.

Furthermore, it was discovered that without the social and political barriers erected by religious establishments, commercial activity was substantially facilitated. Because economic concerns were primary motivators for the exploration and settlement of this continent, ease of commercial interaction excersied considerable impact when deciding what type of

---

[27]Conrad H. Moehlman, *The Wall of Separation Between Church and State* (Boston: Beacon Press, 1951) 100.

government to found. Hence, social and political structures were created that encouraged religious freedom (and commerce) and discouraged religious establishment (and commercial barriers). Moreover, the ideological maxim of the Revolution—freedom and equality—seemed, based upon experience in Europe, to demand the separation of religion and government if that ideal was to achieve any degree of reality.

The successful separation of religion and government in Rhode Island and Pennsylvania provided working models of disestablishment and firsthand evidence of its benefits. Furthermore, the social contract theory formulated by John Locke maintained that religions should not be subject to government. Finally, as Pfeffer wrote, separation provided a convenient compromise between the theological orthodoxy of the Protestant sects on the one hand and the deism and skepticism that had been imported from France on the other.

The American experiment in separation was not motivated by antireligious sentiment or political hostility to religion. Indeed, many of the prominent individuals who worked most effectively for religious freedom were devoutly religious. Rather, the experiment resulted from the twofold realization that establishment inhibits social interaction and progress, but religious freedom contributes to social cohesion, development, and prosperity. As John C. Bennett noted, even the churchmen came to realize that the churches were better off when on their own,[28] free to grow and exercise influence on the basis of their intrinsic merit. In short, the much maligned secular outlook appeared the best solution both for religion and government as the two related in a free society.

One can reduce the motivations for the religion clauses of the First Amendment to two fairly simple and straightforward incentives. First, there was the fervent desire to establish and protect the freedoms of individual citizens to the maximum degree possible in a political state. Second, there was an equally

---

[28]John C. Bennett, *Christians and the State* (New York: Charles Scribner's Sons, 1958) 209.

intense desire to avoid the evils experienced when a religion is established. It was apparent from European and some colonial experience that the fragile experiment in representative democracy was doomed to failure unless establishment was avoided. In their deliberations, the Founding Fathers were not considering an abstract social theory or remote possibility; they were responding to a condition that they had unhappily experienced. Indeed, one writer has noted that the "whole movement of the Enlightenment inclusive of democracy was a rebellion against and a desire for freedom from a monolithic church."[29]

Charles Smith argued that, contrary to much popular wisdom, there is nothing in the Constitution itself or in the records of its adoption that would support the contention that the Founding Fathers intended to construct the government on the basis of some specific form of Christianity.[30] While a most stimulating scholarly activity, arguments concerning the "Christian nature" of this country at the time of its founding have little relevance for the contemporary situation. The facts with which present discussion must deal are: (1) religious freedom is a fact of constitutional injunction, and (2) contemporary American society is characterized by a religious heterogeneity far more diverse and complex than could have been anticipated at the end of the eighteenth century.

The personal piety of the Founding Fathers is immaterial to the contemporary debate concerning religion and public education, or religion and government. Whatever the nature and quality of the Founding Fathers' faith, their writings and actions demonstrate their dedication to eliminating even a trace of religious establishment. Their experience had led them to understand the significance of religious freedom for society. Their personal faith in no way swayed them from their intent to disestablish the Christian church at the national level and, over

---

[29]Charles B. Smith, "Keeping Public Schools Secular," *Educational Forum* 29 (November 1964): 73.

[30]Ibid., 75.

a period of but a few years, at the state level. Apparently, the establishment of religion and the concomitant loss of religious liberty was completely inconsistent with their religious dedication. The oft-cited public expressions of religious devotion by some of the nation's early leaders were not a compromise of this dedication. Indeed, the public expression of personal religious faith by political figures has never been a sociopolitical danger. Danger is only present when, in whatever way, individual citizens are forced to agree with the religious beliefs of political leaders or join those leaders in public expressions of allegiance to that belief. Piety, including codes of ethics directly reflecting that piety, cannot be forced upon the public sector.

The bankruptcy of establishment and the general appeal of separation is illustrated in developments immediately surrounding the adoption of the First Amendment. In 1791, the year in which the First Amendment was adopted, four states—Massachusetts, Connecticut, New Hampshire, and Maryland—had partial establishments relating primarily to taxation. Citizens of those states were taxed for the support of religion, but each taxpayer was free to designate the sect or denomination to benefit from his contribution. However, disestablishment at the state level was complete when Massachusetts amended its statutes in 1833. Furthermore, this process of disestablishment was completed apart from the direct influence of the federal Constitution, for it was not until ratification of the Fourteenth Amendment, in 1868, that constitutional regulations were made directly applicable to state law. The evils of establishment had been experienced by the founders of this nation, and federal legislation was not needed to make the state legislatures set aside all vestiges of such a potentially divisive and destructive practice. It should also be noted that all of the states joining the Union after the Revolution wrote clauses into their constitutions prohibiting the establishment of religion.[31] Apparently the idea that separation was best for the young nation was one whose time had come. The early colonists who

---

[31]Pfeffer, *Church, State, and Freedom,* 126-27.

risked so much to bring this freedom into existence were not thereby expressing allegiance to a mere political theory or abstract philosophical ideal. They were, rather, reacting against the evils of establishment that they had experienced. Establishment had not worked for the betterment of mankind. It is, moreover, the responsibility of each generation to work out the relationship between religion and government that will best preserve the religious freedoms of its society.

Before turning to a discussion of the dynamics of this interaction as it pertains to public education, a brief potpourri of ideas concerning the governmental structure of the United States as it relates to contemporary religion-government relationships should be reviewed. Such a review might best begin with the fundamental goal of a democracy vis-à-vis religion.

The fundamental goal of American democracy with respect to religion is to establish and protect the freedom of individual citizens to the utmost degree possible while maintaining governmental and social integrity. As Justice Goldberg wrote in his concurring opinion in *Abington*:

> The First Amendment's guarantees, as applied to the States through the Fourteenth Amendment, foreclose not only laws "respecting an establishment of religion" but also those "prohibiting the free exercise thereof." These two proscriptions are to be read together, and in light of the single end which they are designed to serve. The basic purpose of the religion clause of the First Amendment is to promote and assure the fullest possible scope of religious liberty and tolerance for all and to nurture the conditions which secure the best hope of attainment of that end.[32]

However, religious liberty as a goal of government requires a delicate harmony of concerns because government must also ensure the common good. As one prominent Christian scholar noted, the political state evolves from the need of a people in community for order, social cohesion, and continuity of cultural tradition. Moreover, people invest the political state with the power to enforce the rules of order and maintain the general di-

---

[32]*Abington v. Schempp*, 374 U.S. 203, 305 (1963).

rection of society. Yet, such power and authority must always be used as instruments for establishing and maintaining community. "Therefore, we might define the state as the organ of the community which lays down laws and enforces them with supreme power for the purpose of furthering the common life."[33]

Nevertheless, American democracy has been shaped so that government is limited with regard to religion. In fact, the principle of separation of religion and government denies final authority to either institution. The union of religion and government confers a degree of divine sanction upon government and bestows religious blessing on its actions, while religion receives governmental sanction, and with it, exclusive power. The establishment clause of the First Amendment is intended to preclude either possibility.[34] Intentional disestablishment limits both the state and religions in the claims they may make upon the individual.

A fundamental distinction, however, should be drawn between religion and government.[35] Government is universal—the state affects all who reside within its parameters. One's relationship to the state is compulsory and can only be evaded if one leaves the country. On the other hand, religion, in its diversity, is a collection of particulars—religion in a democratic society is a patchwork of diverse sects, denominations, and commitments. Each religion does not enjoy universal allegiance or significance nor does it directly affect each citizen to the same degree or in the same manner. Affiliation with a religion or religious institution is voluntary. This distinction cannot be ignored when attempting to determine the proper relationship of religion to government. One can never forget that the com-

---

[33]George F. Thomas, *Christian Ethics and Moral Philosophy* (New York: Charles Scribner's Sons, 1955) 265.

[34]Philip H. Phenix, *Religious Concerns in Contemporary Education* (New York: Columbia University Teachers College, Bureau of Publications, 1959) 40.

[35]Loren P. Beth, *The American Theory of Church and State* (Gainesville FL: University of Florida Press, 1958) 145.

mon good is and must remain the fundamental concern of government. Government, therefore, cannot become entangled in the affairs of religious institutions nor can it support one theology to the exclusion of others. Individual freedom, however, is not an absolute, and the rights of others and the welfare of society must weigh heavily in governmental deliberations.

In this discussion about the delicate balance between the universal nature of government and the diverse nature of religion, the concept of the "rule of the majority" must be analyzed. Majority rule represents an expedient vehicle for accomplishing the tasks of government through elected representatives. However, the basic documents of our government make it clear that the main concern of government is to safeguard the freedom of the individual, not to advance the rule of the majority.

> . . . democracy is government not only for the people but by the people through representatives responsible to them. Its purpose is to serve the good of individual persons in the community, not subordinate them to a superpersonal entity such as the State or Race. Majority rule is not the essence of democracy; it is a practical method adopted to secure the responsibility of representatives to the people and to make possible the determination of general policy by as large a proportion of the citizens as possible.[36]

Perhaps it is appropriate to note that majority rule is not new in the history of government. The locus of governmental influence historically rests with the most powerful individuals or groups in a particular society. When government is to be controlled by some specific individual or group, the first step in securing political stability is to acquire, by one means or another, the support, or at least the acquiescence, of the majority of those persons to be governed. Political power is then exercised, not *by*, but *through* this majority. The unique element in the American experiment is that political power is bestowed upon that political entity whose rights have never before been broadly recognized or intentionally protected: the individual.

---

[36]Thomas, *Christian Ethics and Moral Philosophy*, 286.

In a democracy, power is extended to those who are typically powerless.

Interest here, however, is not in an analysis of majority rule as a political technique. Rather, analysis of the rule of the majority must be undertaken when majority status is employed in order to gain control of religion in the public sector. The fact that Christianity or a specific expression of Christianity may be the religious persuasion of the majority of persons in a community does not give that group the right to exercise religious control over that community in the public setting. It is not only the liberty of the religious majority of a community that is to be governmentally protected; religious liberty of each individual citizen in a community is the focus of the First Amendment. Public recognition of and preferential treatment for a specific religious expression unquestionably represents a movement in the direction of the establishment of that religion and, therefore, violates the First Amendment, regardless of how many may agree with such a movement. Under the Constitution, religious faith may not be subject to popular vote, political whim, or public authority; it cannot be promoted or inhibited by government.

It follows, therefore, that each religion may be protected only to the degree that it is willing for all religions to be equally protected.

> One basis for prohibiting the establishment of religion in America was and continues to be the great diversity of religious beliefs and religious institutions. Every religion can be protected only as it supports that protection for all other religions and for nonbelievers as well. The individual's responsibility is as fully clear.[37]

As William Temple said, if everyone in our society were a Christian of similar persuasion and equal devotion, the issue of religious freedom would be unimportant. American society, however, is not religiously homogenous. There are believers in

---

[37]Commission on Religion in the Public Schools, *Religion in the Public Schools* (Arlington VA: American Association of School Administrators, 1964) 3.

a variety of religions and equally devout nonbelievers. Even those persons who would qualify as believers have a quality of faith ranging from the saintly to an immaturity of belief appropriate for children but found in adults.[38] It is difficult to understand why those who strive so fervently to gain religious supremacy and control over others, typically employing the "majority rule" argument, never entertain the possibility that they might one day lose control to another religion equally dedicated. History shows that political power, when used to deny human freedom, is a tenuous possession.

The concept of freedom connotes the probability of extensive religious diversity rather than a singleness of religious faith. Those persons sincerely dedicated to human freedom place a high value on diversity.

> Though the stability of a culture depends on how much the conflicts it engenders can be supplied adequate outlets, still the strength of the democratic process is that it not only tolerates but welcomes difference. Democracy is based not upon a single value but upon a subtle and intricate multiple of values. Its strength rests in the balance of social institutions.[39]

So long as this nation remains dedicated to the democratic principles upon which its society is founded, it will be unable and unwilling to force uniformity of viewpoint or belief in anything—including religion. Even the sacred shibboleth that the United States is a "melting pot" for human diversity must be questioned. A free society does not seek a commonality of viewpoint. While the diversity of viewpoints and life-styles in American society must not be allowed to render society impotent, the attempt to subsume difference under one national style must likewise be rejected. Human diversity cannot destroy the freedoms Americans cherish; but one dare not destroy freedom in the attempt to preserve it. We are left with naught but a po-

---

[38]William Temple, *Citizen and Churchman* (London: Eyre and Spottiswoode, Publishers, n.d.) 6.

[39]Clyde Kluckhohn, *Mirror for Man* (New York: McGraw-Hill Book Co., 1949) 241.

litical affirmation of faith that the protection of individual liberty through a humane and judicious rule of law will create a society of sufficient strength and stability to endure despite its heterogeneity. History provides little precedent for such faith, but it provides abundant evidence that the oppression of human freedom leads only to individual and social disaster. Indeed, the history of religious establishments demonstrates that religion, when given governmental sanction and support, suppresses diversity and represses freedom. An establishment, therefore, is antithetical to representative democracy, as the Founding Fathers clearly understood.

Commitment to freedom of thought and belief requires that society be "pluralistic"; it must encourage and not simply tolerate diversity of personal commitment. But there appears to be widespread misunderstanding of the effect pluralism will have on individual belief. Although the concept of pluralism requires the right to divergent belief, it does not require personal respect for or agreement with the content of each belief nor does it require legal toleration of public action resulting from those beliefs.[40] Opponents of pluralism appear to think that the concept requires that they agree with beliefs that differ from their own. But, pluralism in no way jeopardizes the quality or content of one's personal belief. It simply assures the right of each individual to hold whatever personal belief that individual may care to affirm. This is the essence of individual liberty. One may feel and think and believe as one wishes. Moreover, one may communicate one's thoughts, feelings, and beliefs in all but total freedom—the single limitation being that such communication may not harm others or infringe upon their rights. One may also act as one's beliefs dictate so long as one's actions do not harm others, infringe upon the rights of others, or endanger the health, safety, or welfare of society.

To affirm pluralism is not to deny the power, or even the necessity, of the salvation offered by Christianity for those who

---

[40]Michael Scriven, "Cognitive Moral Education," *Phi Delta Kappan* 56 (June 1975): 694.

believe in it. Moreover, if pluralism is affirmed, the missionary or evangelical enterprise that some hold to be a primary duty of the Christian church is not violated. Pluralism, rather, provides an environment of freedom in which Christianity, or any other religion, may proclaim its truth as it chooses without coercion or oppression, either by another religion or by government.

In a pluralistic society, no religion can have its way completely, and compromise and accommodation are required.[41] For example, our society should encourage the moral and compassionate behavior typically associated with religious convictions, but religious belief generally connotes deep personal commitment, and such commitment is typically nonnegotiable. Also, institutional religions often generate absolutes in their doctrinal formulations, and those absolutes are, likewise, not negotiable. The compromise and accommodation required are obvious. While society can genuinely benefit from the ethical conduct and concern generated by religious faith, it cannot allow the nonnegotiable tenets of religious belief to be expressed in obligatory acts of public devotion. Fully conscious of this delicate situation, Reinhold Niebuhr called for a spirit of toleration.

> The spirit of toleration is an absolute necessity for any pluralistic society, for unless men understand the possibility of error lurking in their truth and are prepared to glean some truth in the errors which they combat, there is no possibility of that "limited warfare" which Herbert Butterfield rightly regards as the basis of a democratic society.[42]

The absolutism of religious doctrine is a potential deterrent to religious freedom. The notion that one's views are totally correct and that those who disagree are absolutely incorrect undermines the democratic principles upon which this government is founded if that sentiment is allowed to control public life.

---

[41]Mead, "Religion, Constitutional Federalism, Rights, and the Court," 21.

[42]Reinhold Niebuhr, "A Note on Pluralism," *Pluralism in America*, ed. John Cogley (Mountain View CA: World Publishing Co., 1958) 43.

As Justice Frankfurter pointed out, government must leave religion free to survive on its own merit and concentrate on the needs of the citizens of the state. Both government and religion are dedicated to the welfare of the individual and society, and this dedication typically harmonizes for the benefit of all. At other points, however, significant conflict develops, and there is no constitutional protection for religion from this overlap of concern with government. Government must make every effort to reconcile such conflict, but when conflict persists, the welfare of society in general must take precedence.[43] There can be no "wall of separation" between religion and government. In the complex, contemporary society, total separation is impossible because the realms of religion and government are far too influential in day-to-day social life. Justice Douglas expressed this problem clearly.

> There cannot be the slightest doubt that the First Amendment reflects the philosophy that Church and State should be separated. And so far as interference with the "free exercise" of religion and an "establishment" of religion are concerned, the separation must be complete and unequivocal. The First Amendment within the scope of its coverage permits no exceptions: the prohibition is absolute. The First Amendment, however, does not say that in every and all respects there shall be a separation of Church and State. Rather, it studiously defines the manner, the specific ways, in which there shall be no concert or union or dependency one on the other. That is the common sense of the matter. Otherwise the state and religion would be aliens to each other—hostile, suspicious, and even unfriendly.[44]

A page later, Justice Douglas provides an outstanding summary of our religion-government relationship.

> We are a religious people whose institutions presuppose a Supreme Being. We guarantee the freedom to worship as one chooses. We make room for as wide a variety of beliefs and creeds as the spiritual needs of man deem necessary. We sponsor an attitude on the part of government which shows no partiality to any one group and that lets each flourish according to the zeal of its adherents and the appeal of its dogma. When

---

[43]*McGowan v. State of Maryland*, 366 U.S. 420, 462-63 (1961).

[44]*Zorach v. Clauson*, 343 U.S. at 312 (1952).

the state encourages religious instruction or cooperates with religious authorities by adjusting the schedule of public events to sectarian needs, it follows the best of our traditions. For it then respects the religious nature of our people and accommodates the public service to their spiritual needs. To hold that it may not would be to find in the Constitution a requirement that the government show a callous indifference to religious groups. That would be preferring those who believe in no religion over those who do believe. Government may not finance religious groups nor undertake religious instruction nor blend secular and sectarian education nor use secular institutions to force one or some religion on any person. But we find no constitutional requirement which makes it necessary for government to be hostile to religion and to throw its weight against efforts to widen the effective scope of religious influence. The government may be neutral when it comes to competition between sects. It may not thrust any sect on any person. It may not make a religious observance compulsory. It may not coerce anyone to attend church, to observe a religious holiday, or to take religious instruction. But it can close its doors or suspend its operation as to those who want to repair to their religious sanctuary for worship or instruction.[45]

We are too far removed from the experience to have first-hand knowledge of the excesses to which establishment leads and are inclined to dismiss the evils of establishment as exaggerated, though they be historical fact. Moreover, we seem, in some romantic fashion, to wish to believe that Christianity, the majority religion of the nation, would not again be guilty of its past oppressions or of the excesses one sees in other nations of the modern world. One dare not make such an tragic mistake in judgment. In the quest to maintain a balance between religion and government in the nation, one must exercise extreme care that one of the unique elements of our national life-style is not jeopardized. Sidney Mead compares that balancing act to a game in which the American people risk their freedom.

It is helpful to think of American constitutional government as a game which "we the people" have engaged to play for the high stakes of freedom. The game has defined and known rules that are consented to as a condition of entering the game. The rules define the nature of the game, and set limits to permissible conduct in playing it. Referees or umpires are recognized as having power to interpret the rule-book of

---

[45]Ibid., 313-14.

the game, and their decisions have the sanction of coercive power if necessary. The rules themselves include a provision for modifying them without changing the basic character of the game (the constitutional right to amend). And, of course, it is recognized that the players also have the right if they grow weary of the game, to change to another game with a different set of rules (the revolutionary right). Therefore, it is very important if and when we question the decisions of the recognized referees to be very clear whether we are merely advocating amending the existing rules, or whether we are advocating shifting to a different kind of game.[46]

Frequently the religious desire to save the world is joined by an equal lack of appreciation for the delicate balance in the United States between religion and government. As a result, Americans are recommended to undertake a headlong rush down a path intended to return society to some prior state in which it is assumed that a particular religious faith enjoyed some advantage in its quest to save the world. The path leading back to this advantageous state involves some rather drastic changes in the form of religion-government relationship. Professor Mead was wise to caution that when we "question the decisions of the recognized referee" we must be very clear as to whether we are suggesting a change in the rules, or a change in the game itself. Are Americans seriously willing to change their "game" and surrender their religious liberty in search of a benign establishment which has never existed?

The decisions listed in appendix B show the breadth and complexity of the controversy associated with the religion-government relationship in the nation. The relationship of religion to public education is only a small part of the controversy, but the issues of the total controversy are perhaps more evident in that relationship than in any other. The controversy of the early eighties focused more frequently on religion and public education than on the other areas of religion-government controversy. Now that the background of the religion-government relation-

---

[46]Mead, "Religion, Constitutional Federalism, Rights, and the Court," 26-27.

ship in this country has been reviewed, we must consider the religion-government relationship in the context of public education.

CHAPTER 3

A Legal Definition
of Religion

In performing its responsibility for judicial review, the Supreme Court has announced decisions of great social significance; many have laid the course society must take in order to maintain the integrity of the religion clauses of the First Amendment. In order to understand those decisions that relate to the religion-government relationship, it is necessary to isolate the definition of religion the Court employed. The attempt to isolate this definition will also reveal the manner in which the Court understands the word *religion* as it appears in the First Amendment.

Finding or formulating a definition of religion is an extremely difficult task. Whereas the nuances of definition are extensive, definitions of religion can be reduced to three basic classifications. First, there are those definitions that concentrate upon the external characteristics, or social manifestations, of religion. Religion is defined in terms of those religious elements that constitute part of a commonly shared experience: ecclesiastical structures, institutional forms, dogmas, expressions of piety, codes of ethics, sacred writings and religious traditions, and so forth. The popularity of this definition lies in the fact that the elements of the definition are "objective" in nature; people can share these characteristics of religion through common experience and communication and, therefore, agree upon their "reality." The major difficulty in the definition is its superficiality. Many argue that the true meaning of religion is disregarded when it is defined in this way.

In contrast to the first definition, the second deals with precise identification of that "ultimate" or god toward which man's attention is directed through the religious experience. With this definition, one tries to understand the essence of religion, of that element of religious experience which provides fundamental meaning. This essence has been identified as God, Allah, "the way," a pantheon of divine beings, "the cosmic order," "the universal mind," "the good," "the eternal self," etc. This second approach has merit because it is an attempt to identify the essential focus of religion. The potential problem with this approach is that the more precise one becomes, the more restricted and sectarian one's definition becomes.

The third definition explains religion in terms of the religious experience. Such a definition attends to the dynamics and outcomes of that level of human experience that is identified as "religious" or "spiritual." In this approach one attempts to isolate those perceptions, emotions, awarenesses, or levels of commitment that are common to religious experience. The strength of this alternative is at once its essential weakness: religion is defined in terms of human experience. It may, therefore, be objected that such a definition is not of religion per se, but of that level of experience that humanity has chosen to call religious. Those who find this type of definition appealing would rebut that, when the dynamics of human perception and experience are clearly understood, this is the only approach available.

Formal definitions of religion, therefore, never seem completely satisfying. More often than not, something significant appears to be missing, and there is a nagging sense that one has not understood the full range of meaning involved in religion. Others complain that formal definitions are not sufficiently specific; that such definitions are typically too comprehensive to define anything. As these objections are made by theologians and philosophers, one should not entertain unrealistic expectations of a definition of religion from a legal viewpoint.

Still another objection states that no formal definition sufficiently comprehends the intensely personal significance of religious experience and commitment. It has been said, for example, that one does not *have* a self, one *is* a self. The same may be said of religion: one does not define religion for one *is* one's religion—religion is an expression of one's deepest being.

> . . . the truth of religion . . . is a truth that must penetrate my own personal existence, or it is nothing; and I must struggle to renew it in my life every day. . . . Strictly speaking, subjective truth is not a truth that I *have*, but a truth that I *am*.[1]

The problems encountered in attempting to define religion with social or legal rather than personal applicability are substantial indeed.

Difficulties of definition are compounded by the nature of American society. Issues encountered by the Court in addressing religion-government litigation would be significantly reduced if our society possessed a larger degree of religious homogeneity. Such, however, is not the case. The pluralism of our society reflects the "great" religions of the world along with affirmations of meanings in life that do not fit traditional or orthodox categories of religious identification. In *United States v. Ballard*, Justice Douglas wrote that people often believe what they cannot prove. Persons, in fact, do not respond equally to religious experience. A belief held as an absolute truth by one person may be incomprehensible to another. Indeed, the framers of the Constitution were aware of the "varied and extreme views of religious sects, of the violence of disagreement among them, and of the lack of any one religious creed on which all would agree."[2] When required to address litigation involving religion, courts frequently confront a multitude of differing and

---

[1]William Barrett, *Irrational Man* (Garden City NY: Doubleday and Co., 1958) 171.

[2]*United States v. Ballard*, 322 U.S. 78, 86-87 (1944); see also *McCollum v. Board of Education*, 68 S. Ct., at 468 (1948).

often antagonistic patterns of belief that are held with fervor and singularity of devotion. The potential for conflict is unavoidable.

This diversity of religious expression has compelled the Court to view religion as a uniquely personal, private matter (largely following the third option for formal definition discussed above). It is precisely this personal experience that is protected by our Constitution. Justice Black, in the *Engel* decision, wrote of religion as a sacred, holy, and personal experience, far too holy and personal to come under the control of a civil magistrate.[3] Justice Clark wrote that religion enjoys an exalted status in our society. This exalted status has been maintained through reliance upon the home, the religious institutions, and the individual. Therefore, it was not within the province of government to structure or to regulate the personal religion of the individual.[4]

The individuality of religious experience, from the legal point of view, is clearly expressed in the dissenting opinion of Justice Jackson in the *Ballard* decision.

> Belief in what one may demonstrate to the senses is not faith. All schools of religious thought make enormous assumptions, generally on the basis of revelations authenticated by some sign or miracle. The appeal in such matters is to a very different plane of credulity than is involved by representations of secular fact in commerce. Some who profess belief in the Bible read literally what others read as allegory or metaphor, as they read Aesop's fables. Religious symbolism is even used by some with the same mental reservation one has in teaching of Santa Claus or Uncle Sam or Easter bunnies.[5]

Fundamentally, this illustrates the application of the philosophical notion of nonreferability to religion. As applied to religion, nonreferability would assert that, from any standpoint save one's personal position, nothing in religion is forced, nothing is required; one may believe or disbelieve as one wishes on the

---

[3]*Engel v. Vitale*, 82 S. Ct., at 1267 (1962).

[4]*Abington v. Schempp*, 83 S. Ct., at 1574 (1963).

[5]*United States v. Ballard*, 322 U.S., at 94.

basis of experience. The religious experience and its interpretation are matters of individual judgment and commitment.

In order to protect equally the exalted status of this personal experience and the general welfare of society, the Court has frequently sought to distinguish between religious faith and religiously motivated behavior. The legal precedent seems to have been set by the *Reynolds* decision announced in 1878. In that decision, Chief Justice Waite wrote: "Laws are made for the government of actions, and while they cannot interfere with mere religious belief and opinions, they may with practices."[6] This position was reaffirmed in *Cantwell, Jones,* and *Barnette.*[7] Although this distinction between faith and action may not be satisfactory for many churchmen, its legal necessity is clear.

> Whilst legislation for the establishment of a religion is forbidden, and its free exercise permitted, it does not follow that everything which may be so called can be tolerated. Crime is not the less odious because sanctioned by what any particular sect may designate as religion.[8]

Not only is religion difficult to define, but that undertaking, from a legal standpoint, is complicated by the pluralistic nature of society and the legal commitment that religious belief lies beyond political or social control. Notwithstanding this commitment, action motivated by religious belief can require adjudication, and the Court has found it necessary to employ some concept of religion in its deliberations.

The 1890 decision in *Davis v. Beason* is a good starting point for analyzing the definition of religion the Court has used in rendering its decisions in religion-government litigation. Justice Field wrote:

> The term "religion" has reference to one's views of his relations to his Creator, and to the obligations they impose of reverence for his being

---

[6]*Reynolds v. United States* 98 S. Ct., at 166 (1978).

[7]See *Cantwell v. Connecticut*, 310 U.S. 296, 303-304 (1940); *Jones v. Opelika*, 316 U.S. 618 (1942); and *West Virginia v. Barnett*, 63 S. Ct., at 1188 (1943).

[8]*Davis v. Beason*, 133 U.S. 333, 345 (1890).

and character, and of obedience to his will. It is often confused with the
cultus or form of worship of a particular sect, but is distinguished from
the latter.[9]

Taken literally, this is a broad view of religion; one not necessarily linked to the Judeo-Christian tradition, although the
words "creator" and "his" lead one to suspect that Justice Field
intended such an identification. In short, this is a soundly theistic definition with broad potential for application. It is reminis-
cent of the language employed by the Founding Fathers.

There are some interesting points in Justice Field's definition. First, the personal quality of religion, which has remained
fundamental to the Court's understanding, is apparent. Second,
while the legal distinction is drawn between belief and action,
the Court early recognized the inseparability of the two in the
context of religious commitment and the effect of that commitment upon the life of the individual. Recognition of one's creator typically involves an obligation of obedience to the will of
that creator, and the point of potential legal conflict is, therefore, intrinsic. Third, religion is frequently equated with its institutional forms or characteristics, and Justice Field's caution
to avoid this identification was well taken. The Court has been
fairly successful in following his advice.

Whether or not Justice Field intended the potential inclu-
siveness of his concept of religion, Justice Hughes left little
room for misunderstanding when he spoke of the "essence of religion" in the *Macintosh* decision.

The essence of religion is belief in a relation to God involving duties superior to those arising from any human relation. . . . One cannot speak
of religious liberty, with proper appreciation of its essential and historic
significance, without assuming the existence of a belief in supreme allegiance to the will of God.[10]

This definition expresses a straightforward identification with
the Judeo-Christian tradition and, therefore, allows limited ap-

---

[9]Ibid., 342.

[10]*United States v. Macintosh*, 283 U.S. 605, 633-34 (1931).

plicability beyond that tradition. It illustrates the common tendency to define religion in terms of the dominant religious tradition of a culture. It also illustrates the attempt to define religion in terms of a specific focus (following the second type of definition discussed). Such an understanding would not serve the legal community well in a society characterized by thriving pluralism.

The shift in understanding made necessary by the pluralistic nature of society is unmistakably present in the *Minersville* decision. In this decision, the definition of religion encompasses those who believe in the orthodox sense and those who do not.

> Certainly the affirmative pursuit of one's convictions about the ultimate mystery of the universe and man's relation to it is placed beyond the reach of law. Government may not interfere with organized or individual expressions of belief or disbelief. Propagation of belief—or even of disbelief in the supernatural—is protected, whether in church or chapel, mosque or synagogue, tabernacle or meeting-house.[11]

As this analysis of the Court's reasoning progresses, it will become apparent that the Court has not formulated a precise definition of religion; rather, it discusses the nature of religion in brief statements with little elaboration. Care must be exercised, therefore, in amplifying its statements. Nonetheless, this confrontation with ultimate mystery that Justice Frankfurter wrote of is an aspect of human experience that many theologians, philosophers, and psychologists of religion have referred to as the "spiritual" or "depth" level of human experience. In the Court's view, this spiritual experience may or may not result in an affirmation of the existence of a supernatural power or being. Nonetheless, this profound spiritual experience is to be protected for it is viewed as religious regardless of its orthodoxy.

Justice Frankfurter continued his analysis, writing that the "right to freedom of religious belief, however dissident and however obnoxious to the cherished beliefs of others—even of a majority—is itself the denial of an absolute."[12] Thus, if we are

---

[11]*Minersville School District v. Gobitis*, 310 U.S. 586, 593 (1940).

[12]Ibid., 594.

seriously dedicated to religious freedom in a society characterized by religious heterogeneity, there cannot be an established
absolute that will serve as a bench mark for a legal definition of
religion. According to the Constitution, the Judeo-Christian tradition—or theism itself—cannot be adopted as *the* religious position of government or the standard for legal decisions. To
support pluralism is to affirm that there can be no specific religious absolute that will enjoy the official support, approval, and
protection of government. Through law, the religious experience will be protected and the content of that experience will
not be specified. Furthermore, a religion of the majority may
not exercise legal control nor may such a majority position receive preferential treatment by the government. The Constitution was written to protect the rights and freedoms of the
individual citizen and to structure a government dedicated to
that end.

The Court's prohibition of governmental recognition of one
form of religious expression creates no threat for individual or
institutional commitment to, or expression of, a particular form
of religious experience. What is denied is the right of any individual, group, or institution to force, through political or legal
means, a particular form of religious expression upon other individuals, groups, or institutions in the public context.

In search of a legal definition of religion, the Court has stead-
ily moved away from the first and second types of definition
and has moved toward the third. In *Barnette*, Justice Frankfurter followed this direction in his dissenting opinion. In that
dissent, he quoted with approval, a "definition" of religion formulated by Judge Augustus N. Hand in the ruling of a lower
court.

> And so, when confronted with the task of considering the claims of im-
> munity from obedience to a law dealing with civil affairs because of re-
> ligious scruples, we cannot conceive religion more narrowly than in the
> terms in which Judge Augustus N. Hand recently characterized it: "It is
> unnecessary to attempt a definition of religion; the content of the term
> is found in the history of the human race and is incapable of compres-
> sion into a few words. Religious belief arises from a sense of the inad-
> equacy of reason as a means of relating the individual to his fellow-men

and to his universe. . . . [It] may justly be regarded as a response of the individual to an inward mentor, call it conscience or God, that is for many persons at the present time equivalent to what has been thought a religious impulse. 2 Cir., 133F. 2d. 703, 708."[13]

In the religious experience, human beings confront the limits of their existence; experiencing, in traditional theological terminology, "human finitude." Encountering their own limitations, they may become aware of the ground of being, the "wholly other," the meaning of their existence, or of God. Whatever terms are used to communicate the nature of this experience, it is the religious experience and, as such, lies beyond positive or negative governmental manipulation.

A year later, also in dissent, Justice Jackson reaffirmed the sanctity of the individual's religious experience.

William James, who wrote on these matters as a scientist, reminds us that it is not theology or ceremonies which keep religion going. Its vitality is in the religious experiences of many people. . . . If religious liberty includes, as it must, the right to communicate such experiences to others, it seems to me an impossible task for juries to separate fancied ones from real ones, dreams from happenings, and hallucinations from true clairvoyance. Such experiences, like some tunes and colors, have existence for one, but none at all for another. They cannot be verified to the minds of those whose field of consciousness does not include religious insight.[14]

Thus, religion is a matter of individual perception. While a religious experience might be valid for one person, it may not be for another. The breadth of the Court's definition of religion is attained at the expense of specificity. How is one, in keeping with such a definition, to determine the presence or absence of experience that may be validly understood as religious? Justice Jackson's opinion was that such a determination is not a legitimate legal undertaking; rather, in legal cases, the individual's evaluation of the religious nature of the experience is the material judgment. Legal dispute must address the public actions

---

[13]*West Virginia v. Barnette*, 63 S. Ct., at 1194-95 (1943).

[14]*United States v. Ballard*, 322 U.S., at 93.

of the religious individual, not the legitimacy of the religious experience. When reading the whole of Justice Jackson's opinion,
one senses the anxiety reflected in this tacit admission that
greater specificity could not be attained. Legal difficulty was
certain to be forthcoming. The best of intentions notwithstanding, the Court would be required to consider some criteria by
which to ascertain the presence (but not the legitimacy) of religious experience.

In 1961, discussion in the *McGowan* decision brought the
Court closer to a definition of religion applicable to a pluralistic
society. "By its nature, religion—in the comprehensive sense in
which the Constitution uses that word—is an aspect of human
thought and action which profoundly relates the life of man to
the world in which he lives."[15] This statement contains the essence of the legal definition of religion the Court had been required to formulate as a result of religion-government litigation.
It found it necessary, following the trend set in the *Minersville*
decision, to view religion apart from any specific transcendent,
supernatural, or theistic focus for religious faith or creed.

The Court is clearly seeking a definition that will facilitate legal decision making in the presence of religious diversity. In
Ballard, the Court lamented the difficulty of verifying the content of the religious experience. In *McGowan*, the Court was
seeking an essence that might be common to a variety of religious experiences. It was searching for a functional descriptive
(rather than prescriptive) definition. A prescriptive definition
would indicate a movement toward establishing a legal orthodoxy. Therefore, religion is defined as that level of human feeling, thought, and action that profoundly relates man to his life
in this world. Justice Frankfurter's use of the word *profound*
surely indicates that this relationship is not to be understood su-
perficially, as one resulting from the normal course of daily
events. Though this definition had breadth, it was not sufficiently specific regarding the nature of the religious experience;
and the Court was to find that specificity necessary as it contin-

---

[15]*McGowan v. State of Maryland*, 81 S. Ct., at 1154 (1961).

ued to address litigation brought about by religion-government controversy.

The *Torcaso* decision amplified and reinforced the trend toward the third type of definition expressed in *McGowan* but again failed to provide sufficient specificity.

> We repeat and again reaffirm that neither a State nor a Federal Government can constitutionally force a person "to profess a belief or disbelief in any religion." Neither can constitutionally pass laws or impose requirements which aid all religions as against non-believers, and neither can aid those religions based on a belief in the existence of God as against those religions founded on different beliefs.[16]

Belief and disbelief are equally protected from governmental regulation. The Court's definition of religion is expanded to include those expressions of disbelief present in American culture. While the term *disbelief* is commonly used in a pejorative or negative sense, the Court had no judgmental intention. The word is used, rather, to distinguish those "spiritual" experiences that do not result in traditional or orthodox faith affirmations or in the affirmation of some form of theism. This nontheistic option was acknowledged in *Minersville* and *Barnette*, but the important point in *Torcaso* is that it is inappropriate to view religion—from the legal standpoint—exclusively in terms of belief in God or other theistic or supernatural ultimates (building upon the breadth of *McGowan*). The protection of the Constitution may not be restricted to theistic religions. According to a footnote at the end of the last quotation, those "religions in this country which do not teach what would generally be considered a belief in the existence of God are Buddhism, Taoism, Ethical Culture, Secular Humanism and others."[17] From a legal standpoint, religion may not be defined in terms of one particular ultimate; a crucial stipulation in a pluralistic society dedicated to religious freedom.

It was in the *Seeger* decision that the struggle to attain the specificity heretofore absent in the legal definition of religion

---

[16]*Torcaso v. Watkins*, 367 U.S. 488, 495 (1961).

[17]Ibid., 495.

was concluded. In *Seeger*, the Court was required, by the nature of the litigation, to address the problem of defining the nature of the religious experience while remaining loyal to the breadth of understanding required by the nature of society. Justice Clark, in delivering the opinion of the Court, wrote:

> We have concluded that Congress, in using the expression "Supreme Being" rather than the designation "God," was merely clarifying the meaning of religious training and belief so as to embrace all religions and to exclude essentially political, sociologial, or philosophical views. We believe that under this Constitution, the test of belief "in a relation to a Supreme Being" is whether a given belief that is sincere and meaningful occupies a place in the life of its possessor parallel to that filled by the orthodox belief in God of one who clearly qualifies for the exemption.[18]

Justice Clark's distinction closely parallels the distinction Paul Tillich drew between religion and quasi-religion.[19] Tillich's distinction was based upon the difference between conditioned and unconditioned ultimate concerns and the illustrations used by the Court fit well into his categories. Indeed, the parallel may have been intentional for Justice Clark continued:

> . . . we believe this construction embraces the ever-broadening understanding of the modern religious community. The eminent Protestant theologian, Dr. Paul Tillich, whose views the Government concedes would come within the statute, identifies God not as a projection "out there" or beyond the skies but as the ground of our very being.[20]

In following the third definition of religion, the Court was forced by the nature of the litigation it faced to determine what element of the religious experience distinguishes it from other types of human experience. Having progressively abandoned the attempt to specify the focus of the religious experience (for

---

[18]*United States v. Seeger*, 85 S. Ct., at 854 (1965).

[19]See Paul Tillich, *Christianity and the Encounter of the World Religions* (New York: Columbia University Press, 1963) 5-7.

[20]*United States v. Seeger*, 85 S. Ct., at 861.

obvious legal reasons), some precise quality was nevertheless required for the third definition. Consequently, the Court reasoned that religious experience was present when that experience was involved with or resulted in an ultimate concern (the nature of which would remain unspecified) to which an individual's life was dedicated. Such a concern must fulfill the same function as does an orthodox believer's dedication to God.

Justice Clark continued his analysis and application of the definition of religion.

> Under the 1940 Act it was necessary only to have a conviction based upon religious training and belief; we believe that is all that is required here. Within that phrase would come all sincere religious beliefs which are based upon a power or being, or upon a faith, to which all else is subordinate or upon which all else is ultimately dependent. The test might be stated in these words: A sincere and meaningful belief which occupies in the life of its possessor a place parallel to that filled by the God of those admittedly qualifying for the exemption comes within the statutory definition.[21]

Reading further:

> In summary, Seeger professed "religious belief" and "religious faith." He did not disavow any belief "in a relation to a Supreme Being"; indeed he states that "the cosmic order does, perhaps, suggest a creative intelligence." He decried the tremendous "spiritual" price man must pay for his willingness to destroy human life. In light of his beliefs and the unquestioned sincerity with which he held them, we think the Board, had it applied the test we propose today, would have granted him the exemption. We think it clear that the beliefs which prompted his objection occupy the same place in his life as the belief in a traditional deity holds in the lives of his friends, the Quakers.[22]

McGowan provided the level of precision possible within the limits of a legal definition of religion. Religious belief does indeed help mankind relate to life and to this world, but so do many forms of thought that do not, and would not, claim religious identification. Something, therefore, was missing from

---

[21]Ibid., 859.

[22]Ibid., 864-65.

the concept of religion in *McGowan*. That missing element was the ultimate commitment of the life of the individual who has been involved with what has historically been called a religious experience. Religious experience involves this element of commitment to an ultimate concern beyond the individual, a concern that conditions all else, to which all else is subordinated, and from which the meaning of life is derived. Mere sincerity of feeling is not the deciding factor. In his concurring opinion, Justice Douglas said:

> The words "a Supreme Being" have no narrow technical meaning in the field of religion. Long before the birth of our Judeo-Christian civilization the idea of God had taken hold in many forms. Mention of only two—Hinduism and Buddhism—illustrates the fluidity and evanescent scope of the concept.[23]

Justice Douglas could not have selected two more appropriate illustrations: the teachings of Buddha were originally nontheistic while Hinduism is polytheistic.

Application of this definition of religion may be seen in a 1970 decision addressing conscientious objection. In delivering the opinion of the Court, Justice Black wrote:

> If an individual deeply and sincerely holds beliefs that are purely ethical or moral in source and content but that nevertheless impose upon him a duty of conscience to refrain from participation in any war at any time, those beliefs certainly occupy in the life of that individual "a place parallel to that filled by . . . God" in traditionally religious persons. Because his beliefs function as a religion in his life, such an individual is as much entitled to a "religious" conscientious objector exemption . . . as is someone who derives his conscientious opposition to war from traditional religious convictions.[24]

In *Welsh*, Justice Black described the controlling factor for a legal, rather than a theological, understanding of the concept of ultimate concern: the "duty of conscience" imposed upon the individual; and the nature and quality of an individual's behavior as a result of the presence of this ultimate commitment. In

---

[23]Ibid., 865.

[24]*Welsh v. United States*, 90 S. Ct., at 1796 (1970).

effect, the religious priority may rest with the nature of an individual's ultimate concern, but the legal priority remains focused upon the behavior of an individual as a result of commitment to an ultimate concern. From a legal perspective, the nature of the ultimate concern is not material; the significant matter is the effect of the ultimate upon the life of an individual.

Early in this chapter, three options for defining religion were presented. The discussion has demonstrated the integral relationship of the second and third options: that it is difficult to analyze the religious experience apart from its ultimate, and vice versa. Therefore, while there are three options for definition, there are two options for viewing religion: the external perspective represented by the first definition and the internal perspective represented by the second and the third definitions.

Reference to the religion-government decisions listed in appendix B will show that the Court has been forced to utilize both viewpoints in addressing religion-government controversy. The Court will interpret religion in keeping with the manner in which religion is presented in litigation; for example, when addressing litigation related to religious institutions, the Court will view religion from an external perspective; when addressing problems related to religious belief,[25] the Court will view religion from an internal perspective.

Litigation involving religious belief has caused the Court to move toward its current definition of religion. In such litigation, the Court has attempted to define religion as a phenomenon of human experience, thereby defining the essence of religion from a human perspective in order that legal problems might be addressed. Those persons who view religion in terms of a specific configuration of characteristics (the first option discussed in

---

[25]See for example, those decisions listed in appendix B under the headings Religion and Taxation, Church Governance, and The State and Sectarian Education for illustrations of the external viewpoint; consult decisions under the headings Religious Freedom and Religion and Military Service for illustrations of the internal approach.

the opening of this chapter) or who define religion in terms of a specific ultimate (the second option) will find little in the Court's definition with which they can agree.

Irrespective of the popular support a legal definition of religion may enjoy, theological thought supports such a point of view—the Court has not created its experiential understanding ex *nihilo*. Modern-day theologians have wrestled with the nature of the religious experience and the dynamics of the relationship of that experience to its ultimate. Joachim Wach discussed four criteria for defining the religious experience. First, the religious experience represents man's response to what he conceives to be ultimate reality—a reality that gives meaning and structure to life. Second, religious experience has a holistic quality—it involves the total human being and his or her behavior. Third, religious experience is the most meaningful experience that an individual can have. Fourth, religious experience directly affects an individual's commitments and, consequently, the nature, quality, and direction of one's life. Wach believed that all four criteria must be present in a religious experience.[26]

According to modern theological thought, religious experience is that experience or continuum of experiences through which an individual confronts that being, power, structure, process, or concern that provides essential meaning for his life. In religious experience, persons encounter the foundation for the answers to their most profound "why?" questions. It is in religious experience that one progressively attains a meaningful vision of what one's life is all about; of how one as an individual is to relate to one's own being, other persons, and one's world. Religious experience, in short, influences the direction and quality of one's life. In theology, this experience has been identified as the awareness of the "mysterium tremendum,"[27] or a feeling of

---

[26]Joachim Wach, "Universals in Religion," *Religion, Culture and Society*, ed. Louis Schneider (New York: John Wiley and Sons, 1964) 39-40.

[27]Rudolf Otto, *The Idea of the Holy*, trans. J. W. Harvey (New York: Oxford University Press, n.d.) 12.

absolute dependence.[28] Some have characterized it as certainty
that the meaning of experience is open and available to man.[29]
Others have conceptualized this experience as a kind of *a priori*
confidence in the meaning and worth of life.[30] Paul Tillich concluded that the religious experience is unique and that religion,
therefore defies precise classification or inclusion in specific
categories.

> In this situation, without a home . . . religion suddenly realizes that it
> does not need such a place . . . It is at home everywhere, namely, in the
> depth of all functions of man's spiritual life. Religion is the dimension
> of depth in all of them. Religion is the aspect of depth in the totality of
> the human spirit.
>
> What does the metaphor *depth* mean? It means that the religious as-
> pect points to that which is ultimate, infinite, unconditional in man's
> spiritual life. Religion, in the largest and most basic sense of the word,
> is ultimate concern. And ultimate concern is manifest in all creative
> functions of the human spirit.[31]

Religion, from this perspective, is not a specific category of human experience but is the spiritual element in all creative human experiences. Its focus has ultimate meaning for the
individual, shaping and directing that individual more than any
other single experience.

Two quotations, one from Dietrich Bonhoeffer and a second
from J. A. T. Robinson, illustrate this development in theological thought.

> I should like to speak of God not on the borders of life but at its centre,
> not in weakness but in strength, not, therefore, in man's suffering and
> death but in his life and prosperity. On the borders it seems to me better

---

[28]Friedrich Schleiermacher, *The Christian Faith*, ed. H. R. Mackintosh
and S. S. Stewart (New York: Harper and Row, Publishers, n.d.) 1:17-18.

[29]Martin Buber, *Eclipse of God* (New York: Harper and Row, Publishers,
1952) 35.

[30]Schubert M. Ogden, *The Reality of God* (New York: Harper and Row,
Publishers, 1966) 34.

[31]Paul Tillich, *Theology of Culture*, ed. R. C. Kimball (New York: Oxford
University Press, 1959) 7-8.

to hold our peace and leave the problem unsolved. . . . The "beyond" of God is not the beyond of our perceptive faculties. . . . God is the "beyond" in the midst of our life.[32]

God is not 'out there'. He is in Bonhoeffer's words 'the "beyond" in the midst of our life', a depth of reality reached 'not on the borders of life but at its centre', not by a flight of the alone to the alone, but, in Kierkegaard's fine phrase, by a 'deeper immersion in existence'. For the word 'God' denotes the ultimate depth of all our being, the creative ground and meaning of all our existence.[33]

The otherness of God and the individuality of religious experience appear to merge in these formulations. One of the prominent psychologists of the twentieth century summarized the trend as follows:

. . . it is . . . increasingly developing that leading theologians, and sophisticated people in general, define their god, not as person, but as a force, a principle, a gestalt-quality of the whole of Being, an integrating power that expresses the unity and therefore the meaningfulness of the cosmos, the "dimension of depth," etc.[34]

It is on the basis of this kind of reasoning that the Court has come to its current definition of religion when forced, by the nature of the litigation before it, to address religion from an internal perspective.

As both Paul Tillich and Reinhold Niebuhr noted,[35] religion has two dimensions: the vertical and the horizontal. The vertical is that dimension in which man experiences his ultimate concern. The horizontal dimension is the dimension in which self relates to the other. The horizontal dimension is nourished by

---

[32]Dietrich Bonhoeffer, *Letters and Papers from Prison* (Huntington NY: Fontana Books, 1953) 93.

[33]John A. T. Robinson, *Honest to God* (Philadelphia: Westminster Press, 1963) 47.

[34]Abraham H. Maslow, *Religions, Values, and Peak-Experience* (Columbus: Ohio State University Press, 1964) 55.

[35]See Paul Tillich, *The Protestant Era,* trans. J. L. Adams (Chicago: University of Chicago Press, 1957); Reinhold Niebuhr, *The Nature and Destiny of Man* (New York: Charles Scribner's Sons, 1949).

the vertical and, as Martin Buber argued, facilitates encounter with it.[36] The vertical dimension, in these terms, is absolutely protected by the laws of our land. On the other hand, the horizontal dimension of human relationship is the one in which behavior, as motivated by religious experience, may conflict with those legal structures designed to protect the rights of the individual and the welfare of society. It is this horizontal dimension that frequently requires the Court's attention.

In a culture characterized by religious diversity, it is crucial that the Court attempt to define religion in terms of broadest applicability rather than at the level of specific or unique (sectarian) structures or characteristics. It is for this reason that the Court has taken the approach to religion shown in its recent decisions. There is no evidence in the writings of the Court that the justices relish the task of theological investigation and pronouncement. They are and remain jurists, not theologians. Nevertheless, in a thoroughly pluralistic society dedicated to the maintenance of religious liberty, theological discussion is unavoidable in the adjudication of government-religion controversy.

---

[36]See Martin Buber, *I and Thou*, 2d ed., trans. R. G. Smith (New York: Charles Scribner's Sons, 1958).

CHAPTER 4

The Origin and Evolution
of the Religion-Public
Education Relationship

A number of years ago, V. T. Thayer identified an important
social phenomenon when he wrote that no other manifestation
of a people's culture more clearly reflects their hopes and aspirations than does the education they provide for their young.
"Schools reflect what men out of their own experience most sincerely wish for their offspring. In the curriculum and the conduct of schools . . . is written a people's conception of the
essentials of the good life."[1]

Notwithstanding its imperfections, American education is an
accomplishment of which all should be proud. The very presence of this complex and extensive system of education in society demonstrates a unique and commendable dedication to
attaining the best possible life for all members of society. This
chapter will examine the more significant processes and events
that contributed to the contemporary public school system and
its relationship to religion.[2]

---

[1]V. T. Thayer, *Religion in Public Education* (New York: Viking Press,
1947) 26.

[2]For a thorough study of this evolution, see Robert Michaelsen, *Piety in
the Public School* (New York: Macmillan Co., 1970).

The Colonial Beginnings

Education in colonial America clearly bore the characteristics of its European ancestry. With the pressures of establishing a foothold in the wilderness of the New World and winning political independence, little time or thought was devoted to creating an educational system that would facilitate the emerging sociopolitical desires of those first settlers. The colonists, rather, followed the pattern of education common in Europe. While generalizations are often misleading, several broad statements may help to explain the educational theories and practices the settlers brought with them. Except at the most rudimentary level, schooling in Europe was considered a privilege of social class: it was an opportunity generally restricted to those who were blessed with material advantage and, therefore, was considered a matter of private, family responsibility. Institutional schooling was reserved for that small minority who would provide leadership in church or state or who would practice the healing art of medicine. Except for guilds and apprenticeships that emphasized skill development and practical education, European education was classical. Ideas of the past were studied largely for the sake of knowing, not doing. Almost without exception, European education was controlled by the established church. In the few exceptions to that rule, education was privately sponsored.

Protestantism, however, can be credited with creating a substantial change in the pattern of classical, largely elitist schooling—the vernacular school. The vernacular school was intended for the common child (those children who normally had no access to formal schooling) and emphasized training in reading. This schooling resulted from the Protestant belief that each individual was responsible for his or her own salvation before God; a tenet of faith that made it necessary that each individual be able to read the primary source necessary for that salvation—the Bible. The rather novel idea that all human beings needed to be taught the basic academic skills of reading and writing attained some recognition. Although the raison d'être for this education was salvation of the soul, it was none-theless beneficial to individuals. Vernacular schooling, which was free to all but mandatory for none, represented a significant departure from the classical mold of European education. The idea that basic education was a fundamental human need was to come to full fruition in the soil of the New World.

Three broad patterns of education developed in colonial America. In the southern colonies, the education of children re-mained the responsibility of individual families. Towns of any size were few, and town or parochial schools could not find root in the expansive, almost totally agricultural south. The planta-tion owners knew that education was valuable for their children if only because it helped to solidify and perpetuate their chil-dren's social status. The children of this "landed gentry" were educated through one of two ways: some were sent back to Eu-rope to be formally schooled; others were taught at home by a tutor imported (often as an indentured servant) from the Old Country. In either case, this education involved a large invest-ment of family funds. In order to ameliorate the financial drain, the practice developed of gathering the children of several plantation owners at one home where these children could be taught by a single tutor, each family paying what amounted to tuition and fees for the instruction, support, and care of the child. Some "host" plantation owners even erected buildings to facilitate this collective schooling. Most historians of American education believe that the seeds of American private education were thereby planted deeply in the soil of the Southern colonies and in the New World itself.

The situation in the Middle colonies differed markedly. Of all the colonies, the Middle colonies had the greatest religious di-versity. They also contained the bulk of the population. Mem-bers of a variety of religious sects migrated to this central area searching for freedom of religious expression and belief; and for employment in the commercial enterprises that flourished there. There were frequent disputes between the numerous re-ligious sects, and, because there was no establishment, no single educational institution could be developed. Motivated by the same religious beliefs that had prompted the creation of the

Protestant vernacular schools in Europe, the denominations, sects, and individual churches accepted the responsibility for educating the children of their flock. This education provided the foundation for American parochial education.

The type of education that developed in the New England colonies contained the embryo of the American public school. In a monumental break with European tradition, the people of the Massachusetts Bay Colony chose to see education as a public responsibility rather than as a strictly familial one. The goal of "public" education was to guide the young along the paths of religious faith and moral conduct consonant with the Calvinist theology that dominated the social structure. Because orthodoxy is a social or public concern in a theocratic society, learning was not viewed as an end in itself, but as a means to building and deepening the religious commitment of the student. The church totally controlled the state, and the compact New England townships, when influenced by the church-government union and informed by its emphasis upon religious education, created township schools. These township schools became the template for the modern public school. The shift from education as a privilege of class to education as a social necessity was a significant change in educational theory and practice.

At first, the development of township schools in New England was inconsistent. However, in the Law of 1624, the Bay Colony showed its serious intent by enacting legislation that provided for basic education. In 1647, additional legislation compelled all towns of one hundred householders or more to provide elementary education, an education that would teach more than reading. This legislation, which came to be known as the "old deluder Satan Act," read in part as follows:

> It being one chief project of the old deluder, Satan, to keep man from the knowledge of the Scriptures. . .
>
> It is therefore ordered, that every township in this jurisdiction, after the Lord hath increased them to the number of fifty householders, shall then forthwith appoint one within their town to teach all such children as shall resort to him to write and read . . . and it is further ordered, that

where any town shall increase to the number of one hundred families or householders they shall set up a grammar school. . . [3]

The idea of universal education that had found expression in the Protestant vernacular school had attained such support that a legislative act was passed requiring all children of a township be educated at public expense and, in the remarkable embellishment of the act of 1647, required that all towns of one hundred or more provide an elementary education for all children. In a theocratic environment, nothing is purely public or secular; everything is religious in nature and intent. Nevertheless, the idea of an education for every child had been given legislative expression and was to enjoy significant success in the future. The European practice of limiting education to the privileged was renounced; the idea of education as a public responsibility was to shape the educational structure of the nation.

The Development of Public Education

Notwithstanding the development of the township schools in New England, the view of the framers of the Constitution respecting public education remains unclear. Thomas Jefferson clearly expressed his belief in public education in "A Bill for the More General Diffusion of Knowledge."

Whereas it appeareth that however certain forms of government are better calculated than others to protect individuals in the free exercise of their natural rights, and are at the same time themselves better guarded against degeneracy, yet experience hath shewn, that even under the best forms, those entrusted with power have, in time, and by slow operations, perverted it into tyranny; and it is believed that the most effectual means of preventing this would be, to illuminate, as far as practicable, the minds of the people at large, and more especially to give them knowledge of those facts, which history exhibiteth, that, possessed thereby of the experience of other ages and countries, they may be enabled to know ambition under all its shapes, and prompt to exert their natural powers to defeat its purposes. And whereas it is generally true that that people will be happiest whose laws are best, and are best

---

[3]James W. Noll and S. P. Kelly, eds., *Foundations of Education in America* (New York: Harper and Row, Publishers, 1970) 162.

administered, and that laws will be wisely formed, and honestly administered, in proportion as those who form and administer them are wise
and honest; whence it becomes expedient for promoting the public happiness that those persons, whom nature hath endowed with genius and
virtue, should be rendered by liberal education worthy to receive, and
able to guard the sacred deposit of the rights and liberties of their fellow
citizens, and that they should be called to that charge without regard to
wealth, birth or other accidental condition or circumstance, but the in-
digence of the greater number disabling them from so educating, at
their own expense, those of their children whom nature hath fitly
formed and disposed to become useful instruments for the public, it is
better that such should be sought for and educated at the common expense of all, than that the happiness of all should be confided to the
weak or wicked. . . [4]

Jefferson's dedication to the establishment of a just government
in the New World led to the view that education for all at public
expense is required for the public welfare.

The necessity for public education was an idea no longer confined to the Massachusetts Bay Colony. Noah Webster wrote:
"In our American republics, where government is in the hands
of the people, knowledge should be universally diffused by
means of public schools."[5] In spite of such influential support, it
is not known what the framers of the Constitution collectively
thought about public education. All that is known for certain is
that they did not consider education to be the responsibility of
the new national government. The Constitution does not mention education. Rather, Article 10 of the Amendments to the
Constitution reads as follows: "The powers not delegated to the
United States by the Constitution, nor prohibited by it to the
States, are reserved to the States, respectively, or to the people." It is, hence, commonly assumed that the writers of the
Constitution intended to give the responsibility for education to
the states of the new union, if not, in the European tradition, to
the people themselves. Whatever was implied, as history has
shown, the states assumed the responsibility for education, al-

---

[4]Ibid., 143-44.

[5]Ibid., 156.

though there was no rush to undertake the weighty task. By 1800, only seven of the sixteen states had enacted legislation providing for public education.

Although public education had a modest beginning, the idea of public education supported by common tax funds was gaining momentum. As the momentum grew, two factors concerning the religious makeup of the nation required a fundamental departure from the nature of the colonial New England township schools upon which public schools were patterned. The first factor was the broad religious diversity of the nation. This diversity was primarily Protestant but also included growing numbers of Roman Catholics and Jews. As a result, no single religious institution or orthodoxy was capable of providing the religious structure that had nurtured the township schools of Massachusetts. This first factor led to the second: if there was no common religious orthodoxy, which one of the many religious positions would control the religious education undertaken in these public institutions? The conclusion was inevitable: the new public schools would be nonsectarian in control.

As the nonsectarian nature of public schools became apparent, a sense of urgency developed among the Protestant sects. If one sect could not be assured that its fundamental tenets would guide the curriculum of the public schools, it was necessary to be certain that the conflicting tenets of other sects would not guide the curriculum of public schools. Furthermore, the Protestant sects were united in their desire to prevent Roman Catholicism from controlling the public schools. Will Herberg noted that, with respect to the relationship of public schools to religion, "it was not the 'separationist' ban in the First Amendment that stood in the way, but the fragmentation of religion in the country and the mutual hostility and suspicion so rife among religious groups."[6]

---

[6]Will Herberg, "Religion and Education in America," *Religious Perspectives in American Culture*, ed. J. H. Smith and A. L. Jamison, vol. 2 of *Religion in American Life*, 4 vols. (Princeton NJ: Princeton University Press, 1961) 44.

R. Freeman Butts provided a concise and informative discussion of the religious turmoil that gave impetus to the development of secular public education.[7] In his discussion, he isolated three factors that contributed substantially to the development of the secular public schools: (1) the growing legal emphasis in state law upon the separation of religion and government, which included the realization that tax moneys could not be used to support religious instruction; (2) the discord and strife among Protestant sects and denominations; and (3) the growing strength, through immigration, of Roman Catholicism. He summarized these developments as follows:

> With few exceptions the major Protestant denominations turned more and more to the idea of a nonsectarian common school. This was sometimes the result of weariness with sectarian ideological disputes, sometimes in recognition of the added expense of independent denominational effort, sometimes of the need for counteraction against the Catholic threat, and sometimes of a genuine belief in the priority of political community as the goal of training in common citizenship.[8]

The religious considerations were complex indeed, but for whatever reasons, most of the Protestant denominations simply withdrew from their attempts to gain control over public schools.

The option to maintain existing parochial schools and to develop new ones was certainly available, but Protestant denominations typically rejected this alternative. "A lack of trained teachers, a lack of money, a lack of pupils, a lack of strong leadership for parochial schools, and the lassitude of church members were all factors that permitted education to come under the control of the state."[9] Protestants appeared generally to lack the zeal or resources required to found and maintain an ex-

---

[7]See R. Freeman Butts, *Public Education in the United States* (New York: Holt, Rinehart and Winston, 1978) 114-24.

[8]Ibid., 118-19.

[9]Carl S. Meyer, "Development of the American Pattern in Church-State Relations," *Church and State Under God*, ed. A. G. Huegli (St. Louis MO: Concordia Publishing House, 1964) 242.

tensive system of parochial schools. But there may have been another reason for their lack of commitment to parochial education. As Professor Butts pointed out, the Great Awakening had promoted the idea that there was a common Protestant-Christian orthodoxy that transcended all sectarian differences. There also existed a widespread belief that this Protestant orthodoxy was superior to Roman Catholic, Jewish, or nationalistic beliefs. This idea of a common piety enjoyed considerable support among the Protestant faiths of the day.[10] Many Protestants assumed, perhaps, that because of their majority status in the American religious community, this common Protestant orthodoxy would prevail in public schools and that there was, therefore, no need to continue their battle. Their retreat may not have been totally benign in motivation.

As the religious controversy wore on, Roman Catholics, under force of their canon law, largely resorted to establishing parochial schools to serve their children's religious and educational needs. Jews became stalwart defenders of nonsectarian public schools. Some Protestant sects and denominations engaged in local skirmishes among themselves aimed at gaining control of public schools. It became clear to those individuals more interested in the cognitive growth of the young than in sectarian posturing that the new schools could not be subject to sectarian control if they were to be truly public. However, this growing realization did not reflect an intention to drive religion from public schools. As Robert Ulich stated, that was never an intention among those who lead in the design and implementation of public schools. Rather, the nonsectarian public education resulted from social divisiveness brought about by sectarian groups and the growing pluralism of the society the schools were to serve.[11]

---

[10]Butts, *Public Education*, 7.

[11]Robert Ulich, "The Schools and Religion, the Historical Present," *Foundations of American Education*, ed. J. A. Johnson et al., 3d ed. (Boston: Allyn and Bacon, 1975) 239.

Considering that colonial Massachusetts was the setting for the development of the public school template, it is not suprising that extraordinary leadership in public education would come from that state. James G. Carter, Henry Bernard, and Horace Mann provided wise and steadfast direction for the development of public education in Massachusetts. Statements from two of Horace Mann's annual reports to the Massachusetts State Board of Education typify the ideas about education that were gaining strength.

> I believe in the existence of a great, immutable principle of natural law . . . which proves the *absolute right* of every human being that comes into the world to an education; and which, of course, proves the correlative duty of every government to see that the means of that education are provided for all.
>
> . . . it seems clear that the minimum of this education can never be less than such as sufficient to qualify each citizen for the civil and social duties he will be called to discharge; such an education as teaches the individual the great laws of bodily health; as qualifies for the fulfillment of parental duties; as is indispensable for the civil functions of a witness or a juror; as is necessary for the voter in municipal affairs; and finally, for the faithful and conscientious discharge of all those duties which devolve upon the inheritor of a portion of the sovereignty of this great republic.
>
> . . . .
>
> Without undervaluing any other human agency, it may be safely affirmed that the Common School, improved and energized, as it can easily be, may become the most effective and benignant of all forces of civilization.[12]

Americans, on the whole, have shared the belief that most of the ills of society could be cured by applying human reason, honed as it would be through effective public education. Horace Mann was a prominent spokesman for this emerging faith in the power of schooling.

---

[12]Horace Mann, "Tenth Annual Report to the Massachusetts Board of Education, 1846," and "Twelfth Annual Report to the Massachusetts Board of Education, 1848," *Foundations of Education in America*, ed. by J. W. Noll and S. P. Kelly (New York: Harper and Row, Publishers, 1970) 209-10.

However, because of his leadership in establishing secular public schools, Horace Mann has been subject to unwarranted criticism that frequently portrays him as the archenemy of the Christian church and all things sacred. Mann was forced to deal with divisiveness created by the struggles of the religious sects to gain control of the new schools. According to Edward J. Power, Mann's solution in those unfortunate circumstances "was to remove sectarian instruction from the common schools and establish them, not as secular, but as nonsectarian agencies."[13] Mann was not antireligious, but his dedication to a system of public schooling free from sectarian strife and controversy left him no choice.

> . . .the intent of the movement which Mann led was not to exclude all religious subject matter from the educative process as carried on under public auspices. Yet he saw no way to avoid it, and he was ready, apparently, to accept the policy which actually led to that result if that was the only way to keep the schools free from religious controversy.[14]

Mann's own words testify to the depth of his respect for religion. In his "Twelfth Annual Report to the Board of Education" (1848), he wrote:

> In this age of the world, it seems to me that no student of history, or observer of mankind, can be hostile to the precepts and the doctrines of the Christian religion, or opposed to any institutions which expound and exemplify them, and no man who thinks, as I cannot but think, respecting the enduring elements of character, whether public or private, can be willing to have his name mentioned while he is living, or remembered when he is dead, as opposed to religious instruction, and Bible instruction for the young.[15]

Unfortunately, Mann's wish was not realized. Perhaps another section of his report will explain this failure.

---

[13]Edward J. Power. *The Transit of Learning* (Sherman Oaks CA: Alfred Publishing Co., 1979) 180.

[14]Committee on Religion and Education, *The Relation of Religion to Public Education* (Washington DC: American Council on Education, 1947) 8.

[15]Theodore R. Crane, ed. *The Dimensions of American Education* (Reading MA: Addison-Wesley Publishing Co., 1974) 51.

> The elements of a political education are not bestowed upon any school child, for the purpose of making him vote with this or that political party, when he becomes of age, but for the purpose of enabling him to choose for himself, with which party he will vote. So the religious education which a child receives at school, is not imparted to him, for the purpose of making him join this or that denomination, when he arrives at years of discretion, but for the purpose of enabling him to judge for himself, according to the dictates of his own reason and conscience, what his religious obligations are, and whether they lead.[16]

Mann desired political and religious freedom for the students of public schools in order that they might exercise responsible freedom in their maturity. The pedagogical goal was educated judgment—judgment that could responsibly decide what faith would be followed or what vote cast. Because of his pedagogical goal, Mann (along with others who have worked for freedom in American public schools) has been cited as a classic example of the type of leader that has caused public schools to "go astray." For many opponents of nonsectarian public education, freedom of thought is apparently an inappropriate goal. The controversy Mann had to deal with was much like the disputes characterizing the last quarter of this century. Sooner or later, people must realize that those who wish to control human beings in any manner cannot support freedom of thought. The attitude Mann faced is largely the same we now confront: if one possesses the Truth, what is there to think about?

The controversy of Mann's day centered upon the question of sectarian content in public school curricula (the issue of control of those schools was settled largely by default, an outcome of disestablishment). In Europe and in the colonies, education generally had been controlled by the church. Subject to ecclesiastical patronage, it was natural and proper that curriculum materials contain sectarian doctrine selected by the sect supporting education. The battle that Mann and his colleagues fought was to prevent this selective religious material from remaining in public school curricula.

---

[16]Ibid., 52.

. . .while the early public school movement was vigorously opposed to any form of denominationalism it was by no means antireligious. Mann himself approved of Bible reading and other nonsectarian religious exercises in the public school. The McGuffey Readers, which for so long set the tone of public-school education, were almost sermonic in style and content. The public school teacher was expected to be as much an exemplar of morality as was the clergyman. It was common practice to recruit public school teachers and administrators from among graduates of seminaries and denominational colleges.[17]

The pluralism of Mann's day was a pluralism primarily restricted to Christian sects and denominations; it was not a pluralism running the gamut of the world's great religions and a variety of less orthodox religious expressions. However, despite its rather modest nature, it proved impossible to find a common core of religious doctrine that could be called orthodox. Hence, depending upon developments in each community, either the religious content of public school curricula remained broadly sectarian, or all religious content was stricken from the curriculum. It would be a century later, when the Supreme Court would address the issue of prayer in the public schools, that religious content in the curriculum would almost cease to exist. That result was one that Mann would have regretted and that the Court did not intend. Horace Mann was dedicated to the development of schooling that would be open to all and that would have no sectarian curriculum materials that would exclude or offend anyone. Because of this haphazard and unplanned sequence of events, the problem of religious content in public school curricula remains unresolved.

The essence of the controversy Mann faced, and that is faced today, is that strong religious beliefs are typically nonnegotiable. The notion of nonsectarianism, therefore, is an affront (if not a perversion) to many devoted sectarians. The word *fundamentalist* is an apt phrase to describe this point of view. The fundamentals of doctrine, tradition, and piety cannot be com-

---

[17]Arnold C. Mueller, "Religion in the Public Schools," *Church and State Under God*, ed. A. G. Huegli (St. Louis MO: Concordia Publishing House, 1964) 301.

promised because to the believers they constitute the one true expression of religion and are therefore applicable to everyone regardless of their personal preference. For example, to the fundamentalist, Christianity, as interpreted, is the only true religion and the only pathway to salvation. If government refuses to align itself with this fundamentalist belief, for whatever reason, that government is antireligious. To fundamentalists, nonsectarianism is impossible—one is either for or against this absolute truth.

This singleness of dedication has been, is, and will remain at the heart of much religion-government controversy in the United States so long as government continues to support nonsectarianism in public schools and certain segments of the religious community continue to try to impose their faith on everyone. Can people continue to ignore the fact that fundamentalist Christianity, based upon its own record and its own pronouncements, is a closed system that will not tolerate compromise? Moreover, can people close their eyes to the knowledge that fundamentalism will view the educational goal of freedom of thought as religious heresy?

In order to lend credence to the idea that sectarian religion belongs in public schools, fundamentalists stress the fervent religious faith of the early settlers of this country. Though the intensity and influence of that faith has been highly romanticized, the colonists' ideas of religious liberty must not be overlooked. Many of those who did possess a deep religious commitment came to the New World to escape religious persecution. Curiously enough, those persons responded to the colonial milieu in two ways: like the Puritans of the Massachusetts Bay Colony, they erected theocracies and persecuted those of divergent belief; or, like the settlers of Rhode Island, they realized that the essence of religious freedom and integrity was religious liberty for everyone. The Puritan response vividly demonstrated the evil of establishment; the nonsectarian response of the Rhode Island settlers prevailed as the only reasonable means for preserving religious liberty.

As Will Herberg pointed out, public education is government education. As education for the masses became an urgent concern, it became obvious that individuals or independent groups lacked the resources to provide the complex form of mass education required. To accomplish the task, education established, financed, and maintained by government was required. Herberg called this a subsidiary function: "government is justified in taking over a general social function only if it is a function that must be performed in the common interest but cannot be adequately performed by individuals or voluntary non-governmental agencies." Government has not and should not take over the field of education, but it must provide for that segment of the population not involved in private or parochial schooling.[18]

It is from this perspective that the legal status of public education in the United States should be understood. One of the leading school-law authorities describes the legal position of the public schools.

> Public education is not merely a function of government, it is of government. Power to maintain a system of public schools is an attribute of government in much the same sense as is the police power or the power to administer justice or to maintain military forces or to tax. . . . The primary function of the public school, in legal theory at least, is not to confer benefits upon the individual as such, the school exists as a state institution because the very existence of civil society demands it. The education of youth is a matter of such vital importance to the democratic state and to the public weal that the state may do much, may go very far indeed, by way of limiting the control of the parent over the education of his child.[19]

Public education is "of government," more precisely of state government. The Federal government may become involved in public education when, for example, violation of the Constitution is alleged, but it is state government which, through legislation, funds the public schools and requires attendance in

---

[18]Will Herberg, "Religion, Democracy, and Public Education," *Religion in America*, ed. John Cogley (Mountain View CA: World Publishing Co., 1958) 119.

[19]Newton Edwards, *The Courts and the Public Schools*, rev. ed. (Chicago: University of Chicago Press, 1955) 23-24.

those schools or in some approved alternative form of schooling. To say that the public schools are of state government is to say that the public schools belong to the people, to all the people. It is this very fact of common possession which requires the delicacy of the relationship between religion and public education.

While more frequently used in an analysis of the relationship of government to private and parochial education, *Pierce v. Society of Sisters* is reproduced, in edited form, in appendix C because of its fundamental importance in discussions concerning the relationship of government to education. Informed by other decisions of the Supreme Court (see chapter 5 and those decisions listed in appendix B under "The State and Sectarian Education"), but primarily following the dicta of *Pierce*, the following appears to be true of the relationship of government to education. The provision of public education is not a constitutional requirement. But, if state government so chooses, education may be provided at public expense, and attendance at such schools may be required by statute. However, states, in exercising this legislative right, may not restrict student attendance to public schools. They must allow parents and students the freedom to choose alternative forms of education, such as private and parochial schools. According to *Pierce*, states may exercise reasonable control over private and parochial schools to ensure that they provide a basic secular education and that they attend to the state's educational goals. While states may not restrict private or parochial education, neither are they required to make such education available. Public education is, in fact, an alternative, made available at the discretion of the state, to private or parochial education. The provision or maintenance of private or parochial education is not a state responsibility. Lastly, students' constitutional rights may not be violated while attending public school.

A number of goals have contributed directly to the establishment and maintenance of public schools. Two have prompted formal education since antiquity: the goal of cognitive growth and the goal of transmitting the culture of a people from one generation to the next. These two goals are fundamental to all institutionalized education and, therefore, support the rather distinct cluster of goals that have prompted the development of public education in the United States. The first specific goal for public education was the civic goal: it was judged that a representative democracy could not survive if all persons who would have access to the ballot box or to public office were not educated. American political theory rejected aristocracy of leadership; the leadership of the nation was to rest with the people. It was necessary, therefore, that people be educated in order to ensure sound government. Neither social or economic status, nor religious affiliation could preclude access to public education. Hence public education was necessary, for neither the private nor the parochial sectors had shown the capacity or the inclination to provide such extensive education.

Along with the goals of intellectual growth, cultural transmission, and the development of educated voters and political candidates, two other goals helped define the shape and direction of public schools. One concerned the social lives of students: through education, students should be assisted in becoming positive and contributing members of society. The more complex society becomes, the more education is viewed as an initiation rite required for full social membership. Social concerns ranging from simple personal hygiene to the complexity of marriage and family life were viewed as important components of this social goal. Students must have assistance in appreciating and understanding the complexity of community and the intricacies and dynamics of human relationships. The other goal had to do with the material concerns. Following the example provided by Benjamin Franklin's private academy in Philadelphia, the conviction grew that schooling should provide each individual with those skills required for a productive and self-sustaining life. No longer was institutional education expected to train only the leaders of society, the new public schools were expected to prepare their heterogeneous clientele for the world of work. While emphasis upon vocational education was sporadic, it was to be a counterpart of traditional academic education.

The civic and social goals of American public education reflect a concern for moral and character education. The reason for instituting civic education, for example, was to enable voters to undertake political responsibility with integrity. Social education would emphasize the importance of honesty in social relationships. It is true that the Judeo-Christian tradition was the theoretical foundation for character and moral education in early public schools. However, the growing pluralism of society required that public education gradually shift away from a specifically religious moral foundation toward a quasi-legal or secular morality in the public sector. The contemporary complaint that public schools are immoral typically reflects a dedication to that Christian moral foundation of the earlier era.

The role of moral education in public schools has been a prominent topic in contemporary debate. In order to achieve the civic, social, and material goals of American public education, the time-honored goals of cognitive development and cultural transmission have remained fundamental. And these two basic educational goals have been chosen as the focus of attack by contemporary sectarian critics. Failing to reintroduce mandatory devotional exercises in public schools (at least as of this writing) and apparently judging "study about" religion to be an unsatisfactory option, the sectarian critics direct a general attack against public schools. They charge that public schools are failing miserably in the task of training students in academic skills. Then, having laid this groundwork of doubt concerning public education's competence, they accuse schools of not transmitting the cultural heritage of the American people. The critical element, of course, is that to these sectarian critics the keystone of that heritage is the Judeo-Christian tradition; and, in order to make the criticism more convincing and give it a more general appeal, emphasis is placed on the moral values embedded in that tradition. While parents may not want their children subjected to sectarian religious instruction in the public schools, they certainly do not want their children's morality undermined.

Data from national standardized tests does indicate that public schools have some problems with teaching academic skills, but there is no evidence that private or parochial schools would have any greater success if they had to deal with the same heterogeneous population that attends public schools. When responding to criticism concerning public schools, caution is recommended, for the fundamentalists (who comprise the major force in this criticism) will introduce issues of religious faith into public controversy under the guise of introducing issues of morality. "Creation science" has been urged upon the schools under this guise, and debates concerning the morality of sex education and values clarification have cloaked sectarian interests as well. It is true that public schools are not perfect. From the beginning they have had difficulty in attaining the ambitious goals set for them. Yet, when one considers the goals set for them and the diversity of their clientele, only the most romantic dreamer would demand total success in their first century of existence. However, what would the nation be like today without the pedagogic efforts of public schools during the past century? Notwithstanding the imperfect achievements of public education, can one, in good conscience, seriously consider the alternative that its sectarian critics seem to suggest—a publicly supported system of sectarian Christian education? Will the insertion of sectarian morality into public education improve either the intellectual growth of students or the task of cultural transmission that the schools must undertake? A better option would be to devote our efforts and resources to fulfilling the dream of public education—an education that, with such support, might better achieve those cognitive, cultural, civic, social, and material goals for which such education was created.

Horace Mann and his colleagues fought and largely won the battle for public control of public school curricula, guaranteeing that attendance in public schools would be without sectarian restriction or divisiveness. Public schools were to be a fitting complement to parochial and private schools, sectors of education public schools were never intended to replace. One substantial battle remained to be waged (one that will not be detailed here), a battle for the public funds required to support public schools. One by one, perhaps following the example of New York, the states assumed control of public education and, with tax moneys, augmented local funds to pay the bills for public schooling. The following assumptions were developed as a result of the struggle to establish a public, tax-supported system of education.

> Public education in the United States rests on three fundamental as-
> sumptions: First, that the legislature has the power to tax all—even the
> childless and those whose children attend private schools—in order to
> provide free public education for all; second, that the legislature has the
> power to require every parent to provide for his children a basic edu-
> cation in secular subjects; third, that the education provided by the
> state in the free schools must be secular.[20]

The educational system that would guarantee an education for all citizens was well on its way to becoming a reality by the end of the nineteenth century.

The use of public tax money to support public education is a compelling reason for demanding that public schools remain religiously neutral. One of the more onerous burdens of religious establishment was government taxation for the support of a religious institution or activity with which the taxpayer was not affiliated. To legislate taxation of all in order to support public education—regardless of whether or not an individual taxpayer directly participates in public education—requires that schools so supported not represent a sectarian religious position if that society and its government are dedicated to religious liberty. There may be no better illustration of a practice respecting religious establishment than the allocation of public taxes to public schools representing an official sectarian position. The fact that tax support for public education requires the elimination of officially assumed sectarian positions is no less compelling today than it was a century ago.

Further detail regarding the development of public schools during the last one hundred years is beyond the limits of this discussion.[21] However, two observations regarding that devel-

---

[20]Leo Pfeffer, *Church, State, and Freedom* (Boston: Beacon Press, 1953) 280.

[21]For the reader interested in the details of this development, see: Butts, *Public Education in the United States*, ch. 9 and 11; and Adolphe E. Meyer, *An Educational History of the American People*, 2d ed. (New York: McGraw-Hill Book Co., 1967) ch. 9 and 10.

opment are important as we approach the contemporary educational milieu. First, as Americans were busy creating a system of public education, philosophical reflection on the nature of education was undertaken by European scholars and the ideas of Locke, Rousseau, Herbart, and Pestalozzi considerably influenced educational theory and practice on the Continent. Indeed, some American teachers were influenced by the ideas of Herbart and Pestalozzi. But, for the most part, Americans regarded these philosophical ideas as even further removed from the practical tasks of schooling than the Continent itself was removed from American shores.

> In education the Americans' concern involved them in the making of the common school, fetching sufficient financial support from the taxpayer, devising the mechanism for its operation and control, and carrying the system of free and tax-supported benefits into the higher loft of the secondary learning. As for the nature of education, the philosophic bedrock, its aims and principles, and its sociological meaning and implications, together with the inscrutabilities of the psyche involved in the learning and teaching process—all this by comparison appeared remote and estranged from the everyday business of keeping school.[22]

The American educational establishment has not been particularly aggressive in applying philosophical thought to its pedagogy, reflecting the general American propensity for neglecting theoretical thought in favor of practical. Americans seem far more inclined to ask "how?" than "why?"

This preference for the practical over the theoretical impedes the institution of religion studies in public schools. So long as education ignores the philosophy of education, it will not be inclined to address questions about the meaning of human life and experience. Without philosophical reflection on the meaning of life, religion will contribute little to the teaching-learning process because religion studies make a legitimate contribution only in the context of the struggle to find meaning in life. If American schools ignore such questions, it will be difficult to

---

[22]Adolphe E. Meyer, *An Educational History of the American People*, 2d ed. (New York: McGraw Hill Book Co., 1967) 253.

implement study about religion beyond mere factual presentation.

A second event in the development of public education compounded the problem presented by the neglect of educational theory. As the nineteenth century gave way to the twentieth, the population of this country was significantly increased by European immigration. These immigrants realized that they might not fully achieve the "American dream" but were sure that their children could; and they believed the road to that dream passed directly through the doors of the public schools. The demand for public education was intense, particularly in the cities of the eastern seaboard as these immigrants clamored for education for their children. A heavy burden on the facilities and personnel of the infant schools resulted. Educational uniformity and routine was seen as the best way to educate so many children. An unrelenting attention to the acquisition of facts and the perfection of academic skills became characteristic of public schools. Learning was structured and graded, subjects were precisely classified, and schooling was put on a rigorous schedule.

> . . . teaching was reduced to loading pupils with knowledge, dosing them stiffly with homework and examinations, and, needless to say, prodding the loafers and flogging the wicked. The learners' attainments, such as they were, were translated into marks, the best of which went not necessarily to those who steamed and chugged the hardest, or even to those who once in a blue moon showed the gleam of genius, but rather to those who from the pits of their remembrance could haul up the biggest assemblage of facts.[23]

Without a philosophical foundation, educators resorted to the most obvious and efficient ways to "get the job done." Such a transmissive form of schooling, the bulk of which was accurately described by Meyer, may be unable to accommodate the educational approach that must be followed if religion studies are to be implemented.

---

[23]Ibid., 254.

The Secular Public School

The seeds of American public education had been present in the township schools of the Massachusetts Bay Colony. As the nation grew, the necessity for educating all future citizens became urgent, and the Massachusetts educational model was utilized to an extent beyond anticipation a century earlier. The one major modification of that model was the role religion was to play in schools.

> Believer and agnostic claimed equal rights to define the limits of moral indoctrination, Christian and Jew wrestled with the hard question of how the school could transmit their common ethical heritage without exposing their profound disagreement on the nature and authority of Jesus Christ. Protestant and Roman Catholic found it impossible to agree on which version of the Bible was to be read in the schools if indeed it was to be read at all. A small but influential atheist minority demanded respect for their right to have their children uncontaminated by the "superstition" of religion. Among the almost 40 percent of the nation's population who claimed no church membership the prevailing attitude was that religion is a private matter and that the best way to settle the question of religious or moral instruction was to leave this sort of thing to the family and the church and to let the schools restrict themselves to the transmission of information and the development of skills.[24]

American pedagogy had not been inclined to question the basic nature of learning. Therefore, when confronted with a crisis of demand, its response was characterized by routine and regimentation, by "canned" knowledge and transmissive teaching techniques; by a classical *approach* to education dedicated to non-classical, practical goals. Religion, because it had no single answer or widely accepted points of view, proved difficult to teach through transmissive teaching techniques. Thus, serious religious instruction was relegated to the home, to religious institutions, and to parochial schools where sectarian bias was appropriate. However, religion was still maintained in public schools in the form of devotional exercises.

---

[24]Mueller, "Religion in the Public Schools," 302.

Education for the masses, induction into an industrial society, and nationalism were challenges that claimed the attention of the educational establishment. Developing good citizens appeared to be the nation's educational priority. Through citizenship education, young persons could be indoctrinated with patriotism, trained in the skills that would be required in a complex technological society, and exposed to appropriate cultural treasures of past and present. These concerns replaced concern for religious education and led to what has been called the system of secular public education.

Although religious intolerance acted as a catalyst, the separation of religious education and public education was inevitable. The very idea of separation of church and state demanded the separation of church and state schools; the existence of a secular state required the existence of secular schools.[25]

A decision by the Ohio Supreme Court, announced in 1872, illustrates the development of the latter idea. That decision upheld an action by the Cincinnati Board of Education prohibiting religious instruction and reading of religious materials in public schools. Commenting on that decision, Butts wrote:

> When the court emphasized a religious neutrality of government based upon *human* experience, it defined a *secular* basis for public education, a basis specifically not antireligious or irreligious, but a basis upon which the several religions then might build their own activities free of government interference. But it was to be nearly a hundred years before the Supreme Court of the United States took a similar position.[26]

Reinhold Niebuhr summarized the inevitability of the secularization of public schooling in a secular state.

> The secularization of education is the price we pay for the rigor with which we separate Church and State. I will hazard the opinion that however steep the price, such a separation represents a gain for our public

---

[25]Pfeffer, *Church, State, and Freedom*, 288.

[26]Butts, *Public Education in the United States*, 124.

life since organized religion is bound to be divisive and it is a divisiveness we simply cannot afford.[27]

Social pluralism requires that public schools, as public institutions, remain neutral on ideological matters.[28] Therefore, although diversity of religion and intolerance by religious sects
contributed substantially to the development of a system of secular public education, it is clear that this development was also
demanded by the nature of the government and the composition of society, a composition that naturally resulted from the
freedom guaranteed by the political structure. The secularization of public schools was a logical and predictable result of the
commitment to democracy.

The secular nature of public schools however, does not offer
a solution to this question: must religion be totally absent from
public education? This question is complicated by the fact that,
notwithstanding the demands of constitutional law and the theoretical case for the secularity of public schools, public schools
have never been totally without sectarian religion.[29] Professor
Dierenfield's research indicates that, if there is no public protest
or litigation, public schools will continue to teach sectarian religion and observe devotional exercises during the school day in
some communities. His research also showed that American
public schools are continually experimenting in order to find a
constitutionally sound place for religion. Many thoughtful lead-

---

[27]Reinhold Niebuhr, "A Note on Pluralism," *Religion in America*, ed. John
Cogley (Mountain View CA: World Publishing Co., 1958) 47.

[28]Guntram G. Bischoff, "The Search for Common Definitions of Religion
Studies and Public Education," *Religious Education* 71 (January-February
1976): 71.

[29]For a discussion on the diversity of religious influence in public schools
see: R. B. Dierenfield, "The Extent of Religious Influence in American Public Schools," *Religious Education* 56 (May-June 1961): 173-80; "The Impact
of the Supreme Court Decisions on Religion in Public Schools," *Religious
Education* 62 (September-October 1967): 445-52; and "Religion in Public
Schools: Its Current Status," *Religious Education* 68 (January-February
1973): 96-114.

ers in public education and the religious community disagree
with the proposition that religious neutrality means that religion must be totally absent from public schools. Although sectarianism is inappropriate and unconstitutional, is religion in
general also to be banished?

The search for a legally responsible religion-public education
relationship is seriously complicated by a lack of agreement
within the religious community regarding the meaning of the
term *sectarian*, a confusion that results from a failure to appreciate the sectarian nature of Christianity itself. It is not simply
that public schools cannot officially represent some form of
Protestantism; public schools cannot officially represent any religious position—including Christianity. This confusion is illustrated by the persistent affirmation by some Christians that the
United States was founded as a "Christian nation" and the only
way to ensure national prosperity and power is to return to full
recognition of that status. Furthermore, those Christians argue
that this return will be most effectively accomplished if Christianity becomes the official religion of public education. As interpreted by the Supreme Court, such a utilization of public
schools would require a substantial revision of the First Amendment, regardless of the benefits said to accrue from such a utilization. The revision that would be required is a constitutional
right, but, recalling the "ball game analogy" presented earlier,
Americans must seriously question the results of such a revision. Would the necessary revision merely adjust the rules of
the game a bit or would it alter the fundamental nature of the
game itself? Can the pluralism of American society, a pluralism
invited through constitutional dedication to personal freedom,
be subjected to so drastic a change in sociopolitical commitment? Furthermore, social pluralism is not simply a pluralism
of religious belief, it is a cultural pluralism. If belief is controlled
in any way in any sector of the public arena, what human
thought, judgment, belief, or value will next be challenged? The
rule of law, nurtured by free men in a free society, must remain
constant if human liberty is to be protected.

If it may be said that the God revealed in the Judeo-Christian
tradition has a vested interest in this or in any nation, it may be

so said only to the degree that a nation maintains a solemn dedication to the freedom and dignity of human beings. One cannot read the long story that unfolds in the biblical tradition without realizing that God's will, as revealed therein, is that human beings must live their lives responsibly and compassionately. Inasmuch as any people can claim God's special attention, they may only make such a claim when these qualities are consciously facilitated. If God is all he is believed to be, certainly he cannot be manipulated; and therefore, any divine blessing that a nation may receive will result from the steadfast dedication of its people to freedom and human dignity that will allow each individual to seek God in his or her own way, or to seek no God at all.

It has been shown that the relationship between religion and public education remains unsettled after more than a century. The Supreme Court decisions regarding the devotional presence or sectarianism in public schools in the 1950s caused uncertainty with respect to any place for religion in public education.[30] However, Anson P. Stokes correctly summarized the fundamental concern for many of our citizens.

> In general, Americans are almost equally concerned about two things:
> that sectarianism in every form shall be kept out of our public schools;
> and that the schools shall not be dominated by secularism or irreligion,
> which would be out of keeping with the best American tradition.[31]

Philip H. Phenix argued that two positions must be rejected: the position that the United States was founded on religious principles and that, therefore, public education is historically or naturally tied to a theistic position; and the position that the

---

[30]While the next chapter will clarify this judgment, it is important to note here that this confusion was not the intention of the Court—indeed, had the decisions of the Court been studied, little confusion should have resulted.

[31]Anson P. Stokes, *Church and State in the United States*, 3 vols. (New York: Harper and Brothers, 1950) 2:497.

separation of church and state requires that religion be completely eliminated from public education.[32]

If one cannot advocate the official expression of a traditional form of Christianity in public schools and, on the other hand, one does not want to totally eliminate religion from those schools, what is the alternative? The most obvious solution is to institute religion studies in public schools, teaching *about* religion. While not a satisfactory solution to either the sectarian or to the secularist, teaching about religion does provide a legal and potentially constructive place for religion in public schools.

The legal understanding of religion, discussed in the previous chapter, clearly indicates the path religion study must follow. Phenix, for example, recommended that religion be defined as *"comprehensive life-orientation*, or again, as *the pattern or organization of life in relation to values regarded as ultimate . . .* "[33] In public education, the goal must be understanding the fundamental nature of religion as it affects individual life and the quality and direction of society. The goal for religion studies is not that a student accept any specific sectarian expression, but that a student understand its importance to people and society.

While religion study may represent a potential solution to the problem, the rationale for the study will have enormous effect upon the legality and propriety of the program.

> A proposal is suspect if it is made on the grounds that the influence of the family and church has lessened, so the school must take up the slack in the child's religious development. But a proposal for familiarization with the Bible, for example, or with the impact of religion on man's affairs, will meet the test if the instruction is clearly to increase understanding and to bring a representative variety of views to bear, avoiding

---

[32]Philip H. Phenix, *Religious Concerns in Contemporary Education* (New York: Columbia University Teachers College, Bureau of Publications, 1959) 41-42.

[33]Philip H. Phenix, "Religion in American Public Education," *Contemporary American Education*, ed. Stan Dropkin et al., 2d ed. (New York: Macmillan Co., 1970) 555.

indoctrination against or for a religion. This is a tough test, but a crucial one.[34]

If understanding religion as a significant component of history and of culture is the goal, public education may support religion studies without violating the First Amendment.

> The case for the study of religion in the public school cannot be successfully argued unless it can be shown that such study is called for by the very principles on which public school education rests and in terms of which its didactic objectives are conceived.[35]

Public schools may teach about religion as long as the public nature of those schools and their teaching goals are maintained.

The Place of Religion in Public Education

Early on, the Committee on Religion in Education stated that the schools have an obligation to help students gain an appreciation and understanding of Western culture. This obligation, it said, cannot be met unless the ideals and values the culture cherishes are taught. In its view, a program of general education is incomplete if it omits any large and important segment of human concern.[36] Because religion is a significant component of culture, the committee believed that "No person is fully educated who has not gained a knowledge of the faiths men live by."[37]

Notwithstanding the importance of religion in American culture, Anson Stokes believed that much religious education must be left to the home and to religious institutions. The kind of re-

---

[34]Archibald B. Shaw, "Religion in the Public Schools: An Educator's Concern," *Religion and Public School Curriculum*, ed. R. U. Smith (New York: Religious Education Association, 1972) 47.

[35]Bischoff, "Search for Common Definitions," 70.

[36]Committee on Religion and Education, *The Relation of Religion to Public Education* (Washington DC: American Council on Education Studies, 1947) 27-28.

[37]Ibid., 19.

ligious instruction that is appropriate in public school is not the kind that would significantly contribute to religious development in a sectarian or confessional sense; but it would contribute to the development of a broad understanding of the nature of religion. Stokes believed that young people need to be taught more effectively about the history and teachings of religion and that this education may be undertaken by public schools.[38] Perhaps, the most realistic goal for religion studies in public schools is understanding the nature of religion. Theodore M. Greene provided a forthright and fundamentally sound summary of the nature of religion studies from this perspective.

> ... the school should scrupulously maintain an attitude of official neutrality in this, as on all other, controversial matters. This neutrality should not, however, be confused with neglect or indifference. Religion should not be ignored; on the contrary, it should be studied and discussed, in its Far Eastern forms as well as in its more familiar Hebraic and Christian forms. It should be studied and taught, however, always in the liberal spirit of honest inquiry followed by free individual decision. The one and only attitude that should be deliberately inculcated in our students is the attitude of profound concern for whatever can give meaning and value to human life and of profound respect for all sincerely and openly held ultimate beliefs, however much they may differ from our own.[39]

The unavoidable fact is that religion is a controversial subject—as are many other subjects of study. To say that a subject is controversial is simply to acknowledge that "answers" in that area have not been commonly agreed upon. Yet, like beauty, controversy is in the eye of the beholder. Many may resent the classification of religion as controversial, particularly when this classification includes their religion. In spite of such objections, religion seems to fit well in the classification of controversial subjects. It does not follow, however, that because religion is a

---

[38]Stokes, *Church and State in the United States*, 494.

[39]Theodore M. Greene, "A Liberal Christian Idealist Philosophy of Education," *Modern Philosophies and Education, The Fifty-fourth Yearbook of the National Society for the Study of Education*, ed. N. B. Henry (Chicago: University of Chicago Press, 1955) 135.

controversial subject, it should be omitted from public school curricula. It is common belief that students must be introduced to those controversial subjects that are of import to society, as well as taught factual knowledge. How will students, as adults, cope with those social and cultural problems for which there are no commonly accepted answers if they have not been introduced to such problems in the supportive environment of school? Is it not, therefore, a fundamental responsibility of school to introduce students to the dynamics of such issues, particularly when one considers the political and social goals of public education? The mere fact that a subject is controversial does not constitute a reason, *ipso facto*, for omitting that subject from public school curricula.

> Hopefully we may one day recognize that on most crucial questions it may be necessary to present the various issues and sides of a question to pupils without being able to provide a clear definitive answer. For all too long we have tended to examine only those questions which can be handled objectively and therefore neutrally, scientifically and also safely. The desire to avoid personal involvement, commitment and controversy reflects a set of values which may be inadequate for those involved in public education to utilize if the aims of education are to be realized in a period when the questions and concerns raised by teachers as well as pupils challenge the heretofore socially established and accepted value norms.[40]

Perhaps discussions of controversial issues are at odds with the prevailing philosophy of public education, but, if that is the case, it must be seriously questioned whether public education is adequately preparing students for lives as enlightened adults and citizens.

At a number of points, this discussion has flirted with the topic of neutrality. In fact, the word *neutrality* has found its way into discussions of the relationship of religion to public education with such regularity as to have become a cliché: its significance has been diminished thereby and its meaning clouded. Neutrality has frequently been understood as requiring that all

---

[40]Harold Stahmer, "Religion and Moral Values in the Public Schools," *Religious Education* 61 (January-February 1966): 23.

study of religion be omitted from public school, but such an interpretation causes a serious problem. According to John C. Bennett, "when all specific forms of religion are omitted from the world of the school, this is itself a negative form of religious teaching; it strongly implies that religion is peripheral and dispensable as a matter of human concern."[41] Public school administrators expressed the same concern.

> A curriculum which ignored religion would itself have serious religious implications. It would seem to proclaim that religion has not been as real in men's lives as health or politics or economics. By omission it would appear to deny that religion has been and is important in man's history—a denial of the obvious. In day-to-day practice, the topic can not be avoided. As an integral part of man's culture, it must be included.[42]

The concept of neutrality does not require that religion studies be omitted from the curriculum, but it does have two implications. First, a school may not indoctrinate with respect to religious belief nor may it assume an official sectarian position. Second, a school should not ignore religion but should teach about it whenever and wherever it is necessary, either for a full understanding of the secular topic of study, or for a complete secular education. Neutrality, therefore, means that schools will acknowledge the controversial nature of religion, present all the relevant answers in any area of controversy, and steadfastly refuse to advocate any specific solution. Philip H. Phenix summarized the implications of neutrality in religion studies.

> In public schools in a free and pluralistic society such as the United States it is clearly not appropriate for the teachers to offer any religious interpretation as the correct and preferred one. It is not the function of the public schools to propagate particular traditions of religious faith and practice. It is appropriate for the teacher to help students, first, to understand better what is believed and practiced in traditional reli-

---

[41]John C. Bennett, *Christians and the State* (New York: Charles Scribner's Sons, 1958) 236-37.

[42]American Association of School Administrators, *Religion in the Public Schools* (Arlington VA: American Association of School Administrators, 1964) 55.

gions, second, to reflect constructively and critically about these traditions, and third, to see the relevance of various religious ideas to the understanding of "secular" concerns comprehensively and in depth.[43]

Not only does omitting religion study give religion a negative connotation, but the vacuum thereby created may be filled by some other ideology. Many academic subjects, particularly at the middle grades and secondary levels, provide the opportunity to address, explicitly or implicitly, the meaning of human life. If the alternatives represented by religion are not available in such discussions, other alternatives may be viewed by the students as the "official" or accepted position of the school. Will Herberg wrote that, with the exclusion of Protestantism from public schools, the substitute religion of secularism was introduced. Herberg defined secularism as the theory that human life is self-sufficient. In higher education this new "religion of no-religion" took the form of scientism, positivism, and naturalism. In lower schools, however, it assumed the less philosophical configuration of the "American way of life."[44] ". . . so the religiously neutral education of the public school turned out to be a religious education after all—only the religion was no longer Christianity, but the 'religion of democracy. . .'"[45]

Though representing a legitimate concern, it is particularly difficult to document the presence of a religion of democracy in schools. How does one, for example, distinguish between the fervor of honest and innocent patriotism and the presence of a "religion of democracy"? However, regardless of the difficulty in documenting the presence of civil religion, it is fairly easy to illustrate the potential for criticism of public education if neutrality is interpreted as requiring that religion be omitted from the curriculum. As an agency of the state instituted for public welfare, public education cannot represent sectarian religion. It

---

[43]Philip H. Phenix, *Education and the Worship of God* (Philadelphia: Westminster Press, 1966) 30.

[44]Will Herberg, "Religion and Education in America," 2, 28.

[45]Ibid., 32.

is said, therefore, that topics concerning the betterment of human beings, the preservation and improvement of the social order, and the appreciation of nature and humanity's relationship to it represent the extent to which public schools may deal with issues related to the meaning of human life. If there is no form of religion studies in the curricula, humanity, in a benign sense, becomes the common denominator of the educational process. While most teachers understand these limitations, there is the potential that members of the school community will assume that schools are fostering naturalism, secularism, philosophical humanism, or civil religion. Religion studies undertaken in the true spirit of neutrality would help eliminate the potential for this erroneous assumption (except for the most thoroughgoing sectarian) and would prevent public school students from concluding (falsely) that religion is unimportant to humanity. Through such study, students would be made aware of all the options available to them as they attempt to understand life and their place in the world.

Over the years of struggle, discussion, experimentation, debate, and litigation that arose in the effort to determine a proper relationship for religion to public education, many have come to believe that, although schools cannot teach sectarian religion or conduct devotional exercises, they need to institute an academic study of religion if they are to attain their goals. Accordingly, a number of specific arguments favoring academic study about religion have been formulated.

Representing varying degrees of insight and dedication, the major arguments supporting religion studies in public schools are:

1. Public schools cannot expect to provide a comprehensive education if they omit instruction about any influential component of human commitment such as religion. As both national and world events continue to demonstrate, a student cannot effectively respond to the world in which he lives if he does not understand the powerful role religion plays in human affairs. The ultimate commitments and meanings that constitute religion strongly affect the life-style of individuals and the policies

of nations. If public education is to be truly comprehensive, study about religion cannot be omitted.

2. It is hoped that public school students will develop sensitive insight into religion if they are taught about it in an objective and neutral way. Although both commitment and conversion are inappropriate and totally unconstitutional educational goals for public schools, reducing tension, suspicion, and prejudice that results from a lack of understanding should be seen as an educational goal worthy of our best efforts. People typically fear most and are most suspicious of that which they do not understand and it is anticipated that students, by developing understanding of other beliefs, will be more tolerant and less fearful in their relationships.

3. A number of arguments supporting religion studies in public schools reflect specific curriculum concerns. (a) Religion is an important element of culture;[46] if a major goal of schooling is the transmission of culture, that culture must not be significantly edited by omission of religious studies. (b) Study about religion is essential if students are to understand the past. One cannot study the history of the West without also studying the influence of religion upon that history. As Margherite LaPota has argued, "School systems are charged with a major responsibility to transmit those elements of the philosophy, the ideals, and the knowledge of America's past that remain pertinent to America's future."[47] (c) A complete understanding of literature, art, music, and drama is impossible unless one comprehends religious motifs present in aesthetic expression. Indeed, as literary masterpieces, the Bible, the Koran, the Bhagvad-Gita, and other primary religious literature are worthy of study on the basis of

---

[46]Following the ideas of Kroeber and Parsons, culture is defined as the values, ideas, and meaningful symbols that man has created to bring order to social life. It includes the artifacts of human behavior as they are transmitted from one generation to another. (Alfred L. Kroeber and Talcott Parsons, "The Concepts of Culture and of Social System," *American Sociological Review* 23 (October 1958): 583.

[47]Margherite LaPota, "Religion: Not 'Teaching' but 'Teaching About,' " *Educational Leadership* 31 (October, 1973): 31.

artistic merit alone. From such arguments one can conclude that public school curricula are incomplete without study about religion.

4. When religion is omitted from curricula, this represents a negative position with respect to religion. Omission of religion implies that religion is peripheral and dispensable in modern life. Such a position is itself a religious affirmation—a "religion of no-religion" to use Herberg's fine phrase.

5. One may argue that large segments of the student population have no contact with any religious institution or orientation and that if religion is not studied in public schools, those students will have no experience with religion at all, contributing to a general religious illiteracy which, from this point of view, pervades the land. One should be cautious in employing this argument to support religion studies in public schools. If "religious illiteracy" refers to a lack of contact with or ignorance about specific forms and beliefs of sectarian religion, the argument is inappropriate. Public schools cannot be called upon to act as substitutes for the religious institutions of the community. But if this "illiteracy" reflects lack of knowledge of the historical importance and influence of religion, the argument may be legitimate, but is most appropriately expressed in that context above.

6. One of the more troublesome arguments used to support study about religion in public schools calls for construction of durable convictions and personal commitments, and the development, clarification, and ordering of values. Many parents are firmly convinced that public education infringes upon their parental responsibility when it undertakes specific manipulation of values and commitments. Others claim that large numbers of students have no exposure to a home environment in which values, commitments, and convictions are important.There is truth in both positions, but religion studies should not be used to modify personal convictions and commitments of students.

7. Religion studies in public schools will, it is said, counteract the emphasis upon objectivity and empiricism that presently characterizes much public school education. It is often said that American culture has adopted empiricism and objectivity as the

roads to truth and useful knowledge, ignoring less "provable," subjective approaches or relegating them to an inferior status. For example, in man's search for knowledge, facts are typically viewed as far more important than are emotions and intuitions. Furthermore, as public education has opted for the teaching of facts and the omission of controversial subject matter, it appears that the education students receive in public schools is dedicated to fixed knowledge.

> We have come through a period of hegemony of what Paul Tillich called "scientism." By this he meant a tendency to regard as significant only that which can be measured precisely or proved experimentally and a propensity to elevate scientific hypotheses to the status of dogmas. In this period the rich human world of imagination, ritual, symbol, myth, and religious thought was either ignored or cast into the outer darkness of mystery and/or superstition. . . .
>
> This situation does not now call for a renewal of "the warfare between science and theology." . . . What I do wish to stress is the need for a careful, thoughtful, informed consideration of the nature of religion and of its role in human culture.[48]

Empiricism is a fruitful and efficient approach to knowledge and truth, but it is only one approach among many. Advocates of religion studies should not seek to depreciate empiricism but should advocate a balanced approach that will introduce students to many paths to truth and knowledge, among which are religious tradition and religious experience. Any success attained in solving the most pressing human problems may depend upon the application of non-empirical, more traditionally philosophical forms of analysis.

8. According to D. W. O'Connor, students have a right to know about religion to the same degree that they have the right to know about any other academic area.[49] It has been recognized that the limits of one's world are directly related to the

---

[48]Robert Michaelsen, "Beyond the Ground Rules: Next Steps in the Study of Religion in the Public Schools," *Religious Education* 68 (March-April 1973): 213.

[49]Daniel W. O'Conner, "Should Religion be Taught in the Public School?" *Educational Leadership* 30 (April 1973): 650.

kinds of questions one is allowed to ask about that world. If, in their central academic experience, students are not allowed to ask questions about possibilities, about the mysterious, about personal levels of experience, about the meaning of life, about transcendent reality, the horizons of their world will be limited to that degree.

These are the arguments most frequently used to support religion studies in public schools. The first three are the most valid and potentially fruitful. Those rather superficial arguments that contend, for example, that Americans are a religious people, or that religious faith is the most important aspect of human life, or that the study of religion is necessary for moral development or character education, should be avoided. Such statements do little to clarify the relationship of religion to public education and can contribute to unconstitutional involvement. Care must be taken in employing the First Amendment as a support for religion studies; for the Constitution makes no mention of education. The First Amendment must be used as a guide for religion study, not as a rationale for it. Study about religion is neither constitutionally required nor prohibited.

There are also arguments opposing religion studies. Simplistic arguments such as: there is insufficient time during the school day for religion studies, or the Constitution forbids religion studies, will not make compelling cases against religion studies. However, the following are arguments of substance that the advocate of religion studies must be prepared to address.

1. Many teachers who possess personal religious commitments and values may be unable to approach religion objectively. A teacher's personal commitments and values are certain to come into play and can so easily affect the study of religion and the judgment of students. On the other hand, can an individual without religious commitments be called upon to teach in such a sensitive area?

2. Free inquiry is difficult to employ in elementary and secondary classrooms. Students have learned to expect their teachers to provide answers, and teachers generally are trained to dispense fixed knowledge. Can the typical means of dispensing knowledge be sufficiently adjusted to satisfy the required

neutrality of religion studies? Moreover, how can the community be certain that the free inquiry required in religion studies is actually taking place in the classrooms?

3. Effective and appropriate curriculum materials are difficult to produce for religion studies, particularly when these materials would be used in the study of history, social studies, literature, art, and so forth. In fact, some view the production of such materials as an impossibility. The fact that appropriate curriculum materials are becoming increasingly available may mitigate this argument, but this concern underscores the seriousness of the task of curriculum selection and design.

4. A constant danger is that powerful religious groups in a local community will aggressively seek to control a religion studies program. Based upon the history of the religion-government relationship, there is no reason to anticipate that the religious community will act differently today than it has in the past. According to opponents of religion studies, the introduction of religion studies into public schools will place those schools in a sensitive, highly volatile, potentially divisive position in the community. Is the goal worth the cost?

5. The extensive pluralism of American society makes it impossible to do justice to all the religions found in many communities. There is certain, therefore, to be jealousy and opposition from many of these religions who feel they are not receiving "equal time."

6. Religions and religious positions are closed value systems; open inquiry and critical thought, no matter how objective, will be viewed as negative, potentially destructive approaches to religion and will, therefore, be resented if not resisted. This will be particularly true when young communicants of these religions are involved in religion studies.

7. There is no necessary relationship between the kind of moral education the public school should undertake and the teachings of any specific religion. The moral education that public schools should undertake does not require the study of religion for its implementation and such study, therefore, should be avoided.

8. Objective, nonsectarian teaching about religion will dilute religious belief and commitment. One cannot fully understand religion apart from a stance of faith. To teach all religions from the same perspective is to imply that all religions are basically the same and, therefore, equally valid. Students would come to believe that it makes no difference what religion one follows and the element of personal commitment would be seriously compromised.

These are significant objections, but none of them are fatal to religion studies if such study is undertaken with care and wisdom. It is, however, obvious that any approach to religion studies must take into consideration such objections and take care that a program cannot be legitimately challenged on any of these points.

An excellent illustration of the complicated issues associated with the relationship between religion and public education is the heated controversy between advocates of "scientific creationism" and evolution that ushered in the decade of the eighties. The controversy was begun by fundamentalist Christians who believed that public schools, by teaching a theory of the origin of life and the universe that contradicted the biblical account of creation, were systematically undermining the religious beliefs and doctrines that they taught their children. They believed that the teaching of the theory of evolution violated their religious freedom as guaranteed by the First Amendment. Having failed in the past to force the theory of evolution from public school classrooms, these Christians now resorted to public pressure, legislation, and litigation to introduce a "balanced treatment" of both evolution and "scientific creationism" in the classrooms.

Human behavior is normally the result of complex motivations. There is no doubt that the fundamentalist Christians sincerely believed that their religious rights were being violated, but other concerns were also at work. For one thing, the teaching of "scientific creationism" in public schools would lend immense prestige to their literalistic interpretation of the Bible and to a basic doctrine of their faith. Furthermore, such teaching would provide a very promising evangelical entree into the public schools these Christians had long viewed as "hotbeds of godless secular humanism." Failing these goals, they might accomplish something else: if they could not evangelize the students of public schools, they might add this issue to their list of grievances and so weaken those schools in the eyes of the public that financial support from public funds might be obtained for their private fundamentalist Christian schools—a parochial school movement started almost two decades before the debate over creationism/evolution began.

In many respects, the reaction of the scientific community was equally complex. Obviously, there was reaction against teaching something as science for which there was no recognized scientific evidence. Furthermore, it was obvious that if creationism legislation were sustained, purely fundamentalist religious doctrine would be taught in schools under the guise of science. Notwithstanding these legitimate concerns, much scientific reaction was also directed against entertaining the truth of any theory or proposition that did not yield to empirical verification. The reaction, therefore, was motivated by a perceived challenge to the status and prestige of scientific truth in society. For many scientists and non-scientists alike, empiricism is the only reliable approach to truth, and fundamentalist Christians were to be put in their place for even suggesting that truth might be otherwise attainable.

As is so often the case, public schools were caught in the middle of the verbal crossfire. Public schools must teach the truth—but whose truth? Public schools must communicate knowledge—but what knowledge? Public schools must teach morality and values—but whose values and what morality? Public schools must deal with the good and the beautiful—but by what criterion? If public schools move beyond the most elementary intellectual skills and facts, can conflict with some set of cherished beliefs be avoided? It is often charged that public schools do not teach students to think; it is charged that students are taught to think too much and too well. Given specific situations and teachers, both charges are undoubtedly true as perceived, but what are public schools to do?

It is frequently affirmed (in the spirit of true liberalism—a spirit totally offensive to fundamentalism and often no more than a smoke screen for equally narrow points of view) that all sides of an issue should be considered. Fine. But how many parents, for example, want their children to study all sides of issues like environmental decay, the control of nuclear power, abortion, capital punishment, pornography, euthanasia, genetic engineering, moral decline, minority rights, surrogate parenthood, and so forth? Do parents, for the most part, want all sides of an issue considered or do they want their own answer or position reinforced?

Others argue that schools should be value-free. But elements of human experience are value-free only if they are totally devoid of meaning. To say that it is important for a child to learn to read is to express a value judgment—no matter how broad or benign. A child cannot be led or directed (depending upon one's philosophy of education) from a state of ignorance to a state of knowledge without the minimal value judgment that knowledge is preferable to ignorance. And then there are a multitude of value judgments with respect to the specific knowledge a child should gain from schooling. To complicate matters further, children then exercise value judgments concerning the degree and manner of their learning.

These are terribly complex issues. Solutions considered apart from a specific setting in which these issues arise tend to be abstract and difficult to apply. However, several rather general suggestions toward solving these issues may be made. Public schools should not teach science as religion nor, of course, should religion be taught as science. Through science courses, students should gain an appreciation of the nature of the empirical approach, including its capacities and limitations. Students should be taught that science is one valuable approach to solving problems and acquiring knowledge. Science, however, should not be portrayed as the road to final truth but as one of many avenues to truth. While science may clearly indicate *how* natural events occur, it should never be used as a source for answers to the question of *why* natural events occur. Conversely, schools should also teach about religion, but only in terms of the

Supreme Court's guidelines. Indeed, had religion studies programs been in use, they would have been an appropriate vehicle for addressing creationism or any of the answers humanity has formulated regarding the origin of life and the universe.

The intensity of issues related to the relationship of religion to public education might be lessened if public school personnel became more sensitive to the nature of the community they serve and sought open lines of communication with that community. For example, schools cannot avoid teaching about other cultures even when such instruction might include practices and ideas that are offensive to individuals or groups in the community. On the other hand, little of value is gained if predictably controversial material is employed simply in the name of "academic freedom" or "quality education" when less objectionable material would serve the same educational goals. It is important that open lines of communication be maintained between the schools and the students' parents—lines that encourage both speaking and listening.

The serious attention of educators to value or moral education would also help lessen tension arising from the religion-public education relationship. Public school personnel must be very cautious in assuming moral positions beyond fundamental questions of right and wrong in human relationships. The "morality" of a school as a public institution must clearly incorporate the legal structure of the community, and the laws of the community must be enforced in its schools. An additional area of moral concern would involve those moral and value considerations necessary for the function of an academic community. Cheating, for example, must not be tolerated—but care should be taken that the educational program of the school not be the primary cause of academic dishonesty. A far more difficult area of moral concern relates to the quality of relationships maintained by students in school. Concern might run the gamut from, for example, respect for the rights of others to questions related to dress codes or "offensive" language. An enormously complicated area of morality concerns the values that a teacher subconsciously teaches students, and that students and teacher subconsciously agree upon in their dealings with each other.

Relevant questions here would include: How much attention will be given to the "hidden curriculum" [50] of the schools? Will schools undertake values clarification or any other approach to value education? Are teachers to be officially encouraged or discouraged with respect to discussions of values and morals as these matters relate directly to the subjects being taught? Will subjects such as social studies or literature be dealt with factually, or will they provide a vehicle for discussion of moral issues in keeping with the experiential background of the students involved? How far should teachers and other school professionals go in advising students concerning personal values or moral concerns? As an area of study ladened with value and moral considerations, will religion studies be taught?

While steps may be taken to lessen the likelihood of controversy, the potential for controversy will remain. As institutions of government, public schools cannot avoid pressures for accountability to the public, nor should they. Schools were created and are maintained to serve a public function, and they must be answerable for the degree of success they attain. As public institutions, public schools will continue to encounter the enormous problems associated with serving a heterogeneous clientele and satisfying everyone while offending no one seems impossible. Furthermore, as an institution that children are required to attend, public schools share an extraordinarily delicate responsibility with parents for the positive growth of children. The evangelical fervor of fundamentalist Christians and thoroughgoing secularists alike will be satisfied only when their viewpoints are fully established in public schools. Contro-

---

[50]This concept is succinctly "defined" in the following: ". . . children are taught a host of lessons about values, ethics, morality, character, and conduct every day of the week, less by the content of the curriculum than by the way schools are organized, the ways teachers and parents behave, the way they talk to children and to each other, the kinds of behavior they approve or reward and the kinds they disapprove or punish. These lessons are far more powerful than the verbalizations that accompany them and that they frequently controvert." Charles E. Silberman, *Crisis in the Classroom* (New York: Random House, 1970) 9.

versy generated by these forces, therefore, may be anticipated far into the future. We will now turn to a review of the litigation generated by this controversy that has received the attention of the Supreme Court.

CHAPTER 5

The Rulings
of the Supreme Court

A variety of approaches to the relationship of religion to public education are available: the theological, the cultural, the educational, the sectarian, the secular, the sociological, the historical, the legal. The legal approach, however, recommends itself because of constitutional dedication of this nation to the protection of individual liberty, the legal ramifications of the religion-government relationship, and the fact that the American system of public education is part of government. When a legal approach is selected, the decisions of the highest tribunal in the land assume paramount importance and are, therefore, central to this discussion.

The major decisions announced by the Supreme Court directly addressing the relationship of religion to public education are reproduced in this chapter.[1] The decisions have been edited in that technical legal material, extensive support data, and, oc-

---

[1]The edited text of some typical lower court decisions pertinent to the relationship of religion to public education that the Court dealt with as memorandum decisions will be found in appendix D.

casionally, lengthy elaborative discussion have been omitted. Otherwise, the decisions are quoted directly, omission of material representing the only editing undertaken. In all cases, the attempt has been made to preserve the essence of the Court's decision.

Selected concurring and dissenting opinions are included with the decisions of the Court. Concurring opinions, while in agreement with the opinion of the Court, often expand upon that decision or express another approach to the same conclusion that the Court considered to be a noteworthy alternative. Dissenting opinions are the arguments of the justices who oppose the decision of the Court. Generally evidencing genuine and substantial disagreement, dissenting opinions illustrate the kinds of viewpoints the Court has seriously considered but rejected in its deliberations. Therefore, in the absence of an important change in judicial opinion, dissenting opinions familiarize one with the kinds of arguments the Court will probably reject in future litigation. Concurring and dissenting opinions contribute to an understanding of the position of the Court on any issue.

The following section of this chapter presents the edited decisions of the Court. Each decision will be preceded by a brief introduction to that decision. A concluding section will summarize the major guidelines for the relationship to public education that emerge from the rulings of the Court.

The Decisions

MINERSVILLE SCHOOL DISTRICT v. GOBITIS

In formulating the decision of the Court, Justice Frankfurter dealt with conflict between government and religion caused by governmental regulation that allegedly violated religious conscience. Cultural tradition, including patriotic sensibilities, must be preserved through transmission from one generation to the next. Furthermore, loyalty to that form of government that guarantees freedom for religious belief must be nurtured.

However, while religious freedom is essential, does the Court have the right to interfere with state legislatures when they institute citizenship training in schools? Although a symbolic act, the flag salute is surely an important component of such training. Justice Frankfurter believed that it should be easy for parents to cancel state influence upon their children that conflicted with their (the parents') beliefs. Moreover, to rule that some children could be excused from this aspect of citizenship training could possibly disrupt school discipline. Freedom of belief and the sanctity of the home may be maintained and guaranteed only in an ordered society, a society symbolized by the flag. To preserve the freedoms enjoyed in such a society, Justice Frankfurter concluded that it is appropriate for the state to utilize schools for citizenship education.

Justice Stone, in dissent, contended that, whatever the occasion or motivation, it is a denial of individual liberty to force an individual to a belief that he does not in fact hold. Government must protect and sustain itself, but does that require public affirmations that contradict religious belief? Other, more effective methods of citizenship education are surely available. As the state may require school attendance, it may also require the study of United States history and government. Such instruction would provide citizenship education but would not violate the religious sensibilities of certain segments of the population. The democratic process must be preserved, but individual freedom of mind and spirit cannot be suppressed or violated in the process.

MINERSVILLE SCHOOL DISTRICT v. GOBITIS.

310 U.S. 586

Decided June 3, 1940—one justice dissenting.

Mr. Justice FRANKFURTER delivered the opinion of the Court.

A grave responsibility confronts this Court whenever in course of litigation it must reconcile the conflicting claims of liberty and authority. But when the liberty invoked is liberty of conscience, and the authority is authority to safeguard the nation's fellowship, judicial conscience is put to its severest test. Of such a nature is the present controversy.

Lillian Gobitis, aged twelve, and her brother William, aged ten, were expelled from the public schools of Minersville, Pennsylvania, for refusing to salute the national flag as part of a daily school exercise. The local Board of Education required both teachers and pupils to participate in this ceremony. . . . The Gobitis family are affiliated with "Jehovah's Witnesses", for whom the Bible as the Word of God is the supreme authority. The children had been brought up conscientiously to believe that such a gesture of respect for the flag was forbidden by command of scripture.

The Gobitis children were of an age for which Pennsylvania makes school attendance compulsory. Thus they were denied a free education and their parents had to put them into private schools. To be relieved of the financial burden thereby entailed, their father, on behalf of the children and in his own behalf, brought this suit. He sought to enjoin the authorities from continuing to exact participation in the flag-salute ceremony as a condition of his children's attendance at the Minersville school.

We must decide whether the requirement of participation in such a ceremony, exacted from a child who refuses upon sincere religious grounds, infringes without due process of law the liberty guaranteed by the Fourteenth Amendment.

Centuries of strife over the erection of particular dogmas as exclusive or all-comprehending faiths led to the inclusion of a guarantee for religious freedom in the Bill of Rights. The First Amendment, and the Fourteenth through its absorption of the First, sought to guard against repetition of those bitter religious struggles by prohibiting the establishment of a state religion and by securing to every sect the free exercise of its faith. So pervasive is the acceptance of this previous right that its scope is brought into question, as here, only when the conscience of individuals collides with the felt necessities of society.

Certainly the affirmative pursuit of one's convictions about the ultimate mystery of the universe and man's relation to it is placed beyond the reach of law. Government may not interfere with organized or individual expression of belief or disbelief. Propagation of belief—or even of disbelief in the supernatural—is protected, whether in church or chapel, mosque or synagogue, tabernacle or meetinghouse. Likewise the Constitution assures generous immunity to the individual from imposition of penalties for offending, in the course of his own religious activities, the religious views of others, be they a minority or those who are dominant in government.

But the manifold character of man's relations may bring his conception of religious duty into conflict with the secular interests of his fellow-men. When does the constitutional guarantee compel exemption from doing what society thinks necessary for the promotion of some great common end, or from a penalty for conduct which appears dangerous to the general good? To state the problem is to recall the truth that no single principle can answer all of life's complexities. The right to freedom of religious belief, however dissident and however obnoxious to the cherished beliefs of others—even of a majority—is itself the denial of an absolute. But to affirm that the freedom to follow conscience has itself no limits in the life of a society would deny that very plurality of principles which, as a matter of history, underlies protection of religious toleration. Our present task then, as so often the case with courts, is to reconcile two rights in order to prevent either from destroying the other.

Conscientious scruples have not, in the course of the long struggle for religious toleration, relieved the individual from obedience to a general law not aimed at the promotion or restriction of religious beliefs. The mere possession of religious convictions which contradict the relevant concerns of a political society does not relieve the citizen from the discharge of political responsibilities. The necessity for this adjustment has again and again been recognized.

The ultimate foundation of a free society is the binding tie of cohesive sentiment. Such a sentiment is fostered by all those agencies of the mind and spirit which may serve to gather up the traditions of a people, transmit them from generation to generation, and thereby create that continuity of a treasured common life which constitutes a civilization. "We live by symbols." The flag is the symbol of our national unity, transcending all internal differences, however large, within the framework of the Constitution.

The case before us must be viewed as though the legislature of Pennsylvania had itself formally directed the flag-salute for the children of Minersville; had made no exemption for children whose parents were possessed of conscientious scruples like those of the Gobitis family; and had indicated its belief in the desirable ends to be secured by having its public school children share a common experience at those periods of development when their minds are supposedly receptive to its assimilation, by an exercise appropriate in time and place and setting, and one designed to evoke in them appreciation of the nation's hopes and dreams, its sufferings and sacrifices. The precise issue, then, for us to decide is whether the legislatures of the various states and the authorities in a thousand counties and school districts of this country are barred from determining the appropriateness of various means to evoke that unifying sentiment without which there can ultimately be no liberties, civil or religious.

The wisdom of training children in patriotic impulses by those compulsions which necessarily pervade so much of the educational process is not for our independent judgment. Even were we convinced of the folly of such a measure, such belief would be no proof of its unconstitutionality . . . . the courtroom is not the arena for debating issues of educational policy. It is not our province to choose among competing considerations in the subtle process of securing effective loyalty to the traditional ideals of democracy, while respecting at the same time individual idiosyncracies among a people so diversified in racial origins and religious allegiances. So to hold would in effect make us the school board for the country. That authority has not been given to this Court, nor should we assume it.

We are dealing here with the formative period in the development of citizenship. Great diversity of psychological and ethical opinion exists among us concerning the best way to train children for their place in society. Because of these differences and because of reluctance to permit a single, iron-cast system of education to be imposed upon a nation compounded of so many strains, we have held that, even though public education is one of our most cherished democratic institutions, the Bill of Rights bars a state from compelling all children to attend the public schools. . . . But it is a very different thing for this Court to exercise censorship over the conviction of legislatures that a particular program or exercise will best promote in the minds of children who attend the common schools an attachment to the institutions of their country.

What the school authorities are really asserting is the right to awaken in the child's mind considerations as to the significance of the flag contrary to those implanted by the parent. In such an attempt the state is normally at a disadvantage in competing with the parent's authority, so long—and this is the vital aspect of religious toleration—as parents are unmolested in their right to counteract by their own persuasiveness the wisdom and rightness of those loyalties which the state's educational system is seeking to promote. . . .That the flag-salute is an allowable portion of a school program for those who do not invoke conscientious scruples is surely not debatable. But for us to insist that, though the ceremony may be required, exceptional immunity must be given to dissidents, is to maintain that there is no basis for a legislative judgment that such an exemption might introduce elements of difficulty into the school discipline, might cast doubts in the minds of the other children which would themselves weaken the effect of the exercise.

The preciousness of the family relation, the authority and independence which give dignity to parenthood, indeed the enjoyment of all freedom, presuppose the kind of ordered society which is summarized by our flag. A society which is dedicated to the preservation of these ultimate values of civilization may in self-protection utilize the educational process of inculcating those almost unconscious feelings which bind men together in a comprehending loyalty, whatever may be their lesser differences and difficulties.

Mr. Justice STONE (dissenting).

The law which is thus sustained is unique in the history of Anglo-American legislation. It does more than suppress freedom of speech and more than prohibit the free exercise of religion, which concededly are forbidden by the First Amendment and are violations of the liberty guaranteed by the Fourteenth. For by this law the state seeks to coerce these children to express a sentiment which, as they interpret it, they do not entertain, and which violates their deepest religious convictions. It is not denied that such compulsion is a prohibited infringement of personal liberty, freedom of speech and religion, guaranteed by the Bill of Rights, except in so far as it may be justified and supported as a proper exercise of the state's power over public education.

Concededly the constitutional guaranties of personal liberty are not always absolutes. Government has a right to survive and powers conferred upon it are not necessarily set at naught by the express prohibitions of the Bill of Rights . . . . But it is a long step, and one which I am unable to take, to the position that government may, as a supposed educational measure and as a means of disciplining the young, compel public affirmations which violate their religious conscience.

. . . even if we believe that such compulsions will contribute to national unity, there are other ways to teach loyalty and patriotism which are the sources of national unity, than by compelling the pupil to affirm that which he does not believe and by commanding a form of affirmance which violates his religious convictions. Without recourse to such compulsion the state is free to compel attendance at school and require teaching by instruction and study of all in our history and in the structure and organization of our government, including the guarantees of civil liberty which tend to inspire patriotism and love of country.

The guaranties of civil liberty are but guaranties of freedom of the human mind and spirit and of reasonable freedom and opportunity to express them. They presuppose the right of the individual to hold such opinions as he will and to give them reasonably free expression, and his freedom, and that of the state as well, to teach and persuade others by the communication of ideas. The very essence of the liberty which they guarantee is the freedom of the individual from compulsion as to what he shall think and what he shall say, at least where the compulsion is to bear false witness to his religion. If these guaranties are to have any meaning they must, I think, be deemed to withhold from the state any authority to compel belief or the expression of it where that expression violates religious convictions, whatever may be the legislative view of the desirability of such compulsion.

History teaches us that there have been but few infringements of personal liberty by the state which have not been justified, as they are here, in the name of righteousness and the public good, and few which have not been directed, as they are now, at politically helpless minorities. The framers were not unaware that under the system which they created most governmental curtailments of personal liberty would have the support of a legislative judgment that the public interest would be better served by its curtailment than by its constitutional protection. I cannot conceive that in prescribing, as limitations upon the powers of government, the freedom of the mind and spirit secured by the explicit guaranties of freedom of speech and religion, they intended or rightly could have left any latitude for a legislative judgment that the compulsory expression of belief which violates religious convictions would better serve the public interest than their protection. The Constitution may well elicit expressions of loyalty to it and to the government which it created, but it does not command such expressions or otherwise give any indication that compulsory expressions of loyalty play any such part in our scheme of government as to override the constitutional protection of freedom of speech and religion.

The Constitution expresses more than the conviction of the people that democratic processes must be preserved at all costs. It is also an expression of faith and a command that freedom of mind and spirit must be preserved, which government must obey, if it is to adhere to that justice and moderation without which no free government can exist.

WEST VIRGINIA v. BARNETTE

Justice Jackson faced the demanding task of reevaluating a recent decision of the Court. The issue, according to Justice Jackson, turned on the imposition of a specific confession of belief by the student as a condition of access to public education. Regardless of the alleged value of a ceremony, does our government have the right to force an American citizen to affirm publicly a belief or engage in a ceremony? The presence of religious conviction was not the issue, as the Court in *Gobitis* had assumed it was. The issue, rather, was whether government is empowered to force the expression of opinion or political attitude. The Court believed that the Bill of Rights prohibits such governmental action. No matter how important the motivation for providing education, government must function within the limits of the Bill of Rights. Justice Jackson concluded that, in citizenship education, the rights of the individual as a citizen cannot be violated. We must never lose sight of the fact that our form of government was constituted to protect just such rights.

In this decision, Justice Jackson expressed the view of the Court that the will of the majority simply does not apply in such situations. In fact, to follow the will of a majority in religious matters would be tantamount to the establishment of those religious views. The limitations of the Constitution must, therefore, be maintained "with no fear that freedom to be intellectually and spiritually diverse or even contrary will disintegrate the social organization."

Justice Frankfurter's dissent—an eloquent defense of the *Gobitis* decision—presented a view of the limitations of the judiciary with respect to the legislative power and action of the states. He appeared to believe that state legislatures should be subject only to the will of the people they represent. Legislation, he conceded, cannot promote or restrict religion, but legislators also cannot be denied the right to enact purely civil legislation that only "touches conscientious scruples or religious beliefs of an individual or a group."

WEST VIRGINIA
STATE BOARD OF EDUCATION v. BARNETTE
319 U.S. 624
Decided June 14, 1943—three justices dissenting.

Mr. Justice JACKSON delivered the opinion of the Court.

Following the decision by this Court on June 3, 1940, in Minersville School District v. Gobitis, 310 U.S. 586, 1940, the West Virginia legislature amended its statutes to require all schools therein to conduct courses of instruction in history, civics, and in the Constitutions of the United States and of the State "for the purpose of teaching, fostering and perpetuating the ideals, principles and spirit of Americanism, and increasing the knowledge of the organization and machinery of the government."

The Board of Education on January 9, 1942, adopted a resolution containing recitals taken largely from the Court's Gobitis opinion and ordering that the salute to the flag become "a regular part of the program of activities in the public schools," that all teachers and pupils "shall be required to participate in the salute honoring the Nation represented by the Flag; provided, however, that refusal to salute the Flag be regarded as an Act of insubordination, and shall be dealt with accordingly."

Failure to conform is "insubordination" dealt with by expulsion. Readmission is denied by statute until compliance. Meanwhile the expelled child is "unlawfully absent" and may be proceeded against as a delinquent. His parents or guardians are liable to prosecution. . .

Appellees, citizens of the United States and of West Virginia, brought suit in the United States District Court for themselves and others similarly situated asking its injunction to restrain enforcement of these laws and regulations against Jehovah's Witnesses. The Witnesses are an unincorporated body teaching that the obligation imposed by law of God is superior to that of laws enacted by temporal government.

Children of this faith have been expelled from school and are threatened with exclusion for no other cause. Officials threaten to send them to reformatories maintained for criminally inclined juveniles. Parents of such children have been prosecuted and are threatened with prosecutions for causing delinquency.

This case calls upon us to reconsider a precedent decision, as the Court throughout its history often has been required to do. Before turning to the Gobitis case, however, it is desirable to notice certain characteristics by which this controversy is distinguished.

. . . the refusal of these persons to participate in the ceremony does not interfere with or deny rights of others to do so. Nor is there any question in this case that their behavior is peaceable and orderly. The sole conflict is between authority and rights of the individual. The State asserts power to condition access to public education on making a prescribed sign and profession and at the same time to coerce attendance by punishing both parent and child. The latter stand on a right of self-determination in matters that touch individual opinion and personal attitude.

As the present Chief Justice said in dissent in the Gobitis case, the State may "require teaching by instruction and study of all in our history and in the structure and organization of our government, including the guaranties of civil liberty which tend to inspire patriotism and love of country. . ." Here, however, we are dealing with a compulsion of students to declare a belief. . . . The issue here is whether this slow and easily neglected route to aroused loyalties constitutionally may be short-cut by substituting a compulsory salute and slogan.

There is no doubt that, in connection with the pledges, the flag salute is a form of utterance. Symbolism is a primitive but effective way of communicating ideas. The use of an emblem or flag to symbolize some system, idea, institution, or personality, is a short cut from mind to mind. Causes and nations, political parties, lodges and ecclesiastical groups seek to knit the loyalty of their followings to a flag or banner, a color or design. The State announces rank, function, and authority through crowns and maces, uniforms and black robes; the church speaks through the Cross, the Crucifix, the altar and shrine, and clerical raiment. Symbols of State often convey political ideas just as religious symbols come to convey theological ones. Associated with many of these symbols are appropriate gestures of acceptance or respect: a salute, a bowed or bared head, a bended knee. A person gets from a symbol the meaning he puts into it, and what is one man's comfort and inspiration is another's jest and scorn.

. . . here the power of compulsion is invoked without any allegation that remaining passive during a flag salute ritual creates a clear and present danger that would justify an effort even to muffle expression. To sustain the compulsory flag salute we are required to say that a Bill of Rights which guards the individual's right to speak his own mind, left it open to public authorities to compel him to utter what is not in his mind.

Whether the First Amendment to the Constitution will permit officials to order observance of ritual of this nature does not depend upon whether as a voluntary exercise we would think it to be good, bad or merely innocuous . . . .validity of the asserted power to force an American citizen publicly to profess any statement of belief or to engage in any ceremony of assent to one presents questions of power that must be considered independently of any idea we may have as to the utility of the ceremony in question.

Nor does the issue as we see it turn on one's possession of particular religious views or the sincerity with which they are held. While religion supplies appellees' motive for enduring the discomforts of making the issue in this case, many citizens who do not share these religious views hold such a compulsory rite to infringe constitutional liberty of the individual. It is not necessary to inquire whether nonconformist beliefs will exempt from the duty to salute unless we first find power to make the salute a legal duty.

The Gobitis decision, however, *assumed*, as did the argument in that case and in this, that power exists in the State to impose the flag salute discipline upon school children in general. The Court only examined and rejected a claim based on religious beliefs of immunity from an unquestioned general rule. The question which underlies the flag salute controversy is whether such a ceremony so touching matters of opinion and political attitude may be imposed upon the individual by official authority under powers committed to any political organization under our Constitution.

Government of limited power need not be anemic government. Assurance that rights are secure tends to diminish fear and jealousy of strong government, and by making us feel safe to live under it makes for its better support. Without promise of a limiting Bill of Rights it is doubtful if our Constitution could have mustered enough strength to enable its ratification. To enforce those rights today is not to choose weak government over strong government. It is only to adhere as a means of strength to individual freedom of mind in preference to officially disciplined uniformity for which history indicates a disappointing and disastrous end.

The subject now before us exemplifies this principle. Free public education, if faithful to the ideal of secular instruction and political neutrality, will not be partisan or enemy of any class, creed, party, or faction. If it is to impose any ideological discipline, however, each party or denomination must seek to control, or failing that, to weaken the influence of the educational system. Observance of the limitations of the Constitution will not weaken government in the field appropriate for its exercise.

The Fourteenth Amendment, as now applied to the States, protects the citizen against the State itself and all of its creatures—Boards of Education not excepted. These have, of course, important, delicate, and highly discretionary functions, but none that they may not perform within the limits of the Bill of Rights. That they are educating the young for citizenship is reason for scrupulous protection of Constitutional freedoms of the individual, if we are not to strangle the free mind at its source and teach youth to discount important principles of our government as mere platitudes.

Such Boards are numerous and their territorial jurisdiction often small. But small and local authority may feel less sense of responsibility to the Constitution, and agencies of publicity may be less vigilant in calling it to account. The action of Congress in making flag observance voluntary and respecting the conscience of the objector in a matter so vital as raising the Army contrasts sharply with these local regulations in matters relatively trivial to the welfare of the nation.

The very purpose of a Bill of Rights was to withdraw certain subjects from the vicissitudes of political controversy, to place them beyond the reach of majorities and officials and to establish them as legal principles to be applied by the courts. One's right to life, liberty, and property, to free speech, a free press, freedom of worship and assembly, and other fundamental rights may not be submitted to vote; they depend on the outcome of no elections.

. . . the task of translating the majestic generalities of the Bill of Rights, conceived as part of the pattern of liberal government in the eighteenth century, into concrete restraints on officials dealing with the problems of the twentieth century, is one to disturb self-confidence. These principles grew in soil which also produced a philosophy that the individual was the center of society, that his liberty was attainable through mere absence of governmental restraints, and that government should be entrusted with few controls and only the mildest supervision over men's affairs. We must transplant these rights to a soil in which the *laissez-faire* concept or principle of non-interference has withered at least as to economic affairs, and social advancements are increasingly sought through closer integration of society and through expanded and strengthened governmental controls. These changed conditions often deprive precedents of reliability and cast us more than we would choose upon our own judgment. But we act in these matters not by authority of our competence but by force of our commissions. We cannot, because of modest estimates of our competence in such specialties as public education, withhold the judgment that history authenticates as the function of this Court when liberty is infringed.

National unity as an end which officials may foster by persuasion and example is not in question. The problem is whether under our Constitution compulsion as here employed is a permissable means for its achievement.

Struggles to coerce uniformity of sentiment in support of some end thought essential to their time and country have been waged by many good as well as by evil men. Nationalism is a relatively recent phenomenon but at other times and places the ends have been racial or territorial security, support of a dynasty or regime, and particular plans for saving souls. As first and moderate methods to attain unity have failed, those bent on its accomplishment must resort to an ever increasing severity. As governmental pressure toward unity becomes greater, so strife becomes more bitter as to whose unity it shall be. Probably no deeper division of our people could proceed from any provocation than from finding it necessary to choose what doctrine and whose program public educational officials shall compel youth to unite in embracing. Ultimate futility of such attempts to compel coherence is the lesson of every such effort from the Roman drive to stamp out Christianity as a disturber of its pagan unity, the Inquisition, as a means to religious and dynastic unity, the Siberian exiles as a means to Russian unity, down to the fast failing efforts of our present totalitarian enemies. Those who begin coercive elimination of dissent soon find themselves exterminating dissenters. Compulsory unification of opinion achieves only the unanimity of the graveyard.

It seems trite but necessary to say that the First Amendment to our Constitution was designed to avoid these ends by avoiding these beginnings. There is no mysticism in the American concept of the State or of the nature or origin of its authority. We set up government by consent of the governed, and the Bill of Rights denies those in power any legal opportunity to coerce that consent. Authority here is to be controlled by public opinion, not public opinion by authority.

The case is made difficult not because the principles of its decision are obscure but because the flag involved is our own. Nevertheless, we apply the limitations of the Constitution with no fear that freedom to be intellectually and spiritually diverse or even contrary will disintegrate the social organization. To believe that patriotism will not flourish if patriotic ceremonies are voluntary and spontaneous instead of a compulsory routine is to make an unflattering estimate of the appeal of our institutions to free minds. We can have intellectual individualism and the rich cultural diversities that we owe to exceptional minds only at the price of occasional eccentricity and abnormal attitudes. When they are so harmless to others or to the State as those we deal with here, the price is not too great. But freedom to differ is not limited to things that do not matter much. That would be a mere shadow of freedom. The test of its substance is the right to differ as to things that touch the heart of the existing order.

If there is any fixed star in our constitutional constellation, it is that no official, high or petty, can prescribe what shall be orthodox in politics, nationalism, religion, or other matters of opinion or force citizens to confess by word or act their faith therein. If there are any circumstances which permit an exception, they do not now occur to us.

We think the action of the local authorities in compelling the flag salute and pledge transcends constitutional limitations on their power and invades the sphere of intellect and spirit which it is the purpose of the First Amendment to our Constitution to reserve from all official control.

The decision of this Court in *Minersville School District v. Gobitis* and the holdings of those few per curiam decisions which preceded and foreshadowed it are overruled, and the judgment enjoining enforcement of the West Virginia Regulation is affirmed.

Mr. Justice BLACK and Mr. Justice DOUGLAS, concurring.

We are substantially in agreement with the opinion just read, but since we originally joined with the Court in the Gobitis case, it is appropriate that we make a brief statement of reasons for our change of view.

Reluctance to make the Federal Constitution a rigid bar against state regulation of conduct thought inimical to the public welfare was the controlling influence which moved us to consent to the *Gobitis* decision. Long reflection convinced us that although the principle is sound, its application in the particular case was wrong. . . . We believe that the statute before us fails to accord full scope to the freedom of religion secured to the appellees by the First and Fourteenth Amendments.

The statute requires the appellees to participate in a ceremony aimed at inculcating respect for the flag and for this country. The Jehovah's Witnesses, without any desire to show disrespect for either the flag or the country, interpret the Bible as commanding, at the risk of God's displeasure, that they not go through the form of a pledge of allegiance to any flag. The devoutness of their belief is evidenced by their willingness to suffer persecution and punishment, rather than make the pledge.

No well ordered society can leave to the individuals an absolute right to make final decisions, unassailable by the State, as to everything they will or will not do. The First Amendment does not go so far. Religious faiths, honestly held, do not free individuals from responsibility to conduct themselves obediently to laws which are either imperatively necessary to protect society as a whole from grave and pressingly imminent dangers or which, without any general prohibition, merely regulate time, place or manner or religious activity.

Words uttered under coercion are proof of loyalty to nothing but self-interest. Love of country must spring from willing hearts and free minds, inspired by a fair administration of wise laws enacted by the people's elected representatives within the bounds of express constitutional prohibitions.

Neither our domestic tranquillity in peace nor our martial effort in war depends on compelling little children to participate in a ceremony which ends in nothing for them but a fear of spiritual condemnation. If, as we think, their fears are groundless, time and reason are the proper antidotes for their errors. The ceremonial, when enforced against conscientious objectors, more likely to defeat than to serve its high purpose, is a handy implement for disguised religious persecution. As such, it is inconsistent with our Constitution's plan and purpose. . . .

Mr. Justice FRANKFURTER, dissenting.

One who belongs to the most vilified and persecuted minority in history is not likely to be insensible to the freedoms guaranteed by our Constitution. Were my purely personal attitude relevant I should wholeheartedly associate myself with the general libertarian views in the Court's opinion, representing as they do the thought and action of a lifetime. But as judges we are neither Jew nor Gentile, neither Catholic nor agnostic. We owe equal attachment to the Constitution and are equally bound by our judicial obligations whether we derive our citizenship from the earliest or the latest immigrants to these shores. As a member of this Court I am not justified in writing my private notions of policy into the Constitution, no matter how deeply I may cherish them or how mischievous I may deem their discharge. The duty of a judge who must decide which of two claims before the Court shall prevail, that of a State to enact and enforce laws within its general competence or that of an individual to refuse obedience because of the demands of his conscience, is not that of the ordinary person. It can never be emphasized too much that one's own opinion about the wisdom or evil of a law should be excluded altogether when one is doing one's duty on the bench. The only opinion of our own even looking in that direction that is material is our opinion whether legislators could in reason have enacted such a law. In the light of all the circumstances, including the history of this question in this Court, it would require more daring than I possess to deny that reasonable legislators could have taken the action which is before us for review. Most unwillingly, therefore, I must differ from my brethren with regard to legislation like this.

There is no warrant in the constitutional basis of this Court's authority for attributing different roles to it depending upon the nature of the challenge

to the legislation. Our power does not vary according to the particular provision of the Bill of Rights which is invoked. The right not to have property
taken without just compensation has, so far as the scope of judicial power is
concerned, the same constitutional dignity as the right to be protected
against unreasonable searches and seizures, and the latter has no less claim
than freedom of the press or freedom of speech or religious freedom. In no
instance is this Court the primary protector of the particular liberty that is
invoked. This Court has recognized, what hardly could be denied, that all
the provisions of the first ten Amendments are "specific" prohibitions . . .

When Mr. Justice Holmes, speaking for this Court, wrote that "it must be
remembered that legislatures are ultimate guardians of the liberties and
welfare of the people in quite as great a degree as the courts". . . he went to
the very essence of our constitutional system and the democratic conception
of our society. . . . He was stating the comprehensive judicial duty and role
of this Court in our constitutional scheme whenever legislation is sought to
be nullified on any ground, namely, that responsibility for legislation lies
with legislatures, answerable as they are directly to the people, and this
Court's only and very narrow function is to determine whether within the
broad grant of authority vested in legislatures they have exercised a judgment for which reasonable justification can be offered.

We are not reviewing merely the action of a local school board. The flag
salute requirement in this case comes before us with the full authority of the
State of West Virginia. We are in fact passing judgment on "the power of the
State as a whole." . . . Practically we are passing upon the political power of
each of the forty-eight states. Moreover, since the First Amendment has
been read into the Fourteenth, our problem is precisely the same as it would
be if we had before us an Act of Congress for the District of Columbia. To
suggest that we are here concerned with the heedless action of some village
tyrants is to distort the augustness of the constitutional issue and the reach
of the consequences of our decision.

Under our constitutional system the legislature is charged solely with civil
concerns of society. If the avowed or intrinsic legislative purpose is either to
promote or to discourage some religious community or creed, it is clearly
within the constitutional restrictions imposed on legislatures and cannot
stand. But it by no means follows that legislative power is wanting whenever
a general non-discriminatory civil regulation in fact touches conscientious
scruples or religious beliefs of an individual or a group.

A court can only strike down. It can only say "This or that law is void." It
cannot modify or qualify, it cannot make exceptions to a general requirement. And it strikes down not merely for a day. At least the finding of unconstitutionality ought not to have ephemeral significance unless the
Constitution is to be reduced to the fugitive importance of mere legislation.
When we are dealing with the Constitution of the United States, and more
particularly with the great safeguards of the Bill of Rights, we are dealing

with principles of liberty and justice "so rooted in the traditions and conscience of our people as to be ranked as fundamental"—something without
which "a fair and enlightened system of justice would be impossible."

What one can say with assurance is that the history out of which grew constitutional provisions for religious equality and the writings of the great ex-
ponents of religious freedom—Jefferson, Madison, John Adams, Benjamin
Franklin—are totally wanting in justification for a claim by dissidents of exceptional immunity from civic measures of general applicability, measures
not in fact disguised assaults upon such dissident views. The great leaders of
the American Revolution were determined to remove political support from
every religious establishment. . . . So far as the state was concerned, there
was to be neither orthodoxy nor heterodoxy. And so Jefferson and those who
followed him wrote guaranties of religious freedom into our constitutions.
Religious minorities as well as religious majorities were to be equal in the
eyes of the political state. But Jefferson and the others also knew that minorities may disrupt society. It never would have occurred to them to write
into the Constitution the subordination of the general civil authority of the
state to sectarian scruples.

The constitutional protection of religious freedom terminated disabilities,
it did not create new privileges. It gave religious equality, not civil immunity.
Its essence is freedom from conformity to religious dogma, not freedom from
conformity to law because of religious dogma.

Any person may . . . believe or disbelieve what he pleases. He may practice what he will in his own house of worship or publicly within the limits of
public order. But the lawmaking authority is not circumscribed by the variety of religious beliefs, otherwise the constitutional guaranty would be not
a protection of the free exercise of religion but a denial of the exercise of
legislation.

The essence of the religious freedom guaranteed by our Constitution is
therefore this: no religion shall either receive the state's support or incur its
hostility. Religion is outside the sphere of political government. This does
not mean that all matters on which religious organizations or beliefs may
pronounce are outside the sphere of government. Were this so, instead of the
separation of church and state, there would be the subordination of the state
on any matter deemed within the sovereignty of the religious conscience.

An act compelling profession of allegiance to a religion, no matter how
subtly or tenuously promoted, is bad. But an act promoting good citizenship
and national allegiance is within the domain of governmental authority and
is therefore to be judged by the same considerations of power and of constitutionality as those involved in the many claims of immunity from civil obedience because of religious scruples.

Law is concerned with external behavior and not with the inner life of
man. . . . The individual conscience may profess what faith it chooses. It may
affirm and promote that faith . . . but it cannot thereby restrict community

action through political organs in matters of community concern, so long as the action is not asserted in a discriminatory way either openly or by stealth. One may have the right to practice one's religion and at the same time owe the duty of formal obedience to laws that run counter to one's beliefs.

That which to the majority may seem essential for the welfare of the state may offend the consciences of a minority. But, so long as no inroads are made upon the actual exercise of religion by the minority, to deny the political power of the majority to enact laws concerned with civil matters, simply because they may offend the consciences of a minority, really means that the consciences of a minority are more sacred and more enshrined in the Constitution than the consciences of a majority.

McCOLLUM v. BOARD OF EDUCATION

Justice Black spoke for the Court in these deliberations addressing the constitutionality of the utilization of tax-supported public schools for sectarian religious instruction. The Court concluded that the use of the tax-supported public schools and their compulsory attendance laws for such purposes clearly violated the First Amendment.

A separate opinion, written by Justice Frankfurter and joined by three justices, provided a clearly reasoned analysis of the rationale for the position of the Court along with an informative history of the practice. According to Justice Frankfurter, the issue was not the concept of "released time" or the many programs that fall under that rubric; the issue was the role played by the public schools in the execution of such programs. It was no matter that discrimination did not appear to be present in the plan under judicial review; the crucial problem was the fusion of governmental function with sectarian religion that was so apparent in the "released time" program under review. Moreover, while the program did not discriminate, it did put the weight of the state behind sectarian instruction for students susceptible to peer pressure. Therefore, the plan under review violated the Constitution.

Justice Jackson, in a concurring opinion, plead for some specificity in the ruling of the Court. The plaintiff in the case had asked that the Court "ban every form of teaching which suggests or recognizes that there is a God." Justice Jackson saw the "sweep and detail" of such complaints as a danger signal for future litigation and his foresight was prophetic. Furthermore, Justice Jackson provided some guidelines for the presence of religious content in the curriculum of the public schools that are most important in determining the relationship of religion to public education. The problems associated with such a curricular presence were clear to the justice, but he remained unwilling to concede to the demands of the plaintiff for the complete elimination of religion from public education.

PEOPLE OF STATE OF ILLINOIS ex rel. McCOLLUM v. BOARD
OF EDUCATION OF SCHOOL DIST. NO. 71, CHAMPAIGN
COUNTY, ILL.

333 U. S. 203

Decided March 8, 1948—one justice dissenting.

Mr. Justice BLACK delivered the opinion of the Court.

This case relates to the power of a state to utilize its tax-supported public
school system in aid of religious instruction insofar as that power may be restricted by the First and Fourteenth Amendments to the Federal
Constitution.

The appellant, Vashti McCollum, began this action for mandamus against
the Champaign Board of Education in the Circuit Court of Champaign
County, Illinois. Her asserted interest was that of a resident and taxpayer of
Champaign and of a parent whose child was then enrolled in the Champaign
public schools. Illinois has a compulsory education law which, with exceptions, requires parents to send their children, aged seven to sixteen, to its
tax-supported public schools where the children are to remain in attendance
during the hours when the schools are regularly in session. Parents who violate this law commit a misdemeanor punishable by fine unless the children
attend private or parochial schools which meet educational standards fixed
by the State. District boards of education are given general supervisory
powers over the use of the public school buildings within the school districts.

Appellant's petition for mandamus alleged that religious teachers, employed by private religious groups, were permitted to come weekly into the
school buildings during the regular hours set apart for secular teaching, and
then and there for a period of thirty minutes substitute their religious teaching for the secular education provided under the compulsory education law.
The petitioner charged that this joint public-school religious-group program
violated the First and Fourteenth Amendments to the United States
Constitution.

Although there are disputes between the parties as to various inferences
that may or may not properly be drawn from the evidence concerning the
religious program, the following facts are shown by the record without dispute. In 1940 interested members of the Jewish, Roman Catholic, and a few
of the Protestant faiths formed a voluntary association called the Champaign Council on Religious Education. They obtained permission from the
Board of Education to offer classes in religious instruction to public school
pupils in grades four to nine inclusive. Classes were made up of pupils whose
parents signed printed cards requesting that their children be permitted to
attend; they were held weekly, thirty minutes for the lower grades, forty-
five minutes for the higher. The council employed the religious teachers at
no expense to the school authorities, but the instructors were subject to the

approval and supervision of the superintendent of schools. The classes were taught in three separate religious groups by Protestant teachers, Catholic priests, and a Jewish rabbi . . . Classes were conducted in the regular classrooms of the school building. Students who did not choose to take the religious instruction were not released from public school duties; they were required to leave their classrooms and go to some other place in the school building for pursuit of their secular studies. On the other hand, students who were released from secular study for the religious instructions were required to be present at the religious classes. Reports of their presence or absence were to be made to their secular teachers.

The foregoing facts, without reference to others that appear in the record, show the use of tax-supported property for religious instruction and the close cooperation between the school authorities and the religious council in promoting religious education. The operation of the state's compulsory education system thus assists and is integrated with the program of religious instruction carried on by separate religious sects. Pupils compelled by law to go to school for secular education are released in part from their legal duty upon the condition that they attend the religious classes. This is beyond all question a utilization of the tax-established and tax-supported public school system to aid religious groups to spread their faith. And it falls squarely under the ban of the First Amendment . . .

To hold that a state cannot consistently with the First and Fourteenth Amendments utilize its public school system to aid any or all religious faiths or sects in the dissemination of their doctrines and ideals does not, as counsel urge, manifest a governmental hostility to religion or religious teachings. A manifestation of such hostility would be at war with our national tradition as embodied in the First Amendment's guaranty of the free exercise of religion. For the First Amendment rests upon the premise that both religion and government can best work to achieve their lofty aims if each is left free from the other within its respective sphere.

Here not only are the state's tax-supported public school buildings used for the dissemination of religious doctrines. The State also affords sectarian groups an invaluable aid in that it helps to provide pupils for their religious classes through use of the state's compulsory public school machinery. This is not separation of Church and State.

The cause is reversed and remanded to the State Supreme Court for proceeding not inconsistent with this opinion.

Mr. Justice FRANKFURTER delivered the following opinion, in which Mr. Justice JACKSON, Mr. Justice RUTLEDGE and Mr. Justice BURTON join.

We dissented in Everson v. Board of Education, 330 U.S. 1, because in our view the Constitutional principle requiring separation of Church and State compelled invalidation of the ordinance sustained by the majority. Illinois has here authorized the commingling of sectarian with secular instruction in the public schools. The Constitution of the United States forbids this.

The case, in the light of the Everson decision, demonstrates anew that the mere formulation of a relevant Constitutional principle is the beginning of the solution of a problem, not its answer. . . . We are all agreed that the First and the Fourteenth Amendments have a secular reach far more penetrating in the conduct of Government than merely to forbid an "established church." But agreement, in the abstract, that the First Amendment was designed to erect a "wall of separation between Church and State," does not preclude a clash of views as to what the wall separates.

To understand the particular program now before us as a conscientious attempt to accommodate the allowable functions of Government and the special concerns of the Church within the framework of our Constitution and with due regard to the kind of society for which it was designed, we must put this Champaign program of 1940 in its historic setting. Traditionally, organized education in the Western world was Church education.

The emigrants who came to these shores brought this view of education with them. Colonial schools certainly started with a religious orientation.

The evolution of colonial education, largely in the service of religion, into the public school system of today is the story of changing conceptions regarding the American democratic society, of the functions of State-maintained education in such a society, and of the role therein of the free exercise of religion by the people. The modern public school derived from a philosophy of freedom reflected in the First Amendment. . . . As the momentum for popular education increased and in turn evoked strong claims for State support of religious education, contests not unlike that which in Virginia had produced Madison's Remonstrance appeared in various forms in other States. New York and Massachusetts provide famous chapters in the history that established dissociation of religious teaching from State-maintained schools. In New York, the rise of the common schools led, despite fierce sectarian opposition, to the barring of tax funds to church schools, and later to any school in which sectarian doctrine was taught. In Massachusetts, largely through the efforts of Horace Mann, all sectarian teachings were barred from the common school to save it from being rent by denomination conflict. The upshot of these controversies, often long and fierce, is fairly summarized by saying that long before the Fourteenth Amendment subjected the States to new limitations, the prohibition of furtherance by the State of religious instruction became the guiding principle, in law and feeling, of the American people.

Separation in the field of education, then, was not imposed upon unwilling States by force of superior law. In this respect the Fourteenth Amendment merely reflected a principle then dominant in our national life. To the extent that the Constitution thus made it binding upon the States, the basis of the restriction is the whole experience of our people. Zealous watchfulness against fusion of secular and religious activities by Government itself, through any of its instruments but especially through its educational agencies, was the democratic response of the American community to the particular needs of a young and growing nation, unique in the composition of its people. A totally different situation elsewhere, as illustrated for instance by the English provisions for religious education in State-maintained schools, only serves to illustrate that free societies are not cast in one mould.

It is pertinent to remind that the establishment of this principle of separation in the field of education was not due to any decline in the religious beliefs of the people. Horace Mann was a devout Christian, and the deep religious feeling of James Madison is stamped upon the Remonstrance. The secular public school did not imply indifference to the basic role of religion in the life of the people, nor rejection of religious education as a means of fostering it. . . . The sharp confinement of the public schools to secular education was a recognition of the need of a democratic society to educate its children, insofar as the State undertook to do so, in an atmosphere free from pressures in a realm in which pressures are most resisted and where conflicts are most easily and most bitterly engendered. Designed to serve as perhaps the most powerful agency for promoting cohesion among a heterogeneous democratic people, the public school must keep scrupulously free from entanglement in the strife of sects. The preservation of the community from divisive conflicts, of Government from irreconcilable pressures by religious groups, of religion from censorship and coercion however subtly exercised, requires strict confinement of the State to instruction other than religious, leaving to the individual's church and home, indoctrination in the faith of his choice.

Prohibition of the commingling of sectarian and secular instruction in the public school is of course only half the story. A religious people was naturally concerned about the part of the child's education entrusted "to the family altar, the church, and the private school." The promotion of religious education took many forms. Laboring under financial difficulties and exercising only persuasive authority, various denominations felt handicapped in their task of religious education. . . . But the major efforts of religious inculcation were a recognition of the principle of Separation by the establishment of church schools privately supported. Parochial schools were maintained by various denominations. . . . There were experiments with vacation schools, with Saturday as well as Sunday schools. They all fell short of their purpose.

Out of these inadequate efforts evolved the week-day church school, held on one or more afternoons a week after the close of the public school. But children continued to be children; they wanted to play when school was out, particularly when other children were free to do so. Church leaders decided that if the week-day church school was to succeed, a way had to be found to give the child his religious education during what the child conceived to be his "business hours."

The initiation of the movement may fairly be attributed to Dr. George U. Wenner. The underlying assumption of his proposal, made at the Interfaith Conference on Federation held in New York City in 1905, was that the public school unduly monopolized the child's time and that the churches were entitled to their share of it. Thus, the schools should "release." Accordingly, the Federation, citing the example of the Third Republic of France, urged that upon the request of their parents children be excused from public school on Wednesday afternoon, so that the churches could provide "Sunday school on Wednesday." This was to be carried out on church premises under church authority. Those not desiring to attend church schools would continue their normal classes. Lest these public school classes unfairly compete with the church education, it was requested that the school authorities refrain from scheduling courses or activities of compelling interest or importance.

The proposal aroused considerable opposition and it took another decade for a "released time" scheme to become a part of a public school system. Gary, Indiana, inaugurated the movement. . . . [Superintendent of Schools] Wirt's plan sought to rotate the schedules of the children during the school-day so that some were in class, others were in the library, still others in the playground. And some, he suggested to the leading ministers of the City, might be released to attend religious classes if the churches of the City co-operated and provided them. They did, in 1914, and thus was "released time" begun. The religious teaching was held on church premises and the public schools had no hand in the conduct of these church schools. They did not supervise the choice of instructors or the subject matter taught. Nor did they assume responsibility for the attendance, conduct or achievement of the child in a church school; and he received no credit for it. The period of attendance in the religious schools would otherwise have been a play period for the child, with the result that the arrangement did not cut into public school instruction or truly affect the activities or feelings of the children who did not attend the church schools.

From such a beginning "released time" has attained substantial proportions.

Of course, "released time" as a generalized conception, undefined by differentiating particularities, is not an issue for Constitutional adjudication. Local programs differ from each other in many and crucial respects. . . . It is only when challenge is made to the share that the public schools have in the execution of a particular "released time" program that close judicial scrutiny is demanded of the exact relation between the religious instruction and the public educational system in the specific situation before the Court.

The substantial differences among arrangements lumped altogether as "released time" emphasize the importance of detailed analysis of the facts to which the Constitutional test of Separation is to be applied. How does "released time" operate in Champaign? Public school teachers distribute to their pupils cards supplied by church groups, so that the parents may indicate whether they desire religious instruction for their children. For those desiring it, religious classes are conducted in the regular classrooms of the public schools by teachers of religion paid by the churches and appointed by them, but, as the State court found, "subject to the approval of and supervision of the Superintendent." The courses do not profess to give secular instruction in subjects concerning religion. Their candid purpose is sectarian teaching. While a child can go to any of the religious classes offered, a particular sect wishing a teacher for its devotees requires the permission of the school superintendent "who in turn will determine whether or not it is practical for said group to teach in said school system." If no provision is made for religious instruction in the particular faith of a child, or if for other reasons the child is not enrolled in any of the offered classes, he is required to attend a regular school class, or a study period during which he is often left to his own devices. Reports of attendance in the religious classes are submitted by the religious instructor to the school authorities, and the child who fails to attend is presumably deemed a truant.

Religious education so conducted on school time and property is patently woven into the working scheme of the school. The Champaign arrangement thus presents powerful elements of inherent pressure by the school system in the interest of religious sects. The fact that this power has not been used to discriminate is beside the point. Separation is a requirement to abstain from fusing functions of Government and of religious sects, not merely to treat them all equally. That a child is offered an alternative may reduce the constraint; it does not eliminate the operation of influence by the school in matters sacred to conscience and outside the school's domain. The law of imitation operates, and nonconformity is not an outstanding characteristic of children. The result is an obvious pressure upon children to attend. Again, while the Champaign school population represents only a fraction of the more than two hundred and fifty sects of the nation, not even all the practicing sects in Champaign are willing or able to provide religious instruction. . . . As a result, the public school system of Champaign actively furthers inculcation in the religious tenets of some faiths, and in the process sharpens the consciousness of religious differences at least among some of the children committed to its care.

We do not consider, as indeed we could not, school programs not before us which, though colloquially characterized as "released time," present situations differing in aspects that may well be constitutionally crucial. . . . We do not now attempt to weigh in the Constitutional scale every separate detail or various combination of factors which may establish a valid "released time" program. We find that the basic Constitutional principle of absolute separation was violated when the State of Illinois, speaking through its Supreme Court, sustained the school authorities of Champaign in sponsoring and effectively furthering religious beliefs by its educational arrangement.

Separation means separation, not something less. Jefferson's metaphor in describing the relation between Church and State speaks of a "wall of separation," not of a fine line easily overstepped. The public school is at once the symbol of our democracy and the most pervasive means for promoting our common destiny. In no activity of the State is it more vital to keep out divisive forces than in its schools, to avoid confusing, not to say fusing, what the Constitution sought to keep strictly apart.

We renew our conviction that "we have staked the very existence of our country on the faith that complete separation between the state and religion is best for the state and best for religion.". . . . If nowhere else, in the relation between Church and State, "good fences make good neighbors."

Mr. Justice JACKSON, concurring.

I join the opinion of Mr. Justice FRANKFURTER, and concur in the result reached by the Court, but with these reservations: I think it is doubtful whether the facts of this case establish jurisdiction in this Court, but in any event that we should place some bounds on the demands for interference with local schools that we are empowered or willing to entertain. I make these reservations a matter of record in view of the number of litigations likely to be started as a result of this decision.

A Federal Court may interfere with local school authorities only when they invade either a personal liberty or a property right protected by the Federal Constitution. Ordinarily this will come about in either of two ways:

First. When a person is required to submit to some religious rite or instruction or is deprived or threatened with deprivation of his freedom for resisting such unconstitutional requirement. We may then set him free or enjoin his prosecution.

Second. Where a complainant is deprived of property by being taxed for unconstitutional purposes, such as directly or indirectly to support a religious establishment. We can protect a taxpayer against such a levy.

If . . . jurisdiction is found to exist, it is important that we circumscribe our decision with some care. . . . The plaintiff, as she has every right to be, is an avowed atheist. What she has asked of the courts is that they not only end the "released time" plan but also ban every form of teaching which suggests or recognizes that there is a God. . . . This Court is directing the Illinois courts generally to sustain plaintiff's complaint without exception of any of these grounds of complaint, without discriminating between them and without laying down any standards to define the limits of the effect of our decision.

To me, the sweep and detail of these complaints is a danger signal which warns of the kind of local controversy we will be required to arbitrate if we do not place appropriate limitation on our decision and exact strict compliance with jurisdictional requirements. Authorities list 256 separate and substantial religious bodies to exist in the continental United States. Each of them, through the suit of some discontented but unpenalized and untaxed representative, has as good a right as this plaintiff to demand that the courts compel the schools to sift out of their teaching everything inconsistent with its doctrines. If we are to eliminate everything that is objectionable to any of these warring sects or inconsistent with any of their doctrines, we will leave public education in shreds. Nothing but educational confusion and a discrediting of the public school system can result from subjecting it to constant law suits.

While we may and should end such formal and explicit instruction as the Champaign plan and can at all times prohibit teaching of creed and catechism and ceremonial and can forbid forthright proselyting in the schools, I think it remains to be demonstrated whether it is possible, even if desirable, to comply with such demands as plaintiff's completely to isolate and cast out of secular education all that some people may reasonably regard as religious instruction. Perhaps subjects such as mathematics, physics or chemistry are, or can be, completely secularized. But it would not seem practical to teach either practice or appreciation of the arts if we are to forbid exposure of youth to any religious influences. Music without sacred music, architecture minus the cathedral, or painting without the scriptural themes would be eccentric and incomplete, even from a secular point of view. Yet the inspirational appeal of religion in these guises is often stronger than in forthright sermon. Even such a "science" as biology raises the issue between evolution and creation as an explanation of our presence on this planet. Certainly a course in English literature that omitted the Bible and other powerful uses of our mother tongue for religious ends would be pretty barren. And I should suppose it is a proper, if not an indispensable, part of preparation for a worldly life to know the roles that religion and religions have played in the tragic story of mankind. The fact is that, for good or for ill, nearly everything in our culture worth transmitting, everything which gives meaning to life, is saturated with religious influences, derived from paganism, Judaism, Christianity—both Catholic and Protestant—and other faiths accepted by a large part of the world's peoples. One can hardly respect a system of education that would leave the student wholly ignorant of the currents of religious thought that move the world society for a part in which he is being prepared.

But how one can teach, with satisfaction or even with justice to all faiths, such subjects as the story of the Reformation, the Inquisition, or even the New England effort to found "a Church without a Bishop and a State without a King," is more than I know. It is too much to expect that mortals will teach subjects about which their contemporaries have passionate controversies with the detachment they may summon to teaching about remote subjects such as Confucius or Mohamet. When instruction turns to proselyting and imparting knowledge becomes evangelism is, except in the crudest cases, a subtle inquiry.

The opinions in this case show that public educational authorities have evolved a considerable variety of practices in dealing with the religious problem. Neighborhoods differ in racial, religious and cultural compositions.

... We must leave some flexibility to meet local conditions, some chance to progress by trial and error. While I agree that the religious classes involved here go beyond permissable limits, I also think the complaint demands more than plaintiff is entitled to have granted. So far as I can see this Court does not tell the State court where it may stop, nor does it set up any standards by which the State Court may determine that question for itself.

It is idle to pretend that this task is one for which we can find in the Constitution one word to help us as judges to decide where the secular ends and the sectarian begins in education. Nor can we find guidance in any other legal source. It is a matter on which we can find no law but our own prepossessions. If with no surer legal guidance we are to take up and decide every variation of this controversy, raised by persons not subject to penalty or tax but who are dissatisfied with the way schools are dealing with the problem, we are likely to have much business of the sort. And, more importantly, we are likely to make the legal "wall of separation between church and state" as winding as the famous serpentine wall designed by Mr. Jefferson for the University he founded.

DOREMUS v. HAWTHORNE

The *Doremus* decision, in effect, evaded an issue which the court would later decide because of technicalities of presentation. It would be eleven years before the Court would address the issue of opening the school day with reading from the Bible.

DOREMUS v. BOARD OF EDUCATION OF BOROUGH OF HAWTHORNE

342 U.S. 429

Decided March 3, 1952—three justices dissenting.

Mr. Justice JACKSON delivered the opinion of the Court.

This action for a declaratory judgement on a question of federal constitutional law was prosecuted in the state courts of New Jersey. It sought to declare invalid a statute of that State which provides for the reading, without comment, of five verses of the Old Testament at the opening of each public-school day. ... No issue was raised under the State Constitution, but the Act was claimed to violate the clause of the First Amendment to the Federal Constitution prohibiting establishment of religion.

No trial was held and we have no findings of fact, but the trial court denied relief on the merits on the basis of the pleadings and pretrial conference, of which the record contains meager notes. The Supreme Court of New Jersey, on appeal, rendered its opinion that the Act does not violate the Federal Constitution, in spite of jurisdictional doubts which it pointed out but condoned as follows: "No one is before us asserting that his religious practices have been interfered with or that his right to worship in accordance with the dictates of his conscience has been suppressed. No religious sect is a party to the cause. No representative of, or spokesman for, a religious body has attacked the statute here or below. One of the plaintiffs is 'a citizen and taxpayer'; the only interest he asserts is just that. . . . The other plaintiff, in addition to being a citizen and a taxpayer, has a daughter, aged seventeen, who is a student of the school. Those facts are asserted, but, as in the case of the co-plaintiff, no violated rights are urged. It is not charged that the practice required by the statute conflicts with the convictions of either mother or daughter. Apparently the sole purpose and the only function of plaintiffs is that they shall assume the role of actors so that there may be a suit which will invoke a court ruling upon the constitutionally of the statute. . . ."

The view of the facts taken by the court below, though it is entitled to respect, does not bind us and we may make an independent examination of the record. Doing so, we find nothing more substantial in support of jurisdiction than did the court below. Appellants, apparently seeking to bring themselves within *Illinois ex rel. McCollum v. Board of Education of School Dist. No. 71*, 333 U.S. 203, assert a challenge to the Act in two capacities—one as parent of a child subject to it, and both as taxpayers burdened because of its requirements.

In support of the parent-and-school-child relationship, the complaint alleged that appellant Klein was parent of a seventeen-year-old pupil in Hawthorne High School, where Bible reading was practiced pursuant to the Act. That is all. There is no assertion that she was injured or even offended thereby or that she was compelled to accept, approve or confess agreement with any dogma or creed or even to listen when the Scriptures were read. . . .However . . . this child had graduated from the public school before this appeal was taken to this Court. Obviously no decision we could render now would protect any rights she may once have had, and this Court does not sit to decide arguments after events have put them to rest.

The complaint is similarly niggardly of facts to support a taxpayer's grievance. . . . In this school the Bible is read, according to statute. There is no allegation that this activity is supported by any separate tax or paid for from any particular appropriation or that it adds any sum whatever to the cost of conducting the school. No information is given as to what kind of taxes are paid by appellants and there is no averment that the Bible reading increases any tax they do pay or that as taxpayers they are, will, or possibly can be out of pocket because of it.

It is apparent that the grievance which it is sought to litigate here is not a direct dollars-and-cents injury but is a religious difference. If appellants established the requisite special injury necessary to a taxpayer's case or controversy, it would not matter that their dominant inducement to action was more religious than mercenary. It is not a question of motivation but of possession of the requisite financial interest that is, or is threatened to be, injured by the unconstitutional conduct. We find no such direct and particular financial interest here. If the Act may give rise to a legal case or controversy on some behalf, the appellants cannot obtain a decision from this Court by a feigned issue of taxation.

ZORACH v. CLAUSON

In this decision, the Court addressed a variation on the practice of released time for religious instruction. Just four years prior to this decision, the Court had judged an approach to released time to be in violation of the Constitution. The distinction drawn by the Court between the practice under review here and that decided in *McCollum* was the use of public school classrooms for the religious instruction. As the present program involved no sectarian religious instruction on public school property, the program was held to be constitutional. It was a contention of appellants that public school compulsory-attendance laws operated in the present litigation to the same unconstitutional degree as they had in *McCollum.* The Court, however, found no evidence in the record that students were being coerced into attending religious instruction. It is, according to the Court, not a violation of the Constitution for the public schools to adjust their schedule of operations in order to accommodate the religious needs of the community or of individuals when such religious activity or observance does not involve the use of tax-supported public facilities.

Justice Black, in dissent, viewed the compulsory school-attendance laws, to which children are subject during the public school day, as requiring the invalidation of this approach to sectarian instruction to the same degree as had been true in the *McCollum* decision. In both programs, children were available for religious instruction because their attendance at school was required by law. It was Justice Black's view that this placed the state squarely in the process of religious instruction. Justices Frankfurter and Jackson also wrote dissenting opinions focusing on this same objection—the operation of compulsory school-attendance laws in support of sectarian instruction.

ZORACH V. CLAUSON
343 U. S. 306

Decided April 28, 1952—three justices dissenting.

Mr. Justice DOUGLAS delivered the opinion of the Court.
New York City has a program which permits its public schools to release students during the school day so that they may leave the school buildings

and school grounds and go to religious centers for religious instruction or devotional exercises. A student is released on written request of his parents. Those not released stay in the classrooms. The churches make weekly reports to the schools, sending a list of children who have been released from public school but who have not reported for religious instruction.

This "released time" program involves neither religious instruction in public school classrooms nor the expenditure of public funds. All costs, including the application blanks, are paid by the religious organizations. The case is therefore unlike *McCollum v. Board of Education*, 333 U.S. 203, which involved a "released time" program from Illinois. In that case the classrooms were turned over to religious instructors. We accordingly held that the program violated the First Amendment which . . . prohibits the states from establishing religion or prohibiting its free exercise.

Appellants, who are taxpayers and residents of New York City and whose children attend its public schools, challenge the present law, contending it is in essence not different from the one involved in the *McCollum* case. Their argument, stated elaborately in various ways, reduces itself to this: the weight and influence of the school is put behind a program for religious instruction; public school teachers police it, keeping tab on students who are released; the classroom activities come to a halt while the students who are released for religious instruction are on leave; the school is a crutch on which the churches are leaning for support in their religious training; without the cooperation of the schools this "released time" program, like the one in the *McCollum* case, would be futile and ineffective.

The briefs and arguments are replete with data bearing on the merits of this type of "released time" program. Views *pro* and *con* are expressed, based on practical experience with these programs and with their implications. We do not stop to summarize these materials nor to burden the opinion with an analysis of them. For they involve considerations not germane to the narrow constitutional issue presented. They largely concern the wisdom of the system, its efficiency from an educational point of view, and the political considerations which have motivated its adoption or rejection in some communities. Those matters are of no concern here, since our problem reduces itself to whether New York by this system has either prohibited the "free exercise" of religion or has made a law "respecting an establishment of religion" within the meaning of the First Amendment.

It takes obtuse reasoning to inject any issue of the "free exercise" of religion into the present case. No one is forced to go to the religious classroom and no religious exercise or instruction is brought to the classrooms of the public schools.

There is a suggestion that the system involves the use of coercion to get public school students into religious classrooms. There is no evidence in the record before us that supports that conclusion.

Moreover, apart from that claim of coercion, we do not see how New York by this type of "released time" program has made a law respecting an establishment of religion within the meaning of the First Amendment. . . . There cannot be the slightest doubt that the First Amendment reflects the philosophy that Church and State should be separated. And so far as interference with the "free exercise" of religion and an "establishment" of religion are concerned, the separation must be complete and unequivocal. The First Amendment within the scope of its coverage permits no exception; the prohibition is absolute. The First Amendment, however, does not say that in every and all respects there shall be a separation of Church and State. Rather, it studiously defines the manner, the specific ways, in which there shall be no concert or union or dependency one on the other. That is the common sense of the matter. Otherwise the state and religion would be aliens to each other—hostile, suspicious, and even unfriendly. Churches could not be required to pay even property taxes. Municipalities would not be permitted to render police or fire protection to religious groups. Policemen who helped parishioners into their places of worship would violate the Constitution. Prayers in our legislative halls; the appeals to the Almighty in the messages of the Chief Executive; the proclamations making Thanksgiving Day a holiday; "so help me God" in our courtroom oaths—these and all other references to the Almighty that run through our laws, our public rituals, our ceremonies would be flouting the First Amendment. A fastidious atheist or agnostic could even object to the supplication with which the Court opens each session: "God save the United States and this Honorable Court."

We would have to press the concept of separation of Church and State to these extremes to condemn the present law on constitutional grounds. The nullification of this law would have wide and profound effects. A Catholic student applies to his teacher for permission to leave the school during hours on a Holy Day of Obligation to attend a mass. A Jewish student asks his teacher for permission to be excused for Yom Kippur. A Protestant wants the afternoon off for a family baptismal ceremony. In each case the teacher requires parental consent in writing. In each case, the teacher, in order to make sure the student is not a truant, goes further and requires a report from the priest, the rabbi, or the minister. The teacher in other words cooperates in a religious program to the extent of making it possible for her students to participate in it. Whether she does it occasionally for a few students, regularly for one, or pursuant to a systematized program designed to further the religious needs of all the students does not alter the character of the act.

We are a religious people whose institutions presuppose a Supreme Being. We guarantee the freedom to worship as one chooses. We make room for as wide a variety of beliefs and creeds as the spiritual needs of man deem necessary. We sponsor an attitude on the part of government that shows no partiality to any one group and that lets each flourish according to the zeal of its adherents and the appeal of its dogma. When the state encourages religious instruction or cooperates with religious authorities by adjusting the schedule of public events to sectarian needs, it follows the best of our traditions. For it then respects the religious nature of our people and accommodates the public service to their spiritual needs. To hold that it may not would be to find in the Constitution a requirement that the government show a callous indifference to religious groups. That would be preferring those who believe in no religion over those who do believe. Government may not finance religious groups nor undertake religious instruction nor blend secular and sectarian education nor use secular institutions to force one or some religion on any person. But we find no constitutional requirement which makes it necessary for government to be hostile to religion and to throw its weight against efforts to widen the effective scope of religious influence. The government must be neutral when it comes to competition between sects. It may not thrust any sect on any person. It may not make a religious observance compulsory. It may not coerce anyone to attend church, to observe a religious holiday, or to take religious instruction. But it can close its doors or suspend its operations as to those who want to repair to their religious sanctuary for worship or instruction. No more than that is undertaken here. . . .

In the *McCollum* case the classrooms were used for religious instruction and the force of the public school was used to promote that instruction. Here, as we have said, the public schools do no more than accommodate their schedules to a program of outside religious instruction. We follow the *McCollum* case. But we cannot expand it to cover the present released time program unless separation of Church and State means that public institutions can make no adjustments of their schedules to accommodate the religious needs of the people. We cannot read into the Bill of Rights such a philosophy of hostility to religion.

Mr. Justice BLACK, dissenting.

I see no significant difference between the invalid Illinois system and that of New York here sustained. Except for the use of the school buildings in Illinois, there is no difference between the systems which I consider even worthy of mention. In the New York program, as in that of Illinois, the school authorities release some of the children on the condition that they attend the religious classes, get reports on whether they attend, and hold the other children in the school building until the religious hour is over. As we attempted to make categorically clear, the *McCollum* decision would have been the same if the religious classes had not been held in the school buildings. . . . *McCollum* . . . held that Illinois could not constitutionally manipulate the compelled classroom hours of its compulsory school machinery so as to channel children into sectarian classes. Yet that is exactly what the Court holds New York can do.

Here the sole question is whether New York can use its compulsory education laws to help religious sects get attendants presumably too unenthusiastic to go unless moved to do so by the pressure of this state machinery.

That this is the plan, purpose, design and consequence of the New York program cannot be denied. The state thus makes religious sects beneficiaries of its power to compel children to attend secular schools. Any use of such coercive power by the state to help or hinder some religious sects or to prefer all religious sects over nonbelievers or vice versa is just what I think the First Amendment forbids. In considering whether a state has entered this forbidden field the question is not whether it has entered too far but whether it has entered at all. New York is manipulating its compulsory education laws to help religious sects get pupils. This is not separation but combination of Church and State.

The Court's validation of the New York system rests in part on its statement that Americans are "a religious people whose institutions presuppose a Supreme Being." This was at least as true when the First Amendment was adopted; and it was just as true when eight Justices of this Court invalidated the released time system in *McCollum* on the premise that a state can no more "aid all religions" than it can aid one. It was precisely because Eighteenth Century Americans were a religious people divided into many fighting sects that we were given the constitutional mandate to keep Church and State completely separate. Colonial history had already shown that, here as elsewhere zealous sectarians entrusted with governmental power to further their causes would sometimes torture, maim and kill those they branded "heretics," "atheists" or "agnostics." The First Amendment was therefore to insure that no one powerful sect or combination of sects could use political or governmental power to punish dissenters whom they could not convert to their faith. Now as then, it is only by wholly isolating the state from the religious sphere and compelling it to be completely neutral, that the freedom of each and every denomination and of all nonbelievers can be maintained.

Under our system of religious freedom, people have gone to their religious sanctuaries not because they feared the law but because they loved their God. . . . The spiritual mind of man has thus been free to believe, disbelieve, or doubt, without repression, great or small, by the heavy hand of government. Statutes authorizing such repression have been stricken. Before today, our judicial opinions have refrained from drawing invidious distinctions between those who believe in no religion and those who do believe. The First Amendment has lost much if the religious follower and the atheist are no longer to be judicially regarded as entitled to equal justice under law.

State help to religion injects political and party prejudices into a holy field. It too often substitutes force for prayer, hate for love, and persecution for persuasion. Government should not be allowed, under cover of the soft euphemism of "co-operation," to steal into the sacred area of religious choice.

Mr. Justice FRANKFURTER, dissenting.

The Court tells us that in the maintenance of its public schools, "[The State Government] can close its doors or suspend its operations" so that its citizens may be free for religious devotions or instruction. If that were the issue, it would not rise to the dignity of a constitutional controversy. Of course a State may provide that the classes in its schools shall be dismissed, for any reason, or no reason, on fixed days, or for special occasions. The essence of this case is that the school system did not "close its doors" and did not "suspend its operations." There is all the difference in the world between letting the children out of school and letting some of them out of school into religious classes.

The pith of the case is that formalized religious instruction is substituted for other school activity which those who do not participate in the released-time program are compelled to attend. The school system is very much in operation during this kind of released time. If its doors are closed, they are closed upon those students who do not attend the religious instruction, in order to keep them within the school. That is the very thing which raises the constitutional issue. It is not met by disregarding it. Failure to discuss this issue does not take it out of the case.

. . . the Court relies upon the absence from the record of evidence of coercion in the operation of the system. . . . But the Court disregards the fact that as the case comes to us, there could be no proof of coercion, for the appellants were not allowed to make proof of it. Appellants alleged that "The operation of the released time program has resulted and inevitably results in the exercise of pressure and coercion upon parents and children to secure attendance by the children for religious instruction." This allegation—that coercion was in fact present and is inherent in the system, no matter what disavowals might be made in the operating regulations—was denied by respondents.

If we are to decide this case on the present record, however, a strict adherence to the usage of courts in ruling on the sufficiency of pleadings would require us to take as admitted the facts pleaded in the appellants' complaint, including the fact of coercion, actual and inherent. . . . I cannot see how a finding that coercion was absent, deemed critical by this Court in sustaining the practice, can be made here, when appellants were prevented from making a timely showing of coercion because the courts below thought it irrelevant.

Mr. Justice JACKSON, dissenting.

This released time program is founded upon a use of the State's power of coercion, which, for me, determines its unconstitutionality. Stripped to its essentials, the plan has two stages, first, that the State compel each student to yield a large part of his time for public secular education and, second, that some of it be "released" to him on condition that he devote it to sectarian religious purposes.

No one suggests that the Constitution would permit the State directly to require this "released" time to be spent "under the control of a duly constituted religious body." This program accomplishes that forbidden result by indirection. If public education were taking so much of the pupils' time as to injure the public or the students' welfare by encroaching upon their religious opportunity, simply shortening everyone's school day would facilitate voluntary and optional attendance at Church classes. But that suggestion is rejected upon the ground that if they are made free many students will not go to the Church. Hence, they must be deprived of freedom for this period, with Church attendance put to them as one of the two permissable ways of using it.

The greater effectiveness of this system over voluntary attendance after school hours is due to the truant officer who, if the youngster fails to go to the Church school, dogs him back to the public schoolroom. Here schooling is more or less suspended during the "released time" so that the nonreligious attendants will not forge ahead of the churchgoing absentees. But it serves as a temporary jail for a pupil who will not go to Church. It takes more subtlety of mind than I possess to deny that this is governmental constraint in support of religion. It is as unconstitutional, in my view, when exerted by indirection as when exercised forthrightly.

The day that this country ceases to be free for irreligion it will cease to be free for religion—except for the sect that can win political power. The same epithetical jurisprudence used by the Court today to beat down those who oppose pressuring children into some religion can devise as good epithets tomorrow against those who object to pressuring them into a favored religion.

ENGEL v. VITALE

In this litigation, petitioners challenged the New York State Regents' prayer as a violation of the Constitution. According to Justice Black, who wrote the opinion of the Court, neither the denominational neutrality of the prayer claimed by the state nor the fact that students could be excused from the exercise would free the legislation from the restrictions of the Establishment Clause. As a governmental action, formulation of a prayer to be recited by citizens of the state clearly represents the enactment of a law respecting an establishment of religion. The Court went to some length to indicate that this ruling should not be interpreted as expressing a governmental hostility toward religion.

ENGEL v. VITALE

370 U.S. 421

Decided June 25, 1962—one justice dissenting.

Mr. Justice BLACK delivered the opinion of the Court.

The respondent Board of Education of Union Free School District No. 9, New Hyde Park, New York, acting in its official capacity under state law, directed the School District's principal to cause the following prayer to be said aloud by each class in the presence of a teacher at the beginning of each school day:

> "Almighty God, we acknowledge our dependence upon Thee, and we beg Thy blessings upon us, our parents, our teachers and our Country."

This daily procedure was adopted on the recommendation of the State Board of Regents, a governmental agency created by the State Constitution to which the New York Legislature has granted broad supervisory, executive, and legislative powers over the State's public school system.

Shortly after the practice of reciting the Regents' prayer was adopted by the School District, the parents of ten pupils brought this action in a New York State Court insisting that use of this official prayer in the public schools was contrary to the beliefs, religions, or religious practices of both themselves and their children. Among other things, these parents challenged the constitutionality of both the state law authorizing the School District to direct the use of prayer in public schools and the School District's regulation ordering the recitation of this particular prayer on the ground that these actions of official governmental agencies violate that part of the First Amendment of the Federal Constitution which commands that "Congress shall make no law respecting an establishment of religion"—a command which was "made applicable to the State of New York by the Fourteenth Amendment of the said Constitution."

We think that by using its public school system to encourage recitation of the Regents' prayer, the State of New York has adopted a practice wholly inconsistent with the Establishment Clause. There can, of course, be no doubt that New York's program of daily classroom invocation of God's blessings as prescribed in the Regents' prayer is a religious activity.

The petitioners contended among other things that the state laws requiring or permitting use of the Regents' prayer must be struck down as a violation of the Establishment Clause because that prayer was composed by governmental officials as a part of a governmental program to further religious beliefs. For this reason, petitioners argue, the State's use of the Regents' prayer in its public school system breaches the constitutional wall of separation between Church and State. We agree with that contention since we think that the constitutional prohibition against laws respecting an establishment of religion must at least mean that in this country it is no part of the business of government to compose official prayers for any group of the American people to recite as a part of a religious program carried on by government.

By the time of the adoption of the Constitution, our history shows that there was a widespread awareness among many Americans of the dangers of a union of Church and State. These people knew, some of them from bitter personal experience, that one of the greatest dangers to the freedom of the individual to worship in his own way lay in the Government's placing its official stamp of approval upon one particular kind of prayer or one particular form of religious services. They knew the anguish, hardship and bitter strife that could come when zealous religious groups struggled with one another to obtain the Government's stamp of approval from each King, Queen, or Protector that came to temporary power. The Constitution was intended to avert a part of this danger by leaving the government of this country in the hands of the people rather than in the hands of any monarch. But this safeguard was not enough. Our Founders were no more willing to let the content of their prayers and their privilege of praying whenever they pleased be influenced by the ballot box than they were to let these vital matters of personal conscience depend upon the succession of monarchs. The First Amendment was added to the Constitution to stand as a guarantee that neither the power nor the prestige of Federal Government would be used to control, support or influence the kinds of prayer the American people can say—that the people's religions must not be subjected to the pressures of government for change each time a new political administration is elected to office. Under that Amendment's prohibition against governmental establishment of religion, as reinforced by the provisions of the Fourteenth Amendment, government in this country, be it state or federal, is without power to prescribe by law any particular form of prayer which is to be used as an official prayer in carrying on any program of governmentally sponsored religious activity.

There can be no doubt that New York's state prayer program officially establishes the religious beliefs embodied in the Regents' prayer. The respondents' argument to the contrary, which is largely based upon the contention that the Regents' prayer is "nondenominational" and the fact that the program, as modified and approved by state courts, does not require all pupils to recite the prayer but permits those who wish to do so to remain silent or be excused from the room, ignores the essential nature of the program's constitutional defects. Neither the fact that the prayer may be denominationally neutral nor the fact that its observance on the part of the students is voluntary can serve to free it from the limitations of the Establishment Clause, as it might from the Free Exercise Clause, of the First Amendment, both of which are operative against the States by virtue of the Fourteenth Amendment. . . . The Establishment Clause, unlike the Free Exercise Clause, does not depend upon any showing of direct governmental compulsion and is violated by the enactment of laws which establish an official religion whether those laws operate directly to coerce nonobserving individuals or not. . . . When the power, prestige and financial support of government is placed behind a particular religious belief, the indirect coercive pressure upon religious minorities to conform to the prevailing officially approved religion is plain. But the purposes underlying the Establishment Clause go much further than that. Its first and most immediate purpose rested on the belief that a union of government and religion tends to destroy government and to degrade religion. The history of governmentally established religion, both in England and in this country, showed that whenever government had allied itself with one particular form of religion, the inevitable result had been that it had incurred the hatred, disrespect and even contempt of those who held contrary beliefs. That same history showed that many people had lost their respect for any religion that had relied upon the support of government to spread its faith. The Establishment Clause thus stands as an expression of principle on the part of the Founders of our Constitution that religion is too personal, too sacred, too holy, to permit its "unhallowed perversion" by a civil magistrate. Another purpose of the Establishment Clause rested upon an awareness of the historical fact that governmentally established religions and religious persecutions go hand in hand. . . . It was in large part to get completely away from this sort of systematic religious persecution that the Founders brought into being our Nation, our Constitution, and our Bill of Rights with its prohibition against any governmental establishment of religion. The New York laws officially prescribing the Regents' prayer are inconsistent both with the purposes of the Establishment Clause and with the Establishment Clause itself.

It has been argued that to apply the Constitution in such a way as to prohibit state laws respecting an establishment of religious services in public schools is to indicate a hostility toward religion or toward prayer. Nothing, of course, could be more wrong. The history of man is inseparable from the history of religion. And perhaps it is not too much to say that since the beginning of that history many people have devoutly believed that "More things are wrought by prayer than this world dreams of." . . . And there were men of this same faith in the power of prayer who led the fight for adoption of our Constitution and also for our Bill of Rights with the very guarantees of religious freedom that forbid the sort of governmental activity which New York has attempted here. These men knew that the First Amendment, which tried to put an end to governmental control of religion and of prayer, was not written to destroy either. They knew rather that it was written to quiet well-justified fears which nearly all of them felt arising out of an awareness that governments of the past had shackled men's tongues to make them speak only the religious thoughts that government wanted them to speak and to pray only to the God that government wanted them to pray to. It is neither sacrilegious nor antireligious to say that each separate government in this country should stay out of the business of writing or sanctioning official prayers and leave that purely religious function to the people themselves and to those the people choose to look to for religious guidance.

To those who may subscribe to the view that because the Regents' official prayer is so brief and general there can be no danger to religious freedom in its governmental establishment, however, it may be appropriate to say in the words of James Madison, the author of the First Amendment:

[I]t is proper to take alarm at the first experiment on our liberties. . . . Who does not see that the same authority which can establish Christianity, in exclusion of all other Religions, may establish with the same ease any particular sect of Christians, in exclusion of all other sects? That the same authority which can force a citizen to contribute three pence only of his property for the support of any one establishment, may force him to conform to any other establishment in all cases whatsoever?

The judgment of the Court of Appeals of New York is reversed and the cause remanded for further proceedings not inconsistent with this opinion.

ABINGTON TOWNSHIP v. SCHEMPP

Only a year after the *Engel* decision, the Court again addressed problems related to the devotional presence of sectarian religion in the public schools. Here, in companion cases, the Court faced issues related to both prayer and the devotional reading of the Bible as officially prescribed elements of the opening of the school day. Justice Clark guided the Court through this controversial area. In the context of the decision, a test for constitutional violation was employed by Justice Clark: "What are the purpose and primary effect of the enactment? If the result of legislation was either to advance or to inhibit religion, the legislation was unconstitutional." The practices at bar were held to be in clear violation of such tests. In reaching his conclusion, Justice Clark dealt with many of the most common objections to the unconstitutional nature of required devotional exercises. Notwithstanding these objections, the state must remain neutral with respect to religion.

In this decision, Justice Clark provided additional indication of the constructive and permissible place for religion in public education. Religion may be studied in the public schools when such study is "presented objectively as part of a secular program of education." While the academic study of religion is appropriate in the public schools, the Court did not conclude that such study must be undertaken. The concept of neutrality, from a legal standpoint, is not to be equated with the requirement that objective study of religion be part of a secular program of education.

Justice Brennan provided a most interesting concurring opinion. In it he noted the choice that is open to parents: either to send their children to public schools for secular education or to send them to private or parochial schools which present additional values not found in the public schools. Government, in his opinion, cannot deny this choice, a choice necessitated by the fact that public education must remain secular (as opposed to sectarian). As a part of his opinion, Justice Brennan presented a history of the devotional presence of religion in public education and reviewed many of the most important arguments in favor of this presence. His conclusion has been influential in the development of religion studies for the public schools.

While only one justice dissented in this ruling, that dissent is important. In the opinion, Justice Stewart argued that the Court had not applied the Constitution accurately. His dissent appeared to turn on the lack of coercion upon students to engage in either the prayer or the Bible reading activities as prescribed. In this absence of coercion upon individuals to participate, Justice Stewart was unable to see a constitutional violation upon which the Court could legitimately rule.

SCHOOL DISTRICT OF ABINGTON TOWNSHIP, PENNSYLVANIA v. SCHEMPP.
MURRAY v. CURLETT.
374 U.S. 203

Decided June 17, 1963—one justice dissenting.

Mr. Justice CLARK delivered the opinion of the Court.

Once again we are called upon to consider the scope of the provision of the First Amendment to the United States Constitution which declares that "Congress shall make no law respecting an establishment of religion, or prohibiting the free exercise thereof. . . . " These companion cases present the issues in the context of state action requiring that schools begin each day with readings from the Bible. While raising the basic questions under slightly different factual situations, the cases permit of joint treatment. In light of the history of the First Amendment and of our cases interpreting and applying its requirements, we hold that the practices at issue and the laws requiring them are unconstitutional under the Establishment Clause, as applied to the States through the Fourteenth Amendment.

The Commonwealth of Pennsylvania by law . . . requires that "At least ten verses from the Holy Bible shall be read, without comment, at the opening of each public school on each school day. Any child shall be excused from such Bible reading, or attending such Bible reading, upon the written request of his parent or guardian." The Schempp family, husband and wife and two of their three children, brought suit to enjoin enforcement of the statute, contending that their rights under the Fourteenth Amendment to the Constitution of the United States are, have been, and will continue to be violated unless this statute be declared unconstitutional as violative of these provisions of the First Amendment.

On each school day at the Abington Senior High School between 8:15 and 8:30 a.m., while the pupils are attending their home rooms or advisory sections, opening exercises are conducted pursuant to the statute. The exercises are broadcast into each room in the school building through an intercommunications system and are conducted under the supervision of a teacher by students attending the school's radio and television workshop. Selected students from this course gather each morning in the school's workshop studio for the exercises, which include readings by one of the students of 10 verses of the Holy Bible, broadcast to each room in the building. This is followed by the recitation of the Lord's Prayer . . . Participation in the opening exercises, as directed by the statute, is voluntary. The student reading the verses from the Bible may select the passages and read from any version he chooses, although the only copies furnished by the school are the King James version. . . . During the period in which the exercises have been conducted the King James, the Douay and the Revised Standard versions of the Bible have been used, as well as the Jewish Holy Scriptures. There are no prefatory statements, no questions asked or solicited, no comments or explanations made and no interpretations given at or during the exercises. The students and parents are advised that the student may absent himself from the classroom or, should he elect to remain, not participate in the exercises.

In 1905 the Board of School Commissioners of Baltimore City adopted a rule . . . provided for the holding of opening exercises in the schools of the city, consisting primarily of the "reading, without comment, of a chapter in the Holy Bible and/or the use of the Lord's Prayer." The petitioners, Mrs. Madalyn Murray and her son, William J. Murray III, are both professed atheists. Following unsuccessful attempts to have the respondent school board rescind the rule, this suit was filed for mandamus to compel its rescission and cancellation. It was alleged that William was a student in a public school of the city and Mrs. Murray, his mother, was a taxpayer therein; that it was the practice under the rule to have a reading on each school morning from the King James version of the Bible; that at petitioners' insistence the rule was amended to permit children to be excused from the exercise on request of the parent and that William had been excused pursuant thereto; that nevertheless the rule as amended was in violation of the petitioners' rights "to freedom of religion under the First and Fourteenth Amendments" and in violation of "the principle of separation between church and state, contained therein. . . ." The petition particularized the petitioners' atheistic beliefs and stated that the rule, as practiced, violated their rights

> "in that it threatens their religious liberty by placing a premium on belief as against non-belief and subjects their freedom of conscience to the rule of the majority; it pronounces belief in God as the source of all moral and spiritual values, equating these values with religious values, and thereby renders sinister, alien and suspect the beliefs and ideals of your Petitioners, promoting doubt and question of their morality, good citizenship and good faith."

It is true that religion has been closely identified with our history and government. . . . The fact that the Founding Fathers believed devotedly that there was a God and that the unalienable rights of man were rooted in Him is clearly evidenced in their writings, from the Mayflower Compact to the Constitution itself. This background is evidenced today in our public life through the continuance in our oaths of office from the Presidency to the Alderman of the final supplication, "So help me God." Likewise each House of the Congress provides through its Chaplain an opening prayer, and the sessions of this Court are declared open by the crier in a short ceremony, the final phrase of which invokes the grace of God. Again, there are such manifestations in our military forces, where those of our citizens who are under the restrictions of military service wish to engage in voluntary worship. Indeed, only last year an official survey of the country indicated that 64% of our people have church membership . . . while less than 3% profess no religion whatever. . . . It can be truly said, therefore, that today, as in the beginning, our national life reflects a religious people who, in the words of Madison, are "earnestly praying, as . . . in duty bound, that the Supreme Lawgiver of the Universe . . . guide them into every measure which may be worthy of his [blessing . . .]."

This is not to say, however, that religion has been so identified with our history and government that religious freedom is not likewise as strongly imbedded in our public and private life. Nothing but the most telling of personal experiences in religious persecution suffered by our forebears, could have planted our belief in liberty of religious opinion any more deeply in our heritage. It is true that this liberty frequently was not realized by the colonists, but this is readily accountable by their close ties to the Mother Country. However, the views of Madison and Jefferson, preceded by Roger Williams, came to be incorporated not only in the Federal Constitution but likewise in those of most of our States. This freedom to worship was indispensable in a country whose people came from the four quarters of the earth and brought with them a diversity of religious opinion. Today authorities list 83 separate religious bodies, each with membership exceeding 50,000, existing among our people, as well as innumerable smaller groups.

First, this Court has decisively settled that the First Amendment's mandate that "Congress shall make no law respecting an establishment of religion, or prohibiting the free exercise thereof" has been made wholly applicable to the States by the Fourteenth Amendment.

Second, this Court has rejected unequivocally the contention that the Establishment Clause forbids only governmental preference of one religion over another.

While none of the parties to either of these cases has questioned these basic conclusions of the Court, both of which have been long established, recognized and consistently reaffirmed, others continue to question their history, logic and efficacy. Such contentions, in the light of the consistent interpretation in cases of this Court, seem entirely untenable and of value only as academic exercises.

The wholesome "neutrality" of which this Court's cases speak thus stems from a recognition of the teachings of history that powerful sects or groups might bring about a fusion of governmental and religious functions or a concert or dependency of one upon the other to the end that official support of the State or Federal Government would be placed behind the tenets of one or of all orthodoxies. This the Establishment Clause prohibits. And a further reason for neutrality is found in the Free Exercise Clause, which recognizes the value of religious training, teaching and observance and, more particularly, the right of every person to freely choose his own course with reference thereto, free of any compulsion from the state. This the Free Exercise Clause guarantees. Thus, as we have seen, the two clauses may overlap. As we have indicated, the Establishment Clause has been directly considered by this Court eight times in the past score of years and, with only one Justice dissenting on the point, it has consistently held that the clause withdrew all legislative power respecting religious belief or the expression thereof. The test may be stated as follows: what are the purpose and the primary effect of the enactment? If either is the advancement or inhibition of religion then the enactment exceeds the scope of legislative power as circumscribed by the Constitution. That is to say that to withstand the strictures of the Establishment Clause there must be a secular legislative purpose and a primary effect that neither advances nor inhibits religion. . . . The Free Exercise Clause, likewise considered many times here, withdraws from legislative power, state and federal, the exertion of any restraint on the free exercise of religion. Its purpose is to secure religious liberty in the individual by prohibiting any invasions thereof by civil authority. Hence it is necessary in a free exercise case for one to show the coercive effect of the enactment as it operates against him in the practice of his religion. The distinction between the two clauses is apparent—a violation of the Free Exercise Clause is predicated on coercion while the Establishment Clause violation need not be so attended.

Applying the Establishment Clause principles to the cases at bar we find that the States are requiring the selection and reading at the opening of the school day of verses from the Holy Bible and the recitation of the Lord's Prayer by the students in unison. These exercises are prescribed as part of the curricular activities of students who are required by law to attend school.

They are held in the school buildings under the supervision and with the participation of teachers employed in these schools. . . . We agree with the trial court's finding as to the religious character of the exercises. Given that finding, the exercises and the law requiring them are in violation of the Establishment Clause.

The conclusion follows that in both cases the laws require religious exercises and such exercises are being conducted in direct violation of the rights of the appellees and petitioners. Nor are these required exercises mitigated by the fact that individual students may absent themselves upon parental request, for that fact furnishes no defense to a claim of unconstitutionality under the Establishment Clause. . . . Further, it is no defense to urge that the religious practices here may be relatively minor encroachments on the First Amendment. The breach of neutrality that is today a trickling stream may all too soon become a raging torrent . . .

It is insisted that unless these religious exercises are permitted a "religion of secularism" is established in the schools. We agree of course that the State may not establish a "religion of secularism" in the sense of affirmatively opposing or showing hostility to religion, thus "preferring those who believe in no religion over those who do believe." . . . We do not agree, however, that this decision in any sense has that effect. In addition, it might well be said that one's education is not complete without a study of comparative religion or the history of religion and its relationship to the advancement of civilization. It certainly may be said that the Bible is worthy of study for its literary and historic qualities. Nothing we have said here indicates that such study of the Bible or of religion, when presented objectively as part of a secular program of education, may not be effected consistently with the First Amendment. But the exercises here do not fall into those categories. They are religious exercises, required by the States in violation of the command of the First Amendment that the Government maintain strict neutrality, neither aiding nor opposing religion.

Finally, we cannot accept that the concept of neutrality, which does not permit a State to require a religious exercise even with the consent of the majority of those affected, collides with the majority's right to free exercise of religion. While the Free Exercise Clause clearly prohibits the use of state action to deny the rights of free exercise to *anyone*, it has never meant that a majority could use the machinery of the State to practice its beliefs.

The place of religion in our society is an exalted one, achieved through a long tradition of reliance on the home, the church and the inviolable citadel of the individual heart and mind. We have come to recognize through bitter experience that it is not within the power of government to invade that citadel, whether its purpose or effect be to aid or oppose, to advance or retard.

In the relationship between man and religion, the State is firmly committed to a position of neutrality. Though the application of that rule requires interpretation of a delicate sort, the rule itself is clearly and concisely stated in the words of the First Amendment. Applying that rule to the facts of these cases, we affirm the judgment in No. 142. In No. 119, the judgment is reversed and the cause remanded to the Maryland Court of Appeals for further proceedings consistent with this opinion.

Mr. Justice DOUGLAS, concurring.

I join the opinion of the Court and add a few words in explanation.

These regimes violate the Establishment Clause in two different ways. In each case the State is conducting a religious exercise; and, as the Court holds, that cannot be done without violating the "neutrality" required of the State by the balance of power between individual, church and state that has been struck by the First Amendment. But the Establishment Clause is not limited to precluding the State itself from conducting religious exercises. It also forbids the State to employ its facilities or funds in a way that gives any church, or all churches, greater strength in our society than it would have by relying on its members alone. Thus, the present regimes must fall under that clause for the additional reason that public funds, though small in amount, are being used to promote a religious exercise. Through the mechanism of the State, all of the people are being required to finance a religious exercise that only some of the people want and that violates the sensibilities of others.

The most effective way to establish any institution is to finance it; and this truth is reflected in the appeals by church groups for public funds to finance their religious schools. Financing a church either in its strictly religious activities or in its other activities is equally unconstitutional.

It is not the amount of public funds expended; as this case illustrates, it is the use to which public funds are put that is controlling. For the First Amendment does not say that some forms of establishment are allowed; it says that "no law respecting an establishment of religion" shall be made. What may not be done directly may not be done indirectly lest the Establishment Clause become a mockery.

Mr. Justice BRENNAN, concurring.

The Court's historic duty to expound the meaning of the Constitution has encountered few issues more intricate or more demanding than that of the relationship between religion and the public schools. . . . Americans regard the public schools as a most vital civic institution for the preservation of a democratic system of government. It is therefore understandable that the constitutional prohibitions encounter their severest test when they are sought to be applied in the school classroom. Nevertheless, it is this Court's inescapable duty to declare whether exercises in the public schools of the States, such as those of Pennsylvania and Maryland questioned here, are involvements of religion in public institutions of a kind which offends the First and Fourteenth Amendments.

The fact is that the line which separates the secular from the sectarian in American life is elusive. The difficulty of defining the boundary with precision inheres in a paradox central to our scheme of liberty. While our institutions reflect a firm conviction that we are a religious people, those institutions by solemn constitutional injunction may not officially involve religion in such a way as to prefer, discriminate against, or oppress, a particular sect or religion. Equally the Constitution enjoins those involvements of religious with secular institutions which (a) serve the essentially religious activities of religious institutions; (b) employ the organs of government for essentially religious purposes; or (c) use essentially religious means to serve government ends where secular means would suffice.

I join fully in the opinion and the judgement of the Court. I see no escape from the conclusion that the exercises called in question in these two cases violate the constitutional mandate. The reasons we gave only last Term in *Engel v. Vitale*, 370 U.S. 421, for finding in the New York Regents' prayer an impermissible establishment of religion, compel the same judgement of the practices at bar. . . . It should be unnecessary to observe that our holding does not declare that the First Amendment manifests hostility to the practice or teaching of religion, but only applies prohibitions incorporated in the Bill of Rights in recognition of historic needs shared by Church and State alike. While it is my view that not every involvement of religion in public life is unconstitutional, I consider the exercises at bar a form of involvement which clearly violates the Establishment Clause.

The First Amendment forbids both the abridgment of the free exercise of religion and the enactment of laws "respecting an establishment of religion." The two clauses, although distinct in their objectives and their applicability, emerged together from a common panorama of history. The inclusion of both restraints upon the power of Congress to legislate concerning religious matters shows unmistakably that the Framers of the First Amendment were not content to rest the protection of religious liberty exclusively upon either clause.

It is true that the Framers' immediate concern was to prevent the setting up of an official federal church of the kind which England and some of the Colonies had long supported. But nothing in the text of the Establishment Clause supports the view that the prevention of the setting up of an official church was meant to be the full extent of the prohibitions against official involvements in religion.

Plainly, the Establishment Clause, in the contemplation of the Framers, "did not limit the constitutional proscription to any particular, dated form of state-supported theological venture." "What Virginia had long practiced, and what Madison, Jefferson, and others fought to end, was the extension of civil government's support to religion in a manner which made the two in some degree interdependent, and thus threatened the freedom of each. The purpose of the Establishment Clause was to assure that the national legislature would not exert its power in the service of any purely religious end; that it would not, as Virginia and virtually all of the Colonies had done, make of religion, as religion, an object of legislation. . . . The Establishment Clause withdrew from the sphere of legitimate legislative concern and competence a specific, but comprehensive, area of human conduct: man's belief or disbelief in the verity of some transcendental idea and man's expression in action of that belief or disbelief. . ." *McGowan v. Maryland,* 366 U.S. at 465-66 . . .

In sum, the history which our prior decisions have summoned to aid interpretation of the Establishment Clause permits little doubt that its prohibition was designed comprehensively to prevent those official involvements of religion which would tend to foster or discourage religious worship or belief.

But an awareness of history and an appreciation of the aims of the Founding Fathers do not always resolve concrete problems. . . . A more fruitful inquiry, it seems to me, is whether the practices here challenged threaten those consequences which the Framers deeply feared; whether, in short, they tend to promote that type of interdependence between religion and state which the First Amendment was designed to prevent.

A too literal quest for the advice of the Founding Fathers upon the issues of these cases seems to me futile and misdirected for several reasons: First, on our precise problem the historical record is at best ambiguous, and statements can readily be found to support either side of the proposition.

Second, the structure of American education has greatly changed since the First Amendment was adopted. In the context of our modern emphasis upon public education available to all citizens, any views of the eighteenth century as to whether the exercises at bar are an "establishment" offer little aid to decision.

Third, our religious composition makes us a vastly more diverse people than were our forefathers. They knew differences chiefly among Protestant sects. Today the Nation is far more heterogeneous religiously, including as it does substantial minorities not only of Catholics and Jews but as well of those who worship according to no version of the Bible and those who worship no God at all.

Fourth, the American experiment in free public education available to all children has been guided in large measure by the dramatic evolution of the religious diversity among the population which our public schools serve. The interaction of these two important forces in our national life has placed in bold relief certain positive values in the consistent application to public institutions generally, and public schools particularly, of the constitutional decree against official involvements of religion which might produce the evils the Framers meant the Establishment Clause to forestall. . . . It is implicit in the history and character of American public education that the public schools serve a uniquely *public* function: the training of American citizens in an atmosphere free of parochial, divisive, or separatist influences of any sort—an atmosphere in which children may assimilate a heritage common to all American groups and religions. . . . This is a heritage neither theistic nor atheistic, but simply civic and patriotic.

Attendance at the public schools has never been compulsory; parents remain morally and constitutionally free to choose the academic environment in which they wish their children to be educated. . . . The choice which is thus preserved is between a public secular education with its uniquely democratic values, and some form of private or sectarian education, which offers values of its own. In my judgment the First Amendment forbids the State to inhibit that freedom of choice by diminishing the attractiveness of either alternative . . . The lesson of history . . . is that a system of free public education forfeits its unique contribution to the growth of democratic citizenship when that choice ceases to be freely available to each parent.

The exposition by this Court of the religious guarantees of the First Amendment has consistently reflected and reaffirmed the concerns which impelled the Framers to write those guarantees into the Constitution. It would be neither possible nor appropriate to review here the entire course of our decisions on religious questions.

The issue of what particular activities the Establishment Clause forbids the States to undertake is our more immediate concern. In *Everson v. Board of Education* . . . U.S. 1, a careful study of the relevant history led the Court to the view, consistently recognized in decisions since Everson, that the Establishment Clause embodied the Framer's conclusion that government and religion have discreet interests which are mutually best served when each avoids too close a proximity to the other. It is not only the nonbeliever who fears the injection of sectarian doctrines and controversies into the civil polity, but in as high degree it is the devout believer who fears the secularization of a creed which becomes too deeply involved with and dependent upon the government. It has rightly been said of the history of the Establishment Clause that "our tradition of civil liberty rests not only on the secularism of a Thomas Jefferson but also on the fervent sectarianism . . . of a Roger Williams."

Our decisions on questions of religious education or exercises in the public school have consistently reflected this dual aspect of the Establishment Clause.

The use of prayers and Bible readings at the opening of the school day long antedates the founding of our Republic.

After the Revolution, the new States uniformly continued these long-established practices in the private and the few public grammar schools. . . . As the free public schools gradually supplanted the private academies and sectarian schools between 1800 and 1850, morning devotional exercises were retained with few alterations. Indeed, public pressures upon school administrators in many parts of the country would hardly have condoned abandonment of practices to which a century or more of private religious education had accustomed the American people. The controversy centered, in fact, principally about the elimination of plainly sectarian practices and textbooks, and led to the eventual substitution of nonsectarian, though still religious, exercises and materials.

Statutory provision for daily religious exercises is, however, of quite recent origin. At the turn of this century, there was but one State—Massachusetts—which had a law making morning prayer or Bible reading obligatory. Statutes elsewhere either permitted such practices or simply left the question to local option. It was not until after 1910 that 11 more States, within a few years joined Massachusetts in making one or both exercises compulsory. . . . In no State has there ever been a constitutional or statutory prohibition against the recital of prayers or the reading of Scriptures, although a number of States have outlawed these practices by judicial decision or administrative order. What is noteworthy about the panoply of state and local regulations from which these cases emerge is the relative recency of the statutory codification of practices which have ancient roots, and the rather small number of States which have ever prescribed compulsory religious exercises in the public schools.

The purposes underlying the adoption and perpetuation of these practices are somewhat complex. It is beyond question that the religious benefits and values realized from daily prayer and Bible reading have usually been considered paramount, and sufficient to justify the continuation of such practices. To Horace Mann, embroiled in an intense controversy over the role of *sectarian* instruction and textbooks in the Boston public schools, there was little question that the regular use of the Bible—which he thought essentially nonsectarian—would bear fruit in the spiritual enlightenment of his pupils. . . . Wisconsin's Superintendent of Public Instruction, writing a few years later in 1858, reflected the attitude of his eastern colleagues, in that he regarded "with special favor the use of the Bible in public schools, as preeminently first in importance among text-books for teaching the noblest priciples of virtue, morality, patriotism, and good order—love and reverence for God—charity and good will to man."

Such statements reveal the understanding of educators that the daily religious exercises in the schools served broader goals than compelling formal worship of God or fostering church attendance. The religious aims of the educators who adopted and retained such exercises were comprehensive, and in many cases quite devoid of sectarian bias—but the crucial fact is that they were nonetheless religious.

Almost from the beginning religious exercises in the public schools have been the subject of intense criticism, vigorous debate, and judicial or administrative prohibition. Significantly, educators and school boards early entertained doubts about both the legality and the soundness of opening the school day with compulsory prayer or Bible reading. Particularly in the large Eastern cities, where immigration had exposed the public schools to religious diversities and conflicts unknown to the homogeneous academies of the eighteenth century, local authorities found it necessary, even before the Civil War to seek an accommodation.

The last quarter of the nineteenth century found the the courts beginning to question the constitutionality of public school religious exercises. The legal context was still, of course, that of the state constitutions, since the First Amendment had not yet been held applicable to state action. And the state constitutional prohibitions against church-state cooperation or governmental aid to religion were generally less rigorous than the Establishment Clause of the First Amendment. It is therefore remarkable that the courts of a half dozen States found compulsory religious exercises in the public schools in violation of their respective state constitutions. These courts attributed much significance to the clearly religious origins and content of the challenged practices, and to the impossibility of avoiding sectarian controversy in their conduct.

Thus the panorama of history permits no other conclusion than that daily prayers and Bible readings in the public schools have always been designed to be, and have been regarded as, essentially religious exercises. Unlike the Sunday closing laws, these exercises appear neither to have been divorced from their religious origins nor deprived of their centrally religious character by the passage of time. . . . On this distinction alone we might well rest a constitutional decision. But three further contentions have been pressed in the argument of these cases.

First, it is argued that however clearly religious may have been the origins and early nature of daily prayer and Bible reading, these practices today serve so clearly secular educational purposes that their religious attributes may be overlooked. . . .

It is not the business of this Court to gainsay the judgments of experts on matters of pedagogy. Such decisions must be left to the discretion of those administrators charged with the supervision of the Nation's public schools. The limited province of the courts is to determine whether the means which the educators have chosen to achieve legitimate pedagogical ends infringe the constitutional freedoms of the First Amendment. The secular purposes which devotional exercises are said to serve fall into two categories—those which depend upon an immediately religious experience shared by the participating children; and those which appear sufficiently divorced from the religious content of the devotional material that they can be served equally by nonreligious materials. With respect to the first objective, much has been written about the moral and spiritual values of infusing some religious influence or instruction into the public school classroom. To the extent that only *religious* materials will serve this purpose, it seems to me that the purpose as well as the means is so plainly religious that the exercise is necessarily forbidden by the Establishment Clause.

The second justification assumes that religious exercises at the start of the school day may directly serve solely secular ends—for example, by fostering harmony and tolerance among the pupils, enhancing the authority of the teacher, and inspiring better discipline. To the extent that such benefits result not from the content of the readings and recitation, but simply from the holding of such a solemn exercise at the opening assembly or the first class of the day, it would seem that less sensitive materials might equally well serve the same purpose. . . . It has not been shown that readings from the speeches and messages of great Americans, for example, or from the documents of our heritage of liberty, daily recitation of the Pledge of Allegiance, or even the observance of a moment of reverent silence at the opening of class, may not adequately serve the solely secular purposes of the devotional activities without jeopardizing either the religious liberties of any members of the community or the proper degree of separation between the spheres of religion and government. Such substitutes would, I think, be unsatisfactory or inadequate only to the extent that the present activities do in fact serve religious goals. While I do not question the judgment of experienced educators that the challenged practices may well achieve valuable secular ends, it seems to me that the State acts unconstitutionally if it either sets about to attain even indirectly religious ends by religious means, or if it uses religious means to serve secular ends where secular means would suffice.

Second, it is argued that the particular practices involved in the two cases before us are unobjectionable because they prefer no particular sect or sects at the expense of others. . . . The sectarian character of the Holy Bible has been at the core of the whole controversy over religious practices in the public schools throughout its long and often bitter history. To vary the version as the Abington and Baltimore schools have done may well be less offensive than to read from the King James version every day, as once was the practice. But the result even of this relatively benign procedure is that majority sects are preferred in approximate proportion to their representation in the community and in the student body, while the smaller sects suffer commensurate discrimination. So long as the subject matter of the exercise is sectarian in character, these consequences cannot be avoided.

The argument contains, however, a more basic flaw. There are persons in every community—often deeply devout—to whom any version of the Judaeo-Christian Bible is offensive. There are others whose reverence for the Holy Scriptures demands private study or reflection and to whom public reading or recitation is sacrilegious . . .

It has been suggested that a tentative solution to these problems may lie in the fashioning of a "common core" of theology tolerable to all creeds but preferential to none. But as one commentator has recently observed, "[h]istory is not encouraging to" those who hope to fashion a "common denominator of religion detached from its manifestation in any organized church." . . . Engel is surely authority that nonsectarian religious practices, equally with sectarian exercises, violate the Establishment Clause. Moreover, even if the Establishment Clause were oblivious to nonsectarian religious practices, I think it quite likely that the "common core" approach would be sufficiently objectionable to many groups to be foreclosed by the prohibitions of the Free Exercise Clause.

A third element which is said to absolve the practices involved in these cases from the ban of the religious guarantees of the Constitution is the provision to excuse or exempt students who wish not to participate. . . . the short, and to me sufficient, answer is that the availability of excusal or exemption simply has no relevance to the establishment question, if it is once found that these practices are essentially religious exercises designed at least in part to achieve religious aims through the use of public school facilities during the school day.

The more difficult question, however, is whether the availability of excusal for the dissenting child serves to refute challenges to these practices under the Free Exercise Clause. While it is enough to decide these cases to dispose of the establishment questions, questions of free exercise are so inextricably interwoven into the history and present status of these practices as to justify disposition of this second aspect of the excusal issue. The answer is that the excusal procedure itself necessarily operates in such a way as to infringe the rights of free exercise of those children who wish to be excused. We have held in Barnette and Torcaso, respectively, that a State may require neither public school students nor candidates for an office of public trust to profess beliefs offensive to religious principles. By the same token the State could not constitutionally require a student to profess publicly his disbelief as the prerequisite to the exercise of his constitutional right of abstention. . . . by requiring what is tantamount in the eyes of teachers and schoolmates to a profession of disbelief, or at least of nonconformity, the procedure may well deter those children who do not wish to participate for any reason based upon the dictates of conscience from exercising an indisputably constitutional right to be excused. Thus the excusal provision in its operation subjects them to a cruel dilemma. In consequence, even devout children may well avoid claiming their right and simply continue to participate in exercises distasteful to them because of an understandable reluctance to be stigmatized as atheists or nonconformists simply on the basis of their request.

Such reluctance to seek exemption seems all the more likely in view of the fact that children are disinclined at this age to step out of line or to flout "peer-group norms."

To summarize my views concerning the merits of these two cases: The history, the purpose and the operation of the daily prayer recital and Bible reading leave no doubt that these practices standing by themselves constitute an impermissable breach of the Establishment Clause. Such devotional exercises may well serve legitimate nonreligious purposes. To the extent, however, that such purposes are really without religious significance, it has never been demonstrated that secular means would not suffice. Indeed, I would suggest that patriotic or other nonreligious material might provide adequate substitutes—inadequate only to the extent that the purposes now served are indeed directly or indirectly religious. Under such circumstances, the States may not employ religious means to reach a secular goal unless secular means are wholly unavailing.

These considerations bring me to a final contention of the school officials in these cases: that the invalidation of the exercises at bar permits this Court no alternative but to declare unconstitutional every vestige, however slight, of cooperation or accommodation between religion and government. I cannot accept that contention. While it is not, of course, appropriate for this Court to decide questions not presently before it, I venture to suggest that religious exercises in the public schools present a unique problem. For not every involvement of religion in public life violates the Establishment Clause. Our decision in these cases does not clearly forecast anything about the constitutionality of other types of interdependence between religious and other public institutions.

What the Framers meant to foreclose, and what our decisions under the Establishment Clause have forbidden, are those involvements of religious with secular institutions which (a) serve the essentially religious activities of religious institutions; (b) employ the organs of government for essentially religious purposes; or (c) use essentially religious means to serve governmental ends, where secular means would suffice. . . . On the other hand, there may be myriad forms of involvements of government with religion which do not import such dangers and therefore should not, in my judgment, be deemed to violate the Establishment Clause. Nothing in the Constitution compels the organs of government to be blind to what everyone else perceives—that religious differences among Americans have important and pervasive implications for our society. Likewise nothing in the Establishment Clause forbids the application of legislation having purely secular ends in such a way as to alleviate burdens upon the free exercise of an individual's religious beliefs.

The holding of the Court today plainly does not foreclose teaching *about* the Holy Scriptures or about the differences between religious sects in classes in literature or history. Indeed, whether or not the Bible is involved, it would be impossible to teach meaningfully many subjects in the social sciences or the humanities without some mention of religion. To what extent, and at what points in the curriculum, religious materials should be cited are matters which the courts ought to entrust very largely to the experienced officials who superintend our Nation's public schools. They are experts in such matters, and we are not.

Mr. Justice GOLDBERG, with whom Mr. Justice HARLAN joins, concurring.

The First Amendment's guarantees, as applied to the States through the Fourteenth Amendment, foreclose not only laws "respecting an establishment of religion" but also those "prohibiting the free exercise thereof." These two proscriptions are to be read together, and in light of the single end which they are designed to serve. The basic purpose of the religion clause of the First Amendment is to promote and assure the fullest possible scope of religious liberty and tolerance for all and to nurture the conditions which secure the best hope of attainment of that end.

It is said, and I agree, that the attitude of government toward religion must be one of neutrality. But untutored devotion to the concept of neutrality can lead to invocation or approval of results which partake not simply of that noninterference and noninvolvement with the religious which the Constitution commands, but of a brooding and pervasive devotion to the secular and a passive, or even active, hostility to the religious. Such results are not only not compelled by the Constitution, but, it seems to me, are prohibited by it.

Neither government nor this Court can or should ignore the significance of the fact that a vast portion of our people believe in and worship God and that many of our legal, political and personal values derive historically from religious teachings. Government must inevitably take cognizance of the existence of religion and, indeed, under certain circumstances the First Amendment may require that it do so. And it seems clear to me from the opinions in the present and past cases that the Court would recognize the propriety of providing military chaplains and of the teaching *about* religion, as distinguished from the teaching *of* religion, in the public schools. The examples could readily be multiplied, for both the required and the permissible accommodations between state and church frame the relation as one free of hostility or favor and productive of religious and political harmony, but without undue involvement of one in the concerns or practices of the other.

The practices here involved do not fall within any sensible or acceptable concept of compelled or permitted accommodation and involve the state so significantly and directly in the realm of the sectarian as to give rise to those very divisive influences and inhibitions of freedom which both religion clauses of the First Amendment preclude. . . . The pervasive religiosity and direct governmental involvement inhering in the prescription of prayer and Bible reading in the public schools, during and as part of the curricular day, involving young impressionable children whose school attendance is statutorily compelled, and utilizing the prestige, power, and influence of school administration, staff, and authority, cannot realistically be termed simply accommodation, and must fall within the interdiction of the First Amendment. I find nothing in the opinion of the Court which says more than this. . . . The First Amendment does not prohibit practices which by any realistic measure create none of the dangers which it is designed to prevent and which do not so directly or substantially involve the state in religious exercises or in the favoring of religion as to have meaningful and practical impact. It is of course true that great consequences can grow from small beginnings, but the measure of constitutional adjudication is the ability and willingness to distinguish between real threat and mere shadow.

Mr. Justice STEWART, dissenting.

The First Amendment declares that "Congress shall make no law respecting an establishment of religion, or prohibiting the free exercise thereof . . ." It is, I think, a fallacious oversimplification to regard these two provisions as establishing a single constitutional standard of "separation of church and state," which can be mechanically applied in every case to delineate the required boundaries between government and religion. We err in the first place if we do not recognize, as a matter of history and as a matter of the imperatives of our free society, that religion and government must necessarily interact in countless ways. Secondly, the fact is that while in many contexts the Establishment Clause and the Free Exercise Clause fully complement each other, there are areas in which a doctrinaire reading of the Establishment Clause leads to irreconcilable conflict with the Free Exercise Clause.

As a matter of history, the First Amendment was adopted solely as a limitation upon the newly created National Government. The events leading to its adoption strongly suggest that the Establishment Clause was primarily an attempt to insure that Congress not only would be powerless to establish a national church, but would also be unable to interfere with existing state establishments. . . . Each state was left free to go its own way and pursue its own policy with respect to religion.

So matters stood until the adoption of the Fourteenth Amendment, or more accurately, until this Court's decision in Cantwell v. Connecticut, in 1940, 310 U.S. 296 . . . In that case the Court said: "The First Amendment declares that Congress shall make no law respecting an establishment of religion or prohibiting the free exercise thereof. The Fourteenth Amendment has rendered the legislatures of the states as incompetent as Congress to enact such laws."

I accept without question that the liberty guaranteed by the Fourteenth Amendment against impairment by the States embraces in full the right of free exercise of religion protected by the First Amendment, and I yield to no one in my conception of the breadth of that freedom. . . . I accept too the proposition that the Fourteenth Amendment has somehow absorbed the Establishment Clause, although it is not without irony that a constitutional provision evidently designed to leave the States free to go their own way should now have become a restriction upon their autonomy. But I cannot agree with what seems to me the insensitive definition of the Establishment Clause contained in the Court's opinion, nor with the different but, I think, equally mechanistic definitions contained in the separate opinions which have been filed.

That the central value embodied in the First Amendment—and, more particularly, in the guarantee of "liberty" contained in the Fourteenth—is the safeguarding of an individual's right to free exercise of his religion has been consistently recognized.

It is this concept of constitutional protection embodied in our decisions which makes the cases before us such difficult ones for me. For there is involved in these cases a substantial free exercise claim on the part of those who affirmatively desire to have their children's school day open with the reading of passages from the Bible.

It might also be argued that parents who want their children exposed to religious influences can adequately fulfill that wish off school property and outside school time. With all its surface persuasiveness, however, this argument seriously misconceives the basic constitutional justification for permitting the exercises at issue in these cases. For a compulsory state educational system so structures a child's life that if religious exercises are held to be an impermissible activity in schools, religion is placed at an artificial and state-created disadvantage. Viewed in this light, permission of such exercises for those who want them is necessary if the schools are truly to be neutral in the matter of religion. And a refusal to permit religious exercises thus is seen, not as the realization of state neutrality, but rather as the establishment of a religion of secularism, or at the least, as government support of the beliefs of those who think that religious exercises should be conducted only in private.

What seems to me to be of paramount importance, then, is recognition of the fact that the claim advanced here in favor of Bible reading is sufficiently substantial to make simple reference to the constitutional phrase "establishment of religion" as inadequate an analysis of the cases before us as the ritualistic invocation of the nonconstitutional phrase "separation of church and state." What these cases compel, rather, is an analysis of just what the "neutrality" is which is required by the interplay of the Establishment and Free Exercise Clauses of the First Amendment, as imbedded in the Fourteenth.

In the absence of evidence that the legislature or school board intended to prohibit local schools from substituting a different set of readings where parents requested such a change, we should not assume that the provisions before us—as actually administered—may not be construed simply as authorizing religious exercises, nor that the designations may not be treated simply as indications of the promulgating body's view as to the community's preference. . . . In the Schempp case there is evidence which indicates that variations were in fact permitted by the very school there involved, and that further variations were not introduced only because of the absence of requests from parents. And in the Murray case the Baltimore rule itself contains a provision permitting another version of the Bible to be substituted for the King James version.

In the absence of coercion upon those who do not wish to participate . . . such provisions cannot, in my view, be held to represent the type of support of religion barred by the Establishment Clause. For the only support which such rules provide for religion is the withholding of state hostility . . .

I have said that these provisions authorizing religious exercises are properly to be regarded as measures making possible the free exercise of religion. But it is important to stress that, strictly speaking, what is at issue here is a privilege rather than a right. In other words, the question presented is not whether exercises such as those at issue here are constitutionally compelled, but rather whether they are constitutionally invalid. And that issue, in my view, turns on the question of coercion.

The governmental neutrality which the First and Fourteenth Amendments require in the cases before us, in other words, is the extension of even-handed treatment to all who believe, doubt, or disbelieve—a refusal on the part of the State to weight the scales of private choice. In these cases, therefore, what is involved is not state action based on impermissible categories, but rather an attempt by the State to accommodate those differences which the existence in our society of a variety of religious beliefs makes inevitable. The Constitution requires that such efforts be struck down only if they are proven to entail the use of the secular authority of government to coerce a preference among such beliefs.

To be specific, it seems to me clear that certain types of exercises would present situations in which no possibility of coercion on the part of secular officials could be claimed to exist. Thus, if such exercises were held either before or after the official school day, or if the school schedule were such that participation were merely one among a number of desirable alternatives, it could hardly be contended that the exercises did anything more than to provide an opportunity for the voluntary expression of religious belief. On the other hand, a law which provided for religious exercises during the school day and which contained no excusal provision would obviously be unconstitutionally coercive upon those who did not wish to participate.

Viewed in this light, it seems to me clear that the records in both of the cases before us are wholly inadequate to support an informed or responsible decision. Both cases involve provisions which explicitly permit any student who wishes, to be excused from participation in the exercises. There is no evidence in either case as to whether there would exist any coercion of any kind upon a student who did not want to participate.

What our Constitution indispensably protects is the freedom of each of us, be he Jew or Agnostic, Christian or Atheist, Buddhist or Freethinker, to believe or disbelieve, to worship or not worship, to pray or keep silent, according to his own conscience, uncoerced and unrestrained by government. It is conceivable that these school boards, or even all school boards, might eventually find it impossible to administer a system of religious exercises during school hours in such a way as to meet this constitutional standard—in such a way as completely to free from any kind of official coercion those who do not affirmatively want to participate. But I think we must not assume that school boards so lack the qualities of inventiveness and good will as to make impossible the achievement of that goal.

CHAMBERLIN v. DADE COUNTY

This *per curiam* decision (a majority decision that is announced without identification of a specific justice as the spokesman for the Court) is little more than a memorandum decision. Despite its brevity, the decision is significant. The decision held the practice of prayer and Bible reading in the public schools of Florida to be unconstitutional. This put to rest the common wisdom that the *Abington* decision applied only to Pennsylvania and Maryland. The Court, however, did not rule on the other practices included in the appeal: baccalaureate services, the taking of religious census, and a religious test for teachers.

Justice Douglas, with Justice Black, disagreed and wrote that the Court should have considered one of the ignored elements of the appeal—the religious test for teachers. None of the justices apparently saw questions of constitutional substance in relation to the baccalaureate services or the religious census.[2]

CHAMBERLIN v. DADE COUNTY, BOARD OF PUBLIC INSTRUCTION.
377 U.S. 402
Decided June 1, 1964.

PER CURIAM.
The judgment of the Florida Supreme Court is reversed with respect to the issues of the constitutionality of prayer, and of devotional Bible reading

---

[2]To feel safe in assuming that baccalaureate services or a religious census are constitutional, one must be certain to understand the nature of those practices as undertaken in Florida. Furthermore, while speculation might prove inaccurate, perhaps the Court did not address the religious test for teachers because it had already ruled that the requirement of a declaration of belief in God as a prerequisite for holding public office was in violation of the Constitution. (See *Torcaso v. Watkins*, 367 U.S. 488 (1961). Because school teachers are public employees, that judgment could apply to them— as could the principle announced in the *Barnette* decision.

pursuant to a Florida statute . . . in the public schools of Dade County. . . . As to the other questions raised, the appeal is dismissed for want of properly presented federal questions.

Mr. Justice DOUGLAS, with whom Mr. Justice BLACK agrees, concurring in part.

The "other questions raised" which the Court refuses to consider because not "properly presented" involve the constitutionality under the First and Fourteenth Amendments of baccalaureate services in the schools, a religious census among pupils, and a religious test for teachers.

I think . . . that two of those "other questions"—the baccalaureate services and the religious census—do not present substantial federal questions, and so I concur in the dismissal of the appeal as to them. As to the religious test for teachers, I think a substantial question is presented. . . . I would therefore put that question down for argument, postponing the question of jurisdiction to the merits.

Mr. Justice STEWART would note probable jurisdiction of this appeal and set it down for argument on the merits.

EPPERSON v. ARKANSAS

Justice Fortas formulated the opinion of the Court in this dispute with respect to an anti-evolution statute passed by the legislature of Arkansas. The legislation prohibited any teacher in the schools of the state from teaching that humans evolved from lower forms of life. While expressing great hesitancy to involve the Court in matters of school curriculum, Justice Fortas wrote that the Constitution "forbids alike the preference of a religious doctrine or the prohibition of theory which is deemed antagonistic to a particular dogma."

EPPERSON v. ARKANSAS.

393 U.S. 97

Decided November 12, 1968.

Mr. Justice FORTAS delivered the opinion of the Court.

This appeal challenges the constitutionality of the "anti-evolution" statute which the State of Arkansas adopted in 1928 to prohibit the teaching in its public schools and universities of the theory that man evolved from other species of life. The statute was a product of the upsurge of "fundamentalist" religious fervor of the twenties. The Arkansas statute was an adaption of the famous Tennessee "monkey law" which that State adopted in 1925. The constitutionality of the Tennessee law was upheld by the Tennessee Supreme Court in the celebrated *Scopes* case in 1927.

The Arkansas law makes it unlawful for a teacher in any state-supported school or university "to teach the theory or doctrine that mankind ascended or descended from a lower order of animals," or "to adopt or use in any such institution a textbook that teaches" this theory.

According to the testimony, until the events here in litigation, the official textbook furnished for the high school biology course did not have a section on the Darwinian Theory. Then, for the academic year 1965-1966, the school administration, on recommendation of the teachers of biology in the school system, adopted and prescribed a textbook which contained a chapter setting forth "the theory about the origin . . . of man from a lower form of animal."

Susan Epperson . . . was employed by the Little Rock school system in the fall of 1964 to teach 10th grade biology at Central High School. At the start of the next academic year, 1965, she was confronted by the new textbook . . . She faced at least a literal dilemma because she was supposed to use the new textbook for classroom instruction and presumably to teach the statutorily condemned chapter; but to do so would be a criminal offense and subject her to dismissal.

She instituted the present action . . . seeking a declaration that the Arkansas statute is void and enjoining the State and the defendant officials of the Little Rock school system from dismissing her for violation of the statute's provisions.

At the outset, it is urged upon us that the challenged statute is vague and uncertain and therefore within the condemnation of the Due Process Clause of the Fourteenth Amendment.

. . . we do not rest our decision upon the asserted vagueness of the statute. On either interpretation of its language, Arkansas' statute cannot stand. It is of no moment whether the law is deemed to prohibit mention of Darwin's theory, or to forbid any or all of the infinite varieties of communication embraced within the term "teaching." Under either interpretation, the law must be stricken because of its conflict with the constitutional prohibition of state laws respecting an establishment of religion or prohibiting the free exercise thereof. The overriding fact is that Arkansas' law selects from the body of knowledge a particular segment which it proscribes for the sole reason that it is deemed to conflict with a particular religious doctrine; that is, with a particular interpretation of the Book of Genesis by a particular religious group.

Government in our democracy, state and national, must be neutral in matters of religious theory, doctrine, and practice. It may not be hostile to any religion or to the advocacy of no-religion; and it may not aid, foster, or promote one religion or religious theory against another or even against the militant opposite. The First Amendment mandates governmental neutrality between religion and religion, and between religion and nonreligion.

Judicial interposition in the operation of the public school system of the Nation raises problems requiring care and restraint. Our courts, however, have not failed to apply the First Amendment's mandate in our educational system where essential to safeguard the fundamental values of freedom of speech and inquiry and of belief. By and large, public education in our Nation is committed to the control of state and local authorities. Courts do not and cannot intervene in the resolution of conflicts which arise in the daily operation of school systems and which do not directly and sharply implicate basic constitutional values. On the other hand, "[t]he vigilant protection of constitutional freedoms is nowhere more vital than in the community of American schools," Shelton v. Tucker, 364 U.S. 479, 487 (1960).

There is and can be no doubt that the First Amendment does not permit the State to require that teaching and learning must be tailored to the principles or prohibitions of any religious sect or dogma.

While study of religions and of the Bible from a literary and historic viewpoint, presented objectively as part of a secular program of education, need not collide with the First Amendment's prohibition, the State may not adopt programs or practices in its public schools or colleges which "aid or oppose" any religion. . . . This prohibition is absolute. It forbids alike the preference of a religious doctrine or the prohibition of theory which is deemed antagonistic to a particular dogma.

The State's undoubted right to prescribe the curriculum for its public schools does not carry with it the right to prohibit, on pain of criminal penalty, the teaching of a scientific theory or doctrine where that prohibition is based upon reasons that violate the First Amendment.

In the present case, there can be no doubt that Arkansas has sought to prevent its teachers from discussing the theory of evolution because it is contrary to the belief of some that the Book of Genesis must be the exclusive source of doctrine as to the origin of man. . . . It is clear that fundamentalist sectarian conviction was and is the law's reason for existence.

Arkansas' law cannot be defended as an act of religious neutrality. Arkansas did not seek to excise from the curricula of its schools and universities all discussion of the origin of man. The law's effort was confined to an attempt to blot out a particular theory because of its supposed conflict with the Biblical account, literally read. Plainly, the law is contrary to the mandate of the First, and in violation of the Fourteenth, Amendment to the Constitution.

Mr. Justice BLACK, concurring.

It seems to me that in this situation the statute is too vague for us to strike it down on any ground but that: vagueness. Under this statute as construed by the Arkansas Supreme Court, a teacher cannot know whether he is forbidden to mention Darwin's theory, at all or only free to discuss it as long as he refrains from contending that it is true. It is an established rule that a statute which leaves an ordinary man so doubtful about its meaning that he cannot know when he has violated it denies him the first essential of due process. . . . Holding the statute too vague to endorse would not only follow long-standing constitutional precedents but it would avoid having this Court take unto itself the duty of a State's highest court to interpret and mark the boundaries of the State's laws. And, more important, it would not place this Court in the unenviable position of violating the principle of leaving the States absolutely free to choose their own curriculums for their own schools so long as their action does not palpably conflict with a clear constitutional command.

. . . I find it difficult to agree with the Court's statement that "there can be no doubt that Arkansas has sought to prevent its teachers from discussing the theory of evolution because it is contrary to the belief of some that the Book of Genesis must be the exclusive source of doctrine as to the origin of man." It may be instead that the people's motive was merely that it would be best to remove this controversial subject from its schools; there is no reason I can imagine why a State is without power to withdraw from its curriculum any subject deemed too emotional and controversial for its public schools.

A . . . question that arises for me is whether this Court's decision forbidding a State to exclude the subject of evolution from its schools infringes the religious freedom of those who consider evolution an anti-religious doctrine. If the theory is considered anti-religious, as the Court indicates, how can the State be bound by the Federal Constitution to permit its teachers to advocate such an "anti-religious" doctrine to schoolchildren? . . . The Darwinian theory is said to challenge the Bible's story of creation; so too have some of those who believe in the Bible, along with many others, challenged the Darwinian theory. Since there is no indication that the literal Biblical doctrine of the origin of man is included in the curriculum of Arkansas schools, does not the removal of the subject of evolution leave the State in a neutral position toward these supposedly competing religious and anti-religious doctrines? Unless this Court is prepared simply to write off as pure nonsense the views of those who consider evolution an anti-religious doctrine, then this issue presents problems under the Establishment Clause far more troublesome than are discussed in the Court's opinion.

Certainly the Darwinian theory, precisely like the Genesis story of the creation of man, is not above challenge. In fact the Darwinian theory has not merely been criticized by religionists but by scientists, and perhaps no scientist would be willing to take an oath and swear that everything announced in the Darwinian theory is unquestionably true. The Court, it seems to me, makes a serious mistake in bypassing the plain, unconstitutional vagueness of this statute in order to reach out and decide this troublesome, to me, First Amendment question. However wise this Court may be or may become hereafter, it is doubtful that, sitting in Washington, it can successfully supervise and censor the curriculum of every public school in every hamlet and city in the United States. I doubt that our wisdom is so nearly infallible.

Mr. Justice STEWART, concurring in the result.

The States are most assuredly free "to choose their own curriculums for their own schools." A state is entirely free, for example, to decide that the only foreign language to be taught in its public school system shall be Spanish. But would a State be constitutionally free to punish a teacher for letting his students know that other languages are also spoken in the world? I think not.

It is one thing for a State to determine that "the subject of higher mathematics, or astronomy, or biology" shall or shall not be included in its public school curriculum. It is quite another thing for a State to make it a criminal offense for a public school teacher to so much as to mention the very existence of an entire system of respected human thought. That kind of criminal law, I think, would clearly impinge upon the guarantees of free communication contained in the First Amendment, and made applicable to the States by the Fourteenth.

WISCONSIN v. YODER

Chief Justice Burger expressed the Court's opinion in this controversy centering upon the right of members of the Amish faith to prohibit attendance of their children in the public secondary schools of Wisconsin despite that state's compulsory education laws because they believe that such education violates their religious beliefs. While of limited applicability, the ruling is a classic example of the efforts of the Court to protect the religious freedom of individuals within our society. The decision also sheds much light on the legal functions of public education.[3]

WISCONSIN v. YODER.

406 U.S. 205

Decided May 15, 1972—one justice dissenting.

Mr. Chief Justice BURGER delivered the opinion of the Court.

Respondents Jonas Yoder and Wallace Miller are members of the Old Order Amish religion, and respondent Adin Yutzy is a member of the Conser-

---

[3]For an excellent source of brief commentary on the decisions of the Court presented to this point and on a number of other Supreme Court decisions in the area of religion-government controversy, the reader may wish to consult: Thayer S. Warshaw, *Religion, Education, and the Supreme Court* (Nashville: Abingdon, 1979).

vative Amish Mennonite Church. . . . Wisconsin's compulsory school-attendance law required them to cause their children to attend public or private school until reaching age 16 but the respondents declined to send their children, ages 14 and 15, to public school after they completed the eighth grade. The children were not enrolled in any private school, or within any recognized exception to the compulsory-attendance law, and they are conceded to be subject to the Wisconsin statute.

On complaint of the school district administrator for the public schools, respondents were charged, tried, and convicted of violating the compulsory attendance law in Green County Court and were fined the sum of $5 each. Respondents defended on the ground that the application of the compulsory-attendance law violated their rights under the First and Fourteenth Amendments. The trial testimony showed that respondents believed, in accordance with the tenets of Old Order Amish communities generally, that their children's attendance at high school, public or private, was contrary to the Amish religion and way of life. They believed that by sending their children to high school, they would not only expose themselves to the danger of the censure of the church community, but, as found by the county court, also endanger their own salvation and that of their children. The State stipulated that respondents' religious beliefs were sincere.

In support of their position, respondents presented as expert witnesses scholars on religion and education whose testimony is uncontradicted. They expressed their opinions on the relationship of the Amish belief concerning school attendance to the more general tenets of their religion, and described the impact that compulsory high school attendance could have on the continued survival of Amish communities as they exist in the United States today. The history of the Amish sect was given in some detail, beginning with the Swiss Anabaptists of the 16th century who rejected institutionalized churches and sought to return to the early, simple, Christian life de-emphasizing material success, rejecting the competitive spirit, and seeking to insulate themselves from the modern world. As a result of their common heritage, Old Order Amish communities today are characterized by a fundamental belief that salvation requires life in a church community separate and apart from the world and worldly influence. This concept of life aloof from the world and its values is central to their faith.

A related feature of Old Order Amish communities is their devotion to a life in harmony with nature and the soil . . . Amish beliefs require members of the community to make their living by farming or closely related activities. Broadly speaking, the Old Order Amish religion pervades and determines the entire mode of life of its adherents. . . . Adult baptism, which occurs in late adolescence, is the time at which Amish young people voluntarily undertake heavy obligations, not unlike the Bar Mitzvah of the Jews, to abide by the rules of the church community.

Amish objection to formal education beyond the eighth grade is firmly grounded in these central religious concepts. They object to the high school, and higher education generally, because the values they teach are in marked variance with Amish values and the Amish way of life; they view secondary school education as an impermissible exposure of their children to a "worldly" influence in conflict with their beliefs.

Formal high school education beyond the eighth grade is contrary to Amish beliefs, not only because it places Amish children in an environment hostile to Amish beliefs with increasing emphasis on competition in class work and sports and with pressure to conform to the styles, manners, and ways of the peer group, but also because it takes them away from their community, physically and emotionally, during the crucial and formative adolescent period of life. During this period, the children must acquire Amish attitudes favoring manual work and self-reliance and the specific skills needed to perform the adult role of an Amish farmer or housewife. They must learn to enjoy physical labor. Once a child has learned basic reading, writing, and elementary mathematics, these traits, skills, and attitudes admittedly fall within the category of those best learned through example and "doing" rather than in a classroom. And, at this time in life, the Amish child must also grow in his faith and his relationship to the Amish community if he is to be prepared to accept the heavy obligations imposed by adult baptism. In short, high school attendance with teachers who are not of the Amish faith—and may even be hostile to it—interposes a serious barrier to the integration of the Amish child into the Amish religious community.

The Amish do not object to elementary education through the first eight grades as a general proposition because they agree that their children must have basic skills in the "three R's" in order to read the Bible, to be good farmers and citizens, and to be able to deal with non-Amish people when necessary in the course of daily affairs. They view such a basic education as acceptable because it does not significantly expose their children to worldly values or interfere with their development in the Amish community during the crucial adolescent period. While Amish accept compulsory elementary education generally, wherever possible they have established their own elementary schools in many respects like the small local schools of the past. In the Amish belief higher learning tends to develop values they reject as influences that alienate man from God.

On the basis of such considerations, Dr. Hostetler [one of the experts on Amish society] testified that compulsory high school attendance could not only result in great psychological harm to Amish children, because of the conflicts it would produce, but would also, in his opinion, ultimately result in the destruction of the Old Order Amish church community as it exists in the United States today. The testimony of Dr. Donald A. Erickson, an expert witness on education, also showed that the Amish succeed in preparing their high school age children to be productive members of the Amish community.

Although the trial court in its careful findings determined that the Wisconsin compulsory school-attendance law "does interfere with the freedom of the Defendants to act in accordance with their sincere religious belief" it also concluded that the requirement of high school attendance until age 16 was a "reasonable and constitutional" exercise of governmental power, and therefore denied the motion to dismiss the charges. The Wisconsin Circuit Court affirmed the convictions. The Wisconsin Supreme Court, however, sustained respondents' claim under the Free Exercise Clause of the First Amendment and reversed the convictions.

There is no doubt as to the power of a State, having a high responsibility for education of its citizens, to impose reasonable regulations for the control and duration of basic education. . . . Yet even this paramount responsibility was, in *Pierce*, made to yield to the right of parents to provide an equivalent education in a privately operated system. . . . Thus, a State's interest in universal education, however highly we rank it, is not totally free from a balancing process when it impinges on fundamental rights and interests, such as those specifically protected by the Free Exercise Clause of the First Amendment, and the traditional interest of parents with respect to the religious upbringing of their children so long as they, in the words of *Pierce*, "prepare [them] for additional obligations."

It follows that in order for Wisconsin to compel school attendance beyond the eighth grade against a claim that such attendance interferes with the practice of a legitimate religious belief, it must appear either that the State does not deny the free exercise of religious belief by its requirement, or that there is a state interest of sufficient magnitude to override the interest claiming protection under the Free Exercise Clause.

The essence of all that has been said and written on the subject is that only those interests of the highest order and those not otherwise served can overbalance legitimate claims to the free exercise of religion. We can accept it as settled, therefore, that, however strong the State's interest in universal compulsory education, it is by no means absolute to the exclusion or subordination of all other interests.

We come then to the quality of the claims of the respondents concerning the alleged encroachment of Wisconsin's compulsory school-attendance statute on their rights and the rights of their children to the free exercise of the religious beliefs they and their forbears have adhered to for almost three centuries. In evaluating those claims we must be careful to determine whether the Amish religious faith and their mode of life are, as they claim, inseparable and interdependent. A way of life however virtuous and admirable, may not be interposed as a barrier to reasonable state regulation of education if it is based on purely secular considerations; to have the protection of the Religion Clauses, the claims must be rooted in religious belief.

Although a determination of what is "religious" belief or practice entitled to constitutional protection may present a most delicate question, the very concept of ordered liberty precludes allowing every person to make his own standards on matters of conduct in which society as a whole has important interests.

Giving no weight to such secular considerations, however, we see that the record in this case abundantly supports the claim that the traditional way of life of the Amish is not merely a matter of personal preference, but one of deep religious conviction, shared by an organized group, and intimately related to daily living. . . . for the Old Order Amish, religion is not simply a matter of theocratic belief. As the expert witnesses explained, the Old Order Amish religion pervades and determines virtually their entire way of life, regulating it with the detail of the Talmudic diet through the strictly enforced rules of the church community.

The record shows that the respondents' religious beliefs and attitude toward life, family, and home have remained constant—perhaps some would say static—in a period of unparalleled progress in human knowledge generally and great changes in education. The respondents freely concede, and indeed assert as an article of faith, that their religious beliefs and what we would today call "life style" have not altered in fundamentals for centuries.

As the society around the Amish has become more populous, urban, industrialized, and complex, particularly in this century, government regulation of human affairs has correspondingly become more detailed and pervasive. The Amish mode of life has thus come into conflict increasingly with requirements of contemporary society exerting a hydraulic insistence on conformity to majoritarian standards. So long as compulsory education laws were confined to eight grades of elementary basic education imparted in a nearby rural schoolhouse, with a large proportion of students of the Amish faith, the Old Order Amish had little basis to fear that school attendance would expose their children to the worldly influence they reject. But modern compulsory secondary education in rural areas is now largely carried on in a consolidated school, often remote from the student's home and alien to his daily home life. As the record so strongly shows, the values and programs of the modern secondary school are in sharp conflict with the fundamental mode of life mandated by the Amish religion . . . The conclusion is inescapable that secondary schooling, by exposing Amish children to worldly influences in terms of attitudes, goals, and values contrary to beliefs, and by substantially interfering with the religious development of the Amish child and his integration into the way of life of the Amish faith community at the crucial adolescent stage of development, contravenes the basic religious tenets and practice of the Amish faith, both as to the parent and the child.

The impact of the compulsory-attendance law on respondents' practice of the Amish religion is not only severe, but inescapable, for the Wisconsin law affirmatively compels them, under threat of criminal sanction, to perform acts undeniably at odds with fundamental tenets of their religious beliefs. . . . Nor is the impact of the compulsory-attendance law confined to grave interference with important Amish religious tenets from a subjective point of view. It carries with it precisely the kind of objective danger to the free exercise of religion that the First Amendment was designed to prevent. As the record shows, compulsory school attendance to age 16 for Amish children carries with it a very real threat of undermining the Amish community and religious practice as they exist today; they must either abandon belief and be assimilated into society at large, or be forced to migrate to some other and more tolerant region.

In sum, the unchallenged testimony of acknowledged experts in education and religious history, almost 300 years of consistent practice, and strong evidence of a sustained faith pervading and regulating respondents' entire mode of life support the claim that enforcement of the State's requirement of compulsory formal education after the eighth grade would gravely endanger if not destroy the free exercise of respondents' religious beliefs. . . .

Wisconsin concedes that under the Religion Clauses religious beliefs are absolutely free from the State's control, but it argues that "actions," even though religiously grounded, are outside the protection of the First Amendment. . . . It is true that activities of individuals, even when religiously based, are often subject to regulation by the States in the exercise of their undoubted power to promote the health, safety, and general welfare, or the Federal Government in the exercise of its delegated powers. But to agree that religiously grounded conduct must often be subject to the broad police power of the State is not to deny that there are areas of conduct protected by the Free Exercise Clause of the First Amendment and thus beyond the power of the State to control, even under regulations of general applicability. . . . This case, therefore, does not become easier because respondents were convicted for their "actions" in refusing to send their children to the public high school; in this context belief and action cannot be neatly confined in logic-tight compartments.

Nor can this case be disposed of on the grounds that Wisconsin's requirement for school attendance to age 16 applies uniformly to all citizens of the State and does not, on its face, discriminate against religions or a particular religion, or that it is motivated by legitimate secular concerns. A regulation neutral on its face may, in its application, nonetheless offend the constitutional requirement for governmental neutrality if it unduly burdens the free exercise of religion.

The State advances two primary arguments in support of its system of compulsory education. It notes, as Thomas Jefferson pointed out early in our history, that some degree of education is necessary to prepare citizens to participate effectively and intelligently in our open political system if we are to preserve freedom and independence. Further, education prepares individuals to be self-reliant and self-sufficient participants in society. We accept these propositions.

However, the evidence adduced by the Amish in this case is persuasively to the effect that an additional one or two years of formal high school for Amish children in place of their long-established program of informal vocational education would do little to serve those interests. . . . It is one thing to say that compulsory education for a year or two beyond the eighth grade may be necessary when its goal is the preparation of the child for life in modern society as the majority live, but it is quite another if the goal of education be viewed as the preparation of the child for life in the separated agrarian community that is the keystone of the Amish faith.

No one can question the State's duty to protect children from ignorance but this argument does not square with the facts disclosed in the record. Whatever their idiosyncrasies as seen by the majority, this record strongly shows that the Amish community has been a highly successful social unit within our society, even if apart from the conventional "mainstream."

It is neither fair nor correct to suggest that the Amish are opposed to education beyond the eighth grade level. What this record shows is that they are opposed to conventional formal education of the type provided by a certified high school because it comes at the child's crucial adolescent period of religious development.

There can be no assumption that today's majority is "right" and the Amish and others like them are "wrong." A way of life that is odd or even erratic but interferes with no rights or interests of others is not to be condemned because it is different.

The State, however, supports its interest in providing an additional one or two years of compulsory high school education to Amish children because of the possibility that some such children will choose to leave the Amish community, and that if this occurs they will be ill-equipped for life. . . . There is no specific evidence of the loss of Amish adherents by attrition, nor is there any showing that upon leaving the Amish community Amish children, with their practical agricultural training and habits of industry and self-reliance, would become burdens on society because of educational shortcomings. Indeed, this argument of the State appears to rest primarily on the State's mistaken assumption, already noted, that the Amish do not provide any education for their children beyond the eighth grade, but allow them to grow in "ignorance." To the contrary, not only do the Amish accept the necessity for formal schooling through the eighth grade level, but continue to provide what has been characterized by the undisputed testimony of expert educators as an "ideal" vocational education for their children in the adolescent years.

There is nothing in this record to suggest that the Amish qualities of reliability, self-reliance, and dedication to work would fail to find ready markets in today's society. Absent some contrary evidence supporting the State's position, we are unwilling to assume that persons possessing such valuable vocational skills and habits are doomed to become burdens on society should they determine to leave the Amish faith, nor is there any basis in the record to warrant a finding that an additional one or two years of formal school education beyond the eighth grade would serve to eliminate any such problem that might exist.

The Amish alternative to formal secondary school education has enabled them to function effectively in their day-to-day life under self-imposed limitations on relations with the world, and to survive and prosper in contemporary society as a separate, sharply identifiable and highly self-sufficient community for more than 200 years in this country. In itself this is strong evidence that they are capable of fulfilling the social and political responsibilities of citizenship without compelled attendance beyond the eighth grade at the price of jeopardizing their free exercise of religious belief.

This case, of course, is not one in which any harm to the physical or mental health of the child or to the public safety, peace, order, or welfare has been demonstrated or may be properly inferred. The record is to the contrary, and any reliance on that theory would find no support in the evidence.

The State has at no point tried this case on the theory that respondents were preventing their children from attending school against their expressed desires, and indeed the record is to the contrary. The State's position from the outset has been that it is empowered to apply its compulsory-attendance law to Amish parents in the same manner as to other parents—that is, without regard to the wishes of the child. That is the claim we reject today.

The history and culture of Western civilization reflect a strong tradition of parental concern for the nurture and upbringing of their children. This primary role of the parents in the upbringing of their children is now established beyond debate as an enduring American tradition.

However read, the Court's holding in *Pierce* stands as a charter of the rights of parents to direct the religious upbringing of their children. And, when the interests of parenthood are combined with a free exercise claim of the nature revealed by this record, more than merely a "reasonable relation to some purpose within the competency of the State" is required to sustain the validity of the State's requirement under the First Amendment. To be sure, the power of the parent, even when linked to a free exercise claim, may be subject to limitation under *Pierce* if it appears that parental decisions will jeopardize the health or safety of the child, or have a potential for significant social burdens. But in this case, the Amish have introduced persuasive evidence undermining the arguments the State has advanced to support its claims in terms of the welfare of the child and society as a whole.

For the reasons stated we hold, with the Supreme Court of Wisconsin, that the First and Fourteenth Amendments prevent the State from compelling respondents to cause their children to attend formal high school to age 16. Our disposition of this case, however, in no way alters our recognition of the obvious fact that courts are not school boards or legislatures, and are ill-equipped to determine the "necessity" of discrete aspects of a State's program of compulsory education. This should suggest that courts must move with great circumspection in performing the sensitive and delicate task of weighing a State's legitimate social concern when faced with religious claims for exemption from generally applicable educational requirements. It cannot be overemphasized that we are not dealing with a way of life and mode of education by a group claiming to have recently discovered some "progressive" or more enlightened process for rearing children for modern life.

Aided by a history of three centuries as an identifiable religious sect and a long history as a successful and self-sufficient segment of American society, the Amish in this case have convincingly demonstrated the sincerity of their religious beliefs. The interrelationship of belief with their mode of life, the vital role that belief and daily conduct play in the continued survival of Old Order Amish communities and their religious organization, and the hazards presented by the State's enforcement of a statute generally valid as to others. Beyond this, they have carried the even more difficult burden of demonstrating the adequacy of their alternative mode of continuing informal vocational education in terms of precisely those overall interests that the State advances in support of its program of compulsory high school education. In light of this convincing showing, one that probably few other religious groups or sects could make, and weighing the minimal difference between what the State would require and what the Amish already accept, it was incumbent on the State to show with more particularity how its admittedly strong interest in compulsory education would be adversely affected by granting an exemption to the Amish.

Nothing we hold is intended to undermine the general applicability of the State's compulsory school-attendance statutes or to limit the power of the State to promulgate reasonable standards that, while not impairing the free exercise of religion, provide for continuing agricultural vocational education under parental and church guidance by the Old Order Amish or others similarly situated. The States have had a long history of amicable and effective relationships with church-sponsored schools, and there is no basis for assuming that, in this related context, reasonable standards cannot be established concerning the content of the continuing vocational education of Amish children under parental guidance, provided always that state regulations are not inconsistent with what we have said in this opinion.

STONE v. GRAHAM

The last decision to be included is the 1980 *per curiam* decision that held the practice of posting a copy of the Ten Commandments on the walls of public school classrooms in Kentucky to be unconstitutional. While admitting the lasting legal value of many of the commandments, the Court, nevertheless, saw the first four commandments as purely sectarian in nature. Contrary to legislative intent, it was the Court's belief that it is impossible to secularize the Ten Commandments. While four justices dissented, it should be noted that two justices dissented because they would "grant certiorari [would grant a full hearing] and give this case plenary consideration." Their dissent was, therefore, procedural rather than substantive.

STONE v. GRAHAM
449 U.S. 39

Decided November 17, 1980—four justices dissenting.

PER CURIAM

A Kentucky statute requires the posting of a copy of the Ten Commandments, purchased with private contributions, on the wall of each public classroom in the State. Petitioners, claiming that this statute violates the Establishment and Free Exercise Clauses of the First Amendment, sought an injunction against its enforcement.

This Court has announced a three-part test for determining whether a challenged state statute is permissable under the Establishment Clause of the United States Constitution:

> "First, the statute must have a secular legislative purpose; second, its principal or primary effect must be one that neither advances nor inhibits religion . . .; finally, the statute must not foster 'an excessive government entanglement with religion.' "

If a statute violates any of these three principles, it must be struck down under the Establishment Clause. We conclude that Kentucky's statute requiring the posting of the Ten Commandments in public schoolrooms had no secular legislative purpose, and is therefore unconstitutional.

The Commonwealth insists that the statute in question serves a secular legislative purpose, observing that the legislature required the following notation in small print at the bottom of each display of the Ten Commandments: "The secular application of the Ten Commandments is clearly seen in its adoption as the fundamental legal code of Western Civilization and the Common Law of the United States."

The pre-eminent purpose for posting the Ten Commandments on schoolroom walls is plainly religious in nature. The Ten Commandments is undeniably a sacred text in the Jewish and Christian faiths, and no legislative recitation of a supposed secular purpose can blind us to that fact. The Commandments do not confine themselves to arguably secular matters, such as honoring one's parents, killing or murder, adultery, stealing, false witness, and covetousness. . . . Rather, the first part of the Commandments concerns the religious duties of believers; worshiping the Lord God alone, avoiding idolatry, not using the Lord's name in vain, and observing the sabbath day.

This is not a case in which the Ten Commandments are integrated into the school curriculum, where the Bible may constitutionally be used in an appropriate study of history, civilization, ethics, comparative religion, or the like. . . . Posting of religious texts on the wall serves no such educational function. If the posted copies of the Ten Commandments are to have any effect at all, it will be to induce the school children to read, meditate upon, perhaps to venerate and obey, the Commandments. However desirable this might be as a matter of private devotion, it is not a permissible state objective under the Establishment Clause.

The petition for a writ of certiorari is granted and the judgement below is reversed.

The Guidelines

In the years between 1940 and 1980, the Supreme Court, exercising judicial review, announced eleven major decisions (not counting the numerous memorandum decisions) as a result of litigation regarding the relationship of religion to public education. While the nuances are complex and the implications far-reaching, these decisions, taken collectively, present a remarkable clear outline of the nature of this relationship under the Constitution. The fundamental elements of this outline are as follows:

1. Public school attendance may not be predicated upon a confession of belief or opinion by a student.

This guideline results from the *Barnette* decision. There is some parallel between the position of the Court in *Barnette* and other Court rulings holding that assumption of public office may not be contingent upon a statement of religious belief. Thus, participation in the public sector cannot be based upon a required, official affirmation of religious faith. Justice Jackson extended this restriction beyond matters of faith to include "politics, nationalism, religion, or other matters of opinion." In the United States, government may not require an orthodoxy of thought.

2. Public schools may not employ their legal status or utilize their facilities to teach sectarian religion.

3. Public schools may, however, "release" students during the school day for sectarian instruction or devotional exercises if neither public school facilities nor personnel are directly involved in the sectarian activity.

As the Court made clear in both *McCollum* and *Zorach*, the issue was not "released time" per se, but the manner and degree of public school involvement in these programs. However, inconsistency between the two decisions with respect to the role played by compulsory school-attendance laws in released-time programs has caused dispute and confusion. While controversy continues with respect to the precise application of compulsory school-attendance laws,[4] these laws, enacted by the legislatures of the states,[5] require that each child attend some state-approved school that will provide a basic secular education. There is, therefore, an indirect but fundamental sense in which all schooling is subject to the school-attendance laws of the state, and the same compulsory school-attendance laws that operate in released-time programs such as the one in *Zorach* also operate in requiring attendance at parochial schools. *Pierce v. Society of Sisters* (see appendix C) held that alternatives to public education were legal. The state, according to *Pierce*, may require school attendance but may not restrict attendance to public schools. It would appear, the thoughtful arguments of the dissenting justices in *Zorach* notwithstanding, that the released-time plan in the *Zorach* litigation is, therefore, no more unconstitutional than is parochial education from the standpoint of the involvement of compulsory school-attendance laws. Com-

---

[4]See, for example, the *Yoder* decision or review the current literature on "home education."

[5]A recent study indicates the enactment of compulsory school attendance laws in each of the fifty states. See "Compulsory School-Attendance Laws, By State," *Education Week* 2 (6 October 1982): 14-15.

pulsory school-attendance laws mandate school-attendance and apply equally to all children in a state, regardless of the educational alternatives that might be available. Released-time programs that make no use of public school facilities are merely an additional alternative.

While the constitutionality of individual released-time programs, as structured and implemented around the country, remains shrouded in some doubt, it is well to recall that parents have final authority in deciding how (but not whether) their children will be educated. It is, therefore, difficult to envision a released-time plan involving no more than the release of public school students for sectarian instruction or activity that would violate the Constitution.[6] Involvement beyond the release of students by public schools would put such programs in incremental constitutional jeopardy.

4. Government may not create a prayer to be recited by public school students.

5. Sectarian devotional exercises may not be part of the officially prescribed public school day.

While the decisions (*Engel* and *Abington*) from which these two guidelines come are among the most controversial ever announced by the Court, the result of this litigation could have been predicted given the basic thrust of the *Barnette* decision. Government or its agents cannot force children to make public professions of faith nor can they force children to participate in exercises that express a communal affirmation of faith or belief in any "matters of opinion." Moreover, when religious faith or commitment is involved, provisions to excuse children from exercises do not rescue such practices from the restrictions of the religion clauses of the First Amendment.

However, the Court has never ruled that individuals may not, of their own accord, engage in private, voluntary acts of devotion in public school. The school cannot require, sponsor, sup-

---

[6]See *Smith v. Smith*, 523 F 2d. 121, in appendix D.

port, or officially involve itself in obviously devotional acts.[7] Furthermore, it would seem to be the common sense of the matter that acts of private individual devotion cannot disrupt the normal school routine. The same dedication to religious liberty that prohibits official support of religion also prohibits interference with private acts of religious devotion that do not interfere with school functions or violate the rights of others and that do not rely upon school sponsorship or support.

The issue of devotional exercises in the public school continues to be the subject of heated debate, congressional action, and even attempted constitutional amendment; and illustrations of the thoughtlessness and insensitivity associated with this debate are not difficult to find. For example, as a clergyman was heard to say: "What is all the fuss about? Prayer never hurt anybody." Such a comment illustrates the myopic, totally uncharitable and thoughtless attitude common to this issue. Public prayer can "hurt" an individual by compelling him to engage in an act of public sectarian devotion that violates his religious beliefs or by compelling him, in the presence of his peers, to request excusal from the exercise. To say that a public act of religious devotion is not potentially harmful is to imply that such an act is essentially meaningless, devoid of specific religious implication; minus, that is, the completely erroneous position that all persons believe in prayer and share a common understanding of the nature, meaning, and focus of that activity. If these notions are not intended, the only alternative is the

---

[7]Justice Brennan, in his concurring opinion in *Abington*, mentioned, as an alternative to official acts of religious devotion such as prayer or Bible reading, "the observance of a moment of reverent silence at the opening of class" as one method of attaining the *secular* objectives obviously religious acts of devotion are said to fulfill. (See 374 U.S. at 281). Care should be exercised as this practice has not been addressed formally by the Court (the practice has been subject to litigation in Massachusetts and, in 1982, Tennessee enacted legislation permitting the practice), but the mention of this possibility indicates the inviolability of *private* acts of devotion. However, a period of silence could not require bowed heads or closed eyes, nor could it be brought to a close by the pronouncement of "Amen." Furthermore, parents should specify just what their child might do during that period of silence.

affirmation that those persons for whom mandated acts of public sectarian devotion are objectionable have no right to their religious convictions in the public arena. The essence of prayer is not its ritualistic observance; prayer is an act of piety or devotion directed toward a specific transcendent or supernatural focus. Continued activity on behalf of prayer in public schools is motivated by specifically sectarian religious concerns.

Other arguments favoring school prayer are not quite so thoughtless or insensitive. It is objected that so large a block of time in the daily experience of a child should not be without religious devotion. However, to say that the seven-to-eight-hour school day and the five-day school week puts a child at an unusual disadvantage with respect to organized religious devotion or worship is a weak argument. A child is put at no greater disadvantage than is any other regularly employed member of our society, with the exception of the clergy. In fact, the average 180-day school year gives a child a significant break in terms of the domination of her time by her "work." Children have ample time during the day, the week, and the year for organized devotional activity beyond their public school experience.

Others argue that public schools have received unfair attention in this controversy. Why, it is asked, have devotional exercises in public school become so controversial when other public and institutional acts of devotion continue? When military and institutional chaplains are allowed, when the Bible is used in governmental oaths, when government activities of various kinds are opened with public prayer, when the coinage of the nation carries a recognition of God, has not the Supreme Court overreacted in its position on prayer and devotional exercises in public schools? Misunderstanding results, in part, from failure to recognize that public schools (or an appropriate alternative school) are the only institutions in our nation that everyone is required to attend and, moreover, that impact impressionable children whose limited experience has not yet given them a full basis for discretionary judgement. Aside from the obvious difference in maturity between those who attend school and those who attend other government institutions, the difference between public schools and other institutions of gov-

ernment where religious activities are allowed, even encouraged (for example, on military bases or in hospitals and prisons)
is that school attendance is not as confining in terms of time as
is, for example, much military life. Apart from unusual circumstances (as in *Yoder*), public school attendance (that has no officially sponsored sectarian devotional activity) does not
infringe upon the religious freedom of a child, nor upon the parents responsible for the upbringing of a child. School attendance mandated by law is not voluntary; and the involuntary
nature of school attendance coupled with the impressionability
and vulnerability of children subject to these laws is the fundamental reason for protecting all public school students from
the potentially harmful experience of official sectarian positions
and exercises. This special nature of elementary and secondary
schooling has been a central consideration in the Court's decisions regarding government aid to parochial elementary and
secondary schools as opposed to church-related colleges and
universities.[8]

6. Study *about* religion, while not required by the Court, may
be part of the public school curriculum when such study is "presented objectively as part of a secular program of education."

As this guideline concerns the central topic of the following
chapter, comment will be deferred to that discussion.

7. Schools cannot aid or oppose religion, nor may they protect
or espouse any particular or specific religious theory or
doctrine.

This guideline has many implications for the persistent controversy between science and religion regarding the origin of
man and the universe. That government cannot protect religion
from opposing views was clearly expressed in an earlier decision by Justice Clark.

> From the standpoint of freedom of speech and the press, it is enough to
> point out that the state has no legitimate interest in protecting any or all
> religions from views distasteful to them which is sufficient to justify
> prior restraints upon the expression of those views. It is not the business

---

[8]See, for example, *Tilton v. Richardson*, 403 U.S. 672, 685-86 (1971).

of government in our nation to suppress real or imagined attacks upon a particular religious doctrine, whether they appear in publications, speeches, or motion pictures.[9]

To take action intended to protect religious doctrine is to move in a direction respecting an establishment of that doctrine, a movement expressly forbidden by the Constitution.

Whenever man thinks seriously about the universe, the world, and himself, the question of origin arises. Throughout history, in primitive and sophisticated cultures alike, myths and theories abound in the attempt to answer this question, and though many espouse an answer through faith, no one truly knows how it all began. Some proposed "answers," like the theories of science, center on the empirical processes by which man, his world, and the universe came into being. Other approaches, such as the explanations of religion, ask *why* humanity, the world, and the universe came into being.

The present situation, however, is complicated by the fact that religion typically addresses the "why" in terms of original meaning and ultimate purpose, a kind of *a priori* reason for the "how." This approach served well until man turned his attention to the "how" (the question to which religion historically had given little systematic attention), in the attempt to understand this world as it is (following the spirit that developed in the Renaissance). This attempt was sufficiently innocent until conflict developed between the "why" affirmations of religion and the "how" theories of science. Religion follows a set of presuppositions, typically understood to be based upon some form of divine revelation, which provide answers to the "why." These presuppositions are, furthermore, believed to be determinative of the "how." Science, on the other hand, looks first at the "how" and then ponders the meaning of the "how" on the basis of the "facts" that result from scientific research.

Here emerges the problem that has generated the creation/evolution controversy. Modern man generally looks at the "how" and then questions its meaning (reflecting on the "why"

---

[9]*Burstyn v. Wilson*, 343 U.S. at 505 (1952).

of the "how"). This type of reasoning, of course, is threatening to some religious positions for the traditional *a priori* answers to the "why" question are options, in this approach, rather than final truths. An excellent illustration of the results of this modern approach may be seen in the contrast between the ideas of B. F. Skinner and those of Teilhard de Chardin.[10] Looking at the results of the same scientific investigations, de Chardin saw evolution as God's plan and envisioned humanity as moving toward its God-given maturity through that process, while Skinner, in building his theory of operant conditioning, concluded that all reality is objective and that human beings are animals not unlike other animals save for their complexity.

Religion must function as religion; it must make a strong and unencumbered witness to humanity in this world, nourishing man's constant search for ultimate meaning and purpose. Science must likewise function as science and continue to nourish man's insatiable quest for knowledge, for an understanding of how things are and how they operate. Religion as religion cannot address the "how"; science as science cannot finally answer the ultimate "why." When religion attempts to address the "how" questions through a literal interpretation of sacred writings or a final, closed view of some form of revelation, it becomes less than religion and compromises its essential function. Moreover, when science steps beyond "how" questions and begins to address ultimate meaning and value, it becomes an ideology, having moved beyond its legitimate functions.

The biblical account of God's creation of the universe, the world, and humanity clearly was an attempt to understand the purpose and meaning of existence. It is a supremely religious statement. The very first words of the account—"In the beginning God created . . ."[11]—set the unmistakable tone of intent. Except for the statement that creation was the action of God,

---

[10]See Teilhard de Chardin, *The Phenomenon of Man* (New York: Harper and Row, Publishers, 1959); and B. F. Skinner, *Beyond Freedom and Dignity* (New York: Alfred A. Knopf, 1972).

[11]Gen. 1:1.

there is no attempt to address the "how" question. As a matter of fact, for an ancient Jew that question probably paled in significance when compared to the "why" question he was addressing. The only possible way in which the account could be seen as other than a discussion of why is to interpret it literally. Such an interpretation is the right of those who choose it, but it is clearly a religious interpretation and should not be taught in public schools under the guise of science. To teach "creation science" in schools is to take a large step in the direction of establishing that religious doctrine.

It is frequently argued that evolutionary theory is a basic tenet of secular humanism. Ergo, to teach evolution in the public schools is to move in a direction respecting an establishment of religion. While the meaning of "secular humanism" for contemporary fundamentalism is not clear, let it be granted—for the sake of argument—that evolution is a basic postulate of that religion. Notwithstanding this "admission," this has nothing whatsoever to do with teaching evolution as scientific theory. To refuse to teach the scientific theory of evolution because it is also a tenet of some religion would likewise require, for example, that schools not teach that it is wrong to kill another human being—a basic tenet of the Judeo-Christian tradition. The total separation of religion and government in the United States is impossible; some overlap is unavoidable.

Throughout this section, reference has been made to guidelines, not laws. A final observation is, therefore, appropriate regarding the decisions of the Supreme Court and the guidelines derived therefrom. Despite the Court's jurisdiction in controversy concerning the relationship of religion to public education, critics charge that, when the Court's rulings are announced, they are given the status of legislation, a status that exceeds the proper application of such decisions. This objection, if true, has merit, for the responsibility of the courts is the interpretation of law; the responsibility to create law rests with local, state, and federal legislative bodies.

Nonetheless, in legal theory and practice, a judicial judgment may be viewed as a precedent. When a court, particularly the highest court of appeal to address an issue, renders a decision, such a decision may become a precedent for future legal controversy, thereby becoming a kind of legal standard. This is particularly true if, in the view of the legal community, the decision is sound and judicious.

Consequently, while not creating law, the substantial and widely applicable rulings of courts do, and should, act as guidelines for future legislative action and legal interpretation. As rulings by the highest court in the land, the decisions presented in this chapter typically possess precedent status. But, courts do reverse their rulings and, while functioning as guides or standards for legislative action and legal judgment, the decisions of courts should not function as law. The decisions reviewed in this chapter are not laws, but constitutional interpretation by the highest judicial body in the country specifically charged with that responsibility. It is not without reason, then, that state legislatures enact statutes in keeping with these rulings or pass legislation designed to circumvent their applicability or test their legislative reach.

CHAPTER 6

Religion Studies
in Public Schools

Analysis of Supreme Court decisions revealed a number of guidelines for the relationship of religion to public education. Teaching about religion emerges from those guidelines as the legal and academically appropriate place for religion in public schools. Close attention to the brief statements in the Court's decisions regarding religion studies will provide a fundamentally sound idea of the nature of this challenging and promising educational opportunity.

Before proceeding with that investigation, brief attention should be given to the "off campus" option for religious instruction represented by released-time programs, an option thoroughly discussed in *McCollum* and *Zorach*. As all forms of released time have not come before the bar, persons interested in this option should follow those decisions in developing released-time programs.

Apparently, religious organizations involved in released-time programs may provide any type of religious experience approved by the parents of the children involved.[1] Experiences running the gamut from devotional or worship periods to programs of religious education are appropriate. A parent, of course, must request that a student be allowed to participate in the program. Released time, therefore, allows a religious community to extend the time that young congregants can spend in either worship or religious education.

Notwithstanding this option, the results of the last national survey on religion in public education undertaken by R. B. Dierenfield portrayed a rather bleak picture with regard to released-time programs. Of the school systems responding, the number participating in released-time programs between 1960 and 1972 had grown only from 29.6 percent to 32.7 percent.[2] Although the concept of released time has been in existence for some fifty years, Dierenfield remarked that, at the time of the last survey, released-time instruction "does not seem to evidence too much dynamism or vitality." He concluded: "While a small increase is shown in the number of systems with released-time instruction, interest appears to be decreasing and support from school administrators does not seem strong."[3]

Any number of factors may have contributed to the stagnation of released-time program development. Undoubtedly, the administrative problems public school systems encounter when cooperating in these programs is a contributing factor. The minister familiar with the problems of administering a moderately complex religious education program in the parish will sympathize with the problems incurred by the periodic release of groups of students from the public school and its many activities. Another factor is that of a school's legal responsibility for

---

[1]See the opinion of Justice Douglas in *Zorach v. Clauson*, 343 U.S. 306, 314, in which he wrote that the school "can close its doors or suspend its operations as to those who want to repair to their religious sanctuaries for worship or instruction."

[2]R. B. Dierenfield, "Religion in Public Schools: Its Current Status," *Religious Education* 68 (January-February 1973): 110.

[3]Ibid., 111.

students released for religious activity. And, aside from considerations of tort liability, all who administer released-time programs must be concerned for the physical safety of students as they move to and from the place of released time religious activity.

From a religious community's standpoint, perhaps a crucial factor has to do with the amount of released time actually available. In his 1966 survey, Dierenfield found that the majority of released-time programs utilized a period of one hour or less per week.[4] It may be that the amount of time requested or granted for released-time programs has not been judged worth the effort by either religious communities or public school administrators. One is, however, forced to question the seriousness with which religious communities have approached released-time. If a well-reasoned, educationally sound, released-time program were developed; if solid rapport were established with public schools; and if the maximum of cooperation were sought; could more than a minimum, possibly ineffectual one hour or less per week be utilized? On the other hand, if religious institutions would give serious attention to creative and effective use of the time available for religious education in the parish, that additional hour per week might prove satisfactory in terms of the total educational demands, both secular and sectarian, placed upon a child.[5] If a religious community is unwilling to seriously evaluate its own programs of religious education or to consider the potential presented by released time, few demands should be made on public schools for religious education. The option of released time is viable and, based upon a close study of *McCollum* and *Zorach*, provides an opportunity for planning and

---

[4]R. B. Dierenfield, "The Impact of the Supreme Court Decisions on Religion in Public Schools," *Religious Education* 62 (September-October 1967): 449.

[5]If the churches used the time available to them for religious education effectively and if the public schools provided religion studies programs, would even that hour be necessary? The religious institutions must fully and effectively use their existing programs of religious education before turning to the public schools for additional time for sectarian instruction.

development on the part of those religious institutions seriously concerned with improving sectarian religious education.

Religion Studies: Objective and Secular

After this brief discussion of the off-campus option of released time, the on-campus option of religion studies in public schools must be analyzed. Following the dicta of the Supreme Court,[6] religion may be taught about in public schools without conflicting with the religion clauses of the First Amendment. Study about religion may be undertaken (1) in courses of study about religion and/or (2) in the regular school curriculum whenever such study is germane to a full understanding of a secular subject under study. Religion studies, however, must be "presented objectively as part of a secular program of education." That this brief statement represents the substance of the guidance the Court has provided for religion studies is both frustrating and challenging. Regardless of its brevity, it is clear that the Court has not recommended an "anything goes" presence for religion study in public schools. Justice Brennan wrote that the precise nature of religion studies should be left largely to the trained educators who manage public schools, but that such study must comply with the restrictions set forth by the Court with respect to the place of religion in public schools. Although the guideline itself is brief, it must be viewed and implemented in keeping with all the Court has said regarding the place of religion in public education.

Study of that section of the *Abington* decision in which the guidelines of objectivity and secularity were stated leads to the impression that the Court had no intention of providing more precise guidance. Instead, the Court apparently intended to state broad guidelines so that educational and community leaders could tailor programs of teaching about religion for specific

---

[6]The primary references from the decisions of the Supreme Court with regard to religion studies are: *McCollum v. Board of Education*, 333 U.S. 203, 235-36 (Justice Jackson); *Abington v. Schempp*, 374 U.S. 203, 225 (Justice Clark); and *Abington v. Schempp*, 374 U.S. at 300 (Justice Brennan).

communities. As the decisions of the Court frequently demonstrate, the justices do not consider themselves authorities in education or religion. Typically, it has been their practice to leave as much freedom for local initiative as is legally judicious.

The guideline of objectivity is more difficult to implement than it appears. Margherite LaPota believed that the definition of objectivity selected to guide the development of religion studies programs will substantially influence their nature. According to LaPota, one may select from two definitions of objectivity: (1) an intentional search for all relevant facts, interpretations, and attitudes, leaving a student free to decide while respecting differing points of view; or (2) a strict dedication to facts, to looking at things as they are, while entertaining a minimum of interpretation and differing points of view.[7] It shall be the thesis of this discussion that religion studies must be predicated upon the first option.

The difficulty with the second option is that it intentionally minimizes the subjective elements of human experience. The second option would require an impersonal, uninvolved, value-free point of view much like the pure objectivity that the research scientist strives for in the laboratory. However, existential philosophy, by its stress on human subjectivity, has challenged the broad applicability of this concept of objectivity time and time again. As a scientist, Michael Polanyi argued that pure objectivity is a myth, for all human endeavor is undertaken on the basis of subjective choice and from an individual perspective.[8] Human thought itself is a subjective act. Furthermore, many modern psychologists have objected that a human being does not become deeply involved with meaningless tasks or objects. Rather, when one attends to something in one's life with any degree of intensity for any period of time, one does so because of the potential meaning of that experience. One's sub-

---

[7]Margherite LaPota, "Religion: Not 'Teaching' But 'Teaching About,' " *Educational Leadership* 31 (October 1973): 32.

[8]See Michael Polanyi, *Personal Knowledge* (New York: Harper and Row, Publishers, 1962).

jectivity is the basis upon which one makes the decision to approach some element of one's world "objectively."

An illustration of the approach to religion studies that would follow from the second option is in order.

> As a science, religiology is characterized by the scientific point of view, that is, it deals logically and critically with empirically available hence observable and verifiable data. Religion is seen as a human phenomenon, and the religious experience as a human experience. The transcendent gods . . . are empirically available only as part of this experience, not as existing outside of and independent from this experience.[9]

The discussions about the nature of religion to this point indicate the fallacy of this approach. While religion study must begin with human experience, it cannot be impersonal, because religion is personal; it cannot be value free, because religion is value ladened; it cannot be dispassionate, because religion involves the emotions. Moreover, the "data" of religion may not be empirically verifiable. After all, many believe in God, but there is no empirical proof of God's existence. To restrict oneself, in religion studies, to the logical and critical analysis of observable and verifiable data would require the omission of much that is essential to religion. It would appear, therefore, that religion studies from the perspective of the second option might not be a study of religion at all.

The first definition of objectivity recommends itself. David Engel clearly understood the appropriate nature of objectivity when he wrote: ". . . it seems to me that objectivity in religion study has less to do with neutrality than with free inquiry and thorough scholarship."[10] Here is a concept of objectivity that is far more appropriate for non-scientific education. Objectivity, in education, should be defined as the opposite of indoctrina-

---

[9]Guntram G. Bischoff, "The Search for Common Definitions of Religion Studies and Public Education," *Religious Education* 71 (January-February 1976): 74.

[10]David E. Engel, "Objectivity in the Teaching of Religion Studies in Public Schools," *Religious Education* 71 (January-February 1976) 85.

tion; it should be viewed as an open search for knowledge without restriction or precondition. According to Philip Phenix, to be objective is not to be value free, or detached from the focus of human concern. Rather, to be objective is to engage in "disciplined intersubjectivity." This, according to Phenix, is the desire to understand the points of view of others, particularly those viewpoints that differ from one's own. Empathy is an important ingredient in intelligent human behavior.[11] Basically, academic disciplines are developed and maintained in order to provide a set of accepted procedures and concepts that will assist in the attainment of mutual understanding.

Professor Phenix found it difficult to understand how the normal concept of objectivity (the absence of emotion; a devotion to fact; the absence of personal commitment or preference) could apply to any field of study. His belief was that no fact is value free, for the declaration of facticity assigns truth value. In education, objectivity is attained when one is able to transcend one's own particular and limited point of view in order to reflect upon the truth value of other points of view. Objectivity means "involvement in the interests of others and commitment to the community of persons who endeavor to understand the nature of things as they are and not for purposes of group propaganda and advantage." Objectivity is "a process of becoming aware of the subjectivities of others, controlled so as to create common understanding on the part of all inquirers."[12] The viewpoints of Professors Engel and Phenix appropriately define objectivity as it applies to education, at least in religion studies. It would be neither appropriate nor productive to interpret this guideline in a more restrictive manner. Robert Michaelsen expressed the same belief through the paradigm of critical study.

---

[11]Philip H. Phenix, "Religion in Public Education: Principles and Issues," *Religion and Public School Curriculum*, ed. R. U. Smith: (New York: Religious Education Association, 1972) 18-19.

[12]Philip H. Phenix, "The Role of Religion," *Foundations of Education*, ed. G. F. Kneller, 3d ed. (New York: John Wiley and Sons, 1971) 170.

I begin with the assumption that the critical study of religion in the public schools is both constitutionally acceptable and educationally mandatory. By "critical" I mean a) informed, b) appreciative as well as analytical, and c) for educational rather than propagandistic or proselyting purposes.[13]

These three characteristics of critical study provide an excellent summary of the educational qualities of objectivity.

In terms of the rationale for religion studies, the goal of understanding was especially emphasized. The recommended definition of objectivity would facilitate understanding of religion. Understanding the points of view of others, particularly when those viewpoints differ from or contradict one's own, is a compelling educational goal. Although understanding does not require that one agree with another's belief or modify one's own, it may create a degree of tolerance. There can be no more significant result of religion studies in public schools.

Will the religious community favorably regard the unrestricted study of religion in public schools? In a parish, much religious education is transmissive and prescriptive in nature, as it has every right to be. The viewpoints that the learner should accept are decided in advance, and teaching is devoted to promulgating those views. Religious leaders must decide whether they want their young communicants investigating religion from an objective standpoint in public schools. To use a current buzz-word, religion studies involve *value clarification*. As David Engel argued, the goal of "teaching about" is not that the student retain specific material or accept certain viewpoints; the goal is that the student be able to analyze material and ideas and arrive at conclusions that he has scrutinized critically. ". . . this kind of approach is open-minded and open-ended. There are no predetermined, fixed answers. Where answers or conclusions appear, they are critically examined and evaluated in re-

---

[13]Robert Michaelsen, "Beyond the Ground Rules: Next Steps in the Study of Religion in the Public Schools," *Religious Education* 68 (March-April 1973): 212.

lation to other patterns of perception."[14] While seemingly trite at first glance, the difference between teaching *about* and teaching *of* is a significant issue for the religious community.

The extended discussion of "secular" in chapter 2 simplifies analysis of the second guideline for religion studies: religion studies in public schools must be part of a secular program of study. The decisions of the Supreme Court do not reveal any complicated or technical meaning; "secular" is simply used in contrast to "sacred." The goals of public education are cognitive development, cultural transmission, citizenship education, social membership, and material competency, and these goals define secular education. Public education cannot seek sectarian commitment. The secularity of public schools is not antagonistic toward religion; it is a viewpoint required by the pluralism of American society and its dedication to religious liberty. Antagonism would be involved if "secular" was interpreted as requiring the total elimination of religion from the public schools, but such is not the case.

The following policy is an excellent illustration of the proper relationship between religion and public education. A correct interpretation of the second guideline would require an integration or infusion of religion studies into regular public school curricula.

> The desirable policy in the schools, as the Commission sees it, is to deal directly and objectively with religion whenever and wherever it is intrinsic to learning experience in the various fields of study, and to seek out appropriate ways to teach what has been aptly called "the reciprocal relation" between religion and other elements in human culture. The implication of that policy calls for much more than an added course, either for teachers or for the high school curriculum itself. It requires topic-by-topic analysis of the separate courses, and cooperative efforts by the teachers to give appropriate attention to these relationships.[15]

---

[14]David E. Engel, "Toward a Theory of Religion in General Education," *Religious Education* 65 (July-August 1970): 348.

[15]Commission on Religion in the Public Schools, *Religion in the Public Schools* (Arlington VA: American Association of School Administrators, 1964) 60.

Curriculum integration would require that religion be integrated into public school curricula at those points where it is intrinsic to the study of a secular subject and, therefore, to the attainment of secular educational goals.

Philip Phenix employed a phrase that is most useful: the "principle of genuine relevance." He argued that the creation of an artificial place for religion in the curriculum is as academically dishonest as is the perfunctory omission of religion from that curriculum. He employed two illustrations to make his point. First, regardless of an instructor's sincerity, references to the power and majesty of God in a study of astronomy contribute nothing of substance to the study of astronomy *qua* astronomy. On the other hand, a study of colonial America must include discussion of the religious dynamics that shaped that era of national history.[16] These illustrations clarify both the principle of genuine relevance and the second guideline of the Supreme Court: religion should be studied in the context of regular subjects when such study is necessary for a full, meaningful understanding of the subject.

The Commission on Religion in the Public Schools wrote of a reciprocal relationship between religion and culture. Following this line of thought, Phenix pressed his argument beyond genuine relevance to scholarly adequacy. "At the very minimum, merely for scholarly adequacy and quite apart from any consideration of religious dimensions, all curriculum materials should be prepared with due regard for religion as a fact of culture."[17] Religion is an inherent part of American culture, history, social structure, and way of life. To omit religion from the curriculum of the public schools at points of genuine relevance is less than honest. Appropriate curriculum infusion or integra-

---

[16]Philip H. Phenix, *Religious Concerns in Contemporary Education* (New York: Columbia University, Teachers College, Bureau of Publications, 1959) 71-72.

[17]Philip H. Phenix, *Education and the Worship of God* (Philadelphia: Westminster Press, 1966) 185.

tion is absolutely necessary from an academic point of view in a secular program of education. This is not an adjustment which the religious community should request; it is an approach which the educational community should undertake and which the public should expect. There is general agreement with the dicta of the Court that the obvious curriculum areas in which infusion should be undertaken are history, literature, social studies, and the fine arts.[18]

To require that religion studies be secular is to require that religion studies not have sectarian or sacred goals; that religion studies contribute directly to the general education of the student rather than seeking religious commitment or acceptance of sectarian positions by the students. Religion should be integrated into the public school curriculum at those points where it is genuinely relevant to the secular subject under study and can contribute to a complete understanding of that subject.

David Engel added another argument for a positive role for religion studies in a secular program of education: "socio-cultural understanding."[19] What could be more beneficial for our society than to diminish, to whatever degree, fear, hostility, and religious prejudice through the vehicle of understanding? Agreement with the tenets of other religions is not intended in a program of secular education; rather, it is hoped that such study will reduce prejudice and enhance tolerance. "What is needed in our society as a whole, but especially in matters pertaining to our schools, is a spirit of understanding and consideration toward those who hold religious views different from or even contrary to our own."[20] Critical thought is the vehicle by which this understanding is attained as students are encouraged to analyze viewpoints different from their own. Such analysis is the essence of the open-minded and open-ended objective ap-

---

[18]See, for example, the early statement of William C. Bower, *Church and State in Education* (Chicago: University of Chicago Press, 1944) 30-32.

[19]Engel, "Toward a Theory of Religion in General Education," 345.

[20]Sam Duker, *The Public Schools and Religion: The Legal Context* (New York: Harper and Row Publishers, 1966) 228.

proach that must be followed in religion studies, and, in the final analysis, the two guidelines provided by the Supreme Court for religion studies are vitally related. Students must not be required to agree with any predetermined positions; nor must they accept an "answer" as final. If some type of religious commitment does result, it will be the responsibility of the student and an outgrowth of his experience and critical thought.

Not only is it inappropriate to institute a religion studies program in order to influence the religious commitments of students, it is also inappropriate to create these programs in the name of moral reform.

> . . . we call for the inclusion of religion studies in public education curricula in the name of good, sound and complete education, not moral reformation. Moreover, in a pluralistic society such as ours it is not legally legitimate to teach religion in the public schools in a manner which leads directly to moral reform. All we can rightfully and legally hope to achieve is to provide students with an intellectual appreciation of religion in general and its particular expressions in various cultures throughout human history, and to make students aware of the religious value options available to mankind.[21]

Moral education and religion studies are two distinct initiatives. If the public schools are to be responsible for moral education, they cannot meet that responsibility with religion studies. Religion studies may familiarize students with "religious value options," but the goal of religion study is intellectual appreciation and understanding. Due to the sensitive nature of religion study, nothing more can be attempted.

California adopted the following goals for teaching about religion in its public schools. These goals are an excellent summary of what religion studies programs should attempt.

> Students should develop an informed understanding and appreciation of the role of religion in the lives of Americans and the people of other nations;

---

[21]Nicholas Piediscalzi, "Public Education and Religion Studies," *Religion and Public School Curriculum*, ed. R. U. Smith (New York: Religious Education Association, 1972) 82.

Students should be able to recognize and discuss the influence of religious views and values on the social, economic, and political aspects of society;

Students should understand the influence of religion on the development of ideas in Western and Eastern cultures and civilizations;

Students should be aware of the influence of religion on life-styles (such as work, prayer, devotion, ritual, worship and meditation);

Students should appreciate problems of conscience in relation to historical and contemporary issues of religious freedom.[22]

The Curriculum

It would extend this discussion far beyond its intended limits if it covered technical matters regarding curriculum design, implementation, and evaluation for religion studies programs.[23] However, while creativity must be encouraged, three basic designs may be employed in religion studies programs. The first two designs are alternative approaches to curriculum integration: (1) the integration of religious content at any point in the curriculum of the public schools where it is genuinely relevant; and (2) the development of a variety of teaching units or modules addressing, in a more unified and thorough fashion, aspects of religion relevant for a specific subject of study. The third option is the creation of courses of study in religion. Needless to say, the three options are not mutually exclusive and a thorough religion studies program would include all three curriculum-design approaches.

---

[22]Bischoff, "Search for Common Definitions," 76.

[23]For the reader interested in curriculum design and materials evaluation, the following will be valuable sources: Nicholas Piediscalzi and William E. Collie, eds., *Teaching About Religion in Public Schools* (Allen TX: Argus Communications, 1977); and Thayer Warshaw, ed., *Review of Curriculum and Resource Materials* (Lawrence KS: National Council on Religion and Public Education). Extensive resource listings may be found in Lawrence Byrnes, *Religion and Public Education* (New York: Harper and Row Publishers, 1975). One may stay abreast of current developments through membership in the National Council on Religion and Public Education, University of Kansas, Lawrence KS 66045.

It is strongly recommended, however, that religion studies programs be initially restricted to a curriculum integration format. Because religion would be studied in conjunction with a recognized academic discipline, like history or literature, the study would more precisely contribute to the secular goals of public education and, thereby, remain well within the guidelines established by the Supreme Court. For example, a student cannot fully understand the history of Western civilization apart from understanding the role religion has played in that history, and knowledge of Western history is certainly one of the bona fide secular goals of public education. The study of religion as an element in the attainment of that goal would remain within sound constitutional parameters. Furthermore, religion studies in the context of a truly "secular" academic discipline runs far less risk of becoming embroiled in sectarian controversy. If the study is occasioned by relevance to an accepted, standard public school subject-matter area and is restricted to the demands of that secular subject, the emotional and divisive reactions associated with sectarian religious difference may be avoided. Religion studies undertaken in a curriculum integration format, therefore, will have less risk of violating the guideline of objectivity, will be more clearly secular in purpose, and will involve far less potential for sectarian controversy. Wisdom appears to dictate that religion studies begin with curriculum integration. However, while the goal of understanding the relationship of religion to the history and life of Western man may be attained in this fashion, other of the goals for religion studies discussed earlier may require the development of units of study in religion and, to complete the program, elective courses in religion studies.

Once curriculum integration has been accomplished, the development of courses about religion may be considered. The Supreme Court spoke of courses in the history of religion and in comparative religion. Apparently, there will be no legal problems if such courses remain objective in approach and secular in purpose. The goals and objectives developed for each course in religion will clearly reveal its intended nature. Beyond questions of legality, however, a number of additional concerns are frequently expressed regarding religion courses.

One concern has to do with the grade level at which such courses would be taught. This concern stems from the belief that young children are not capable of dealing effectively with the high-level abstraction associated with intense religion study. Considering the nature of religion and what we know about cognitive development,[24] it would be wise to restrict courses in religion studies to adolescents. Whether or not the thinking process of young children is restricted to concrete application, it is obvious that adolescents possesses a richer background of experience and, therefore, will find a concentrated study about religion more meaningful.

Another significant concern is that courses in religion tend to remove religion from the mainstream of academic thought, dissipating the relationship of religion to the other academic disciplines. This problem is reduced if courses in religion studies are not offered until curriculum integration has become an accomplished fact. Perhaps, it might be wise to make courses in religion studies available only to students who have progressed through a program of integrated religion study. This policy would ensure a proper foundation and would maintain perspective.

Another problem is whether courses in religion should be required or elective. Courses in religion studies, by all means, must be elective. Severe legal problems would ensue if students were required to take the most objective and secularly oriented course in religion studies. Apart from fully understanding history, literature, or social structures and customs, no public school student should be required to study about religion per se, no matter how laudable the goals or objective the study. The basic thrust of curriculum integretion is genuine relevance to a

---

[24]See, for example: Barry J. Wadsworth, *Piaget's Theory of Cognitive Development* (New York: David McKay Co., 1971) and Jean Piaget and Barbel Inhelder, *The Psychology of the Child*, trans. Helen Weaver (New York: Basic Books, 1969).

secular subject and religion studies integrated into a recognized secular subject may be required. Religion courses, on the other hand, while appropriate within constitutional guidelines, must not be required because the goal of such courses is the understanding of religion itself. The relevance of courses in religion to the secular goals of public education is far more difficult to establish and maintain than is curriculum integration.

The Teacher

Of the many concerns associated with teaching about religion in the public schools, perhaps the most crucial is the role of the teacher. While it is true that the teaching-learning process is a "triadic relationship"[25] (a balanced and dynamic interaction of pupil, teacher, and subject matter), it is common experience that, in the institutional setting, a teacher more directly influences the nature of the process than any other single element. Motivated students are crucial, as is demonstrated by the extensive learning students undertake successfully outside the school, but the teacher can do much to challenge even lethargic students. Appropriate curriculum materials are essential, but even the best of materials will not help unless properly used. As with any other subject taught in the schools, the expertise, enthusiasm, and integrity of a teacher are crucial in religion studies.

Three types of teaching personnel may be involved in religion studies. One is the teacher who conducts courses in religion. Another is the religion studies supervisor, or resource teacher, who is responsible for one or more schools and might teach units in religion studies for the regular classroom teacher. This supervisor would guide, support, and provide resource information in religion studies for regular classroom teachers. The third is the regular classroom teacher who would be responsible for religion studies instruction whenever and wherever it would be genuinely relevant to the secular subject

---

[25]Ronald T. Hyman, "Teaching: Triadic and Dynamic," *The Educational Forum* 32 (November 1967): 65-69.

matter. As most religion studies teaching would be undertaken by a regular classroom teacher, any school division seriously considering a religion studies program should employ a religion studies supervisor. The addition of religion studies teachers to the faculty should be considered only after the curriculum integration phase has been fully established.

When religion studies are undertaken through curriculum integration, the crucial considerations are the expertise, enthusiasm, and integrity of a teacher, not a teacher's spirituality or quality of religious faith. The expertise of the teacher should make the genuine relevance of religion apparent and will allow the teacher to approach religious content as appropriate for the subject matter and the grade level involved. A teacher's enthusiasm for the secular subject or subjects should also apply to the genuinely relevant religious content. Integrity would require that a teacher approach genuinely relevant religious content with the same degree of academic responsibility as would be reflected in a teacher's approach to the secular subject. Moreover, the teacher's integrity would determine the degree to which the teacher's approach to religion is honest and within the framework of current judicial decisions. If a teacher does not perceive the genuine relevance of religion, that teacher will—and should—skirt or ignore religious content—as is typically the practice with so many controversial elements of the school curriculum.

The level of curriculum integration attained would result from the quality and depth of a teacher's knowledge of the secular subject. A well-prepared and knowledgeable art teacher could address, in an academically sound fashion, those religious themes which are encountered in the study of art, particularly if assisted by a religion studies supervisor. Although some members of the religious community may believe it inaccurate to assume that even a well-prepared teacher could address religious topics appropriate to a secular subject, this is the basic assumption made with respect to the many aspects of all subjects taught in the schools. Furthermore, it must be clear that an art teacher will teach about religion as artist, not as theologian.

The same concerns (professional expertise, enthusiasm, and integrity) apply equally to the supervisor or resource teacher who might teach units in religion, or the religion studies teacher who would be responsible for courses in religion. However, while the piety or quality of religious faith of these teachers should not concern those involved in public education, it does not follow that those teachers should be disinterested in, or uncommitted to, the study of religion. We have all suffered through classes with teachers who were bored with their subject. The religion studies supervisor or religion studies teacher must be deeply interested in religion as an academic area of study and investigation. Any teacher who is involved in religion studies should be enthusiastic about the subject matter, but such enthusiasm must be generated by a teacher's appreciation for the significance of religion in the life, history, and culture of mankind and not by the desire to propagate a sectarian religious perspective or to indoctrinate students in a specific theological system.

An illustration of this process utilizing a secular subject may be helpful. Any English teacher, particularly one who teaches literature in the upper grades, would have a favorite poet and would be, perhaps, more familiar with the work of that poet than with any other. The teacher knows a great deal about the poet's life and feels attuned to the poet's emotions and expression. Of all poets, this is the one most preferred and most enjoyed. When teaching a unit or course for which this beloved poet is appropriate, the teacher may reveal this personal preference to the students. But the teacher should not teach poetry if the teacher refuses to deal with the work of any other poet or degrades all other poets as compared to the favorite. To successfully teach poetry, it is expected that one will have favorite poets, but it is also expected that one will be enthusiastic about and appreciative of poetry in general. We must expect the same of teachers who will teach about religion. We can ask nothing more; we can tolerate nothing less.

Wallace Alcorn illustrated the futility of attempting to classify teachers for religion studies. While his discussion focused on resource teachers or teachers of religion studies courses, his insights are generally applicable. Alcorn discussed four paradigms of the religion studies teacher. The first is a teacher committed to the purely secular viewpoint. Such an individual would seem to be perfect for religion studies because that teacher's dedication would be to understanding religion rather than encouraging commitment to religion. However, a secularist may not have much respect for religion and may, therefore, experience substantial difficulty in avoiding the depreciation of religion. The problem is not the quality of religious faith or the lack of it; the problem is that such a teacher may be devoutly antireligious. We normally do not allow a teacher to teach mathematics if that individual believes that mathematics is irrelevant to education. The same must be true for religion studies teachers.

A second type of teacher is an individual of liberal persuasion. That teacher would seem remarkedly suited for religion studies for she would be willing to put personal convictions and ideas on matters of faith to the test of honest thought and experience. As a liberal, this teacher would be open to new and conflicting ideas and would encourage their expression and investigation. The problem, however, is that liberalism cannot be guaranteed. All of us have encountered self-styled liberals who, under the guise of free thought, are as dogmatic as are the ultraconservatives they oppose. Many liberals seem to have made a fetish of change and controversy, and sound intellectual growth may all but disappear in the academic vacuum thereby created. Furthermore, the liberal may be intolerant of the conservative position and may even attempt to preach in favor of liberalism.

The third type of teacher discussed by Alcorn is the conservative. Perhaps the greatest asset the conservative has is his typical dedication to traditional religion and to the role of religion in history. The conservative most clearly and firmly upholds the value of religion. The major liability is that the conservative's position is closed and inflexible. This individual may deny the validity of any but the position to which he is personally committed. Moreover, the conservative often experiences difficulty with objective academic approaches to religion studies.

A fourth paradigm discussed by Alcorn is the religious professional—the minister, priest, or rabbi.[26] While such persons should possess the academic preparation appropriate for religion studies, it is risky to employ them as religion studies teachers because, even if they are certified and able to teach religion objectively, their identification with a particular sectarian position may cause controversy. While professionals in religion might be excellent religion studies teachers, the sad fact is that "guilt by association" may cause considerable difficulty.

Who, then, should teach in a religion studies program? Alcorn concluded, as have most scholars in this area, that a religion studies teacher should be a fully qualified and certified, regularly employed teacher with academic credentials appropriate for religion studies. Obviously this conclusion does not bring religion studies into any safe pedagogical harbor.

> The religious situation of any person is defined by what he most truly loves, i.e., by what concerns him ultimately. The teacher makes his object of worship known by every indication of what most deeply interests him, of how he measures his successes and failures, of the sources from which he seeks strength and solace, and by his criteria of choice in making important decisions. What counts in the living witness is not primarily an explicit rational system of belief but the implicit values and commitments which govern the actual organization of the person's life.[27]

Here we encounter the hidden curriculum. In the intimacy of the classroom, what the teacher is as a person can be far more influential than what that teacher expresses verbally. The teacher's personality has lasting impact on the students regardless of the subject taught, and fully qualified public school teachers are human beings who may, despite their training, manifest many of the shortcomings just discussed.

No way has yet been devised to guarantee teaching excellence in any classroom or in any subject. Nevertheless, as an ab-

---

[26]Wallace Alcorn, "Who Should Teach Religion in the Public Schools?" *Religious Education* 69 (November-December 1974): 654-55.

[27]Phenix, *Religious Concerns*, 44-45.

solute minimum, religion studies teachers and resource teachers must be academically qualified and accountable to the public school system. With regard to regular classroom teachers who will address religion strictly on the basis of curriculum integration, we can only assume that their academic preparation, integrity, and sense of what is relevant will allow them, particularly with the assistance of religion studies resource teachers, to effectively address religion when germane to the subject(s) for which they are responsible.

Considering the vast array of teaching methodologies employed in schools today, it would be futile to stress a particular teaching method for a religion studies teacher. At any rate, as Arthur Combs recognized, teaching methods, when effective, are very much like the clothes we wear: they are expressions of our personality.[28] The selection and utilization of a teaching method is, therefore, a very personal matter.

However, as has been discussed, religion in public education is a controversial subject. While no precise method of teaching is recommended, a general procedure does recommend itself. When controversial issues are addressed, the students' experience must not be exceeded. Admittedly, it is difficult to determine the nature of a student's experiential background with any precision. Obvious extremes such as the difference between a first grade student and a senior in high school or the difference between a student with absolutely no religious background and a devout member of some religious confession rarely occur in a typical classroom. In approaching a controversial topic, therefore, the teacher must observe all appropriate pedagogical precautions against exceeding that background. Some comfort may result from the realization that this problem is not unique to religion studies; if any learning experience is successful, the subject matter cannot surpass the student's experiential background (the goal of education is to extend this background, but

---

[28]Arthur W. Combs, "The Personal Approach to Good Teaching," *American Education: Foundations and Superstructure*, ed. W. E. Beckner and W. Dumas (Scranton PA: International Textbook Co., 1970) 513.

it may not be extended if it is initially exceeded). The unique problem, however, lies in the fact that controversial issues are not clearly sequential on the basis of prior study as is, for example, language arts. If we want students to learn to think critically, a most worthy "secular" goal, they will have to study issues which have no correct answer (issues of genuine controversy).

> For all too long we have tended to examine only those questions which can be handled objectively and therefore neutrally, scientifically and also safely. The desire to avoid personal involvement, commitment and controversy reflects a set of values which may be inadequate for those involved in public education to utilize if the aims of education are to be realized in a period when the questions and concerns raised by teachers as well as pupils challenge the heretofore socially established and accepted value norms.[29]

In approaching the study of controversial issues, a teacher must be certain that a sound factual basis is laid. A common error occurs when, ignoring this guideline, one launches into study of the controversial area and, in dismay, discovers that the study resulted in little more than a pooling of ignorance or, as an outgrowth of the ensuing frustration, an acceptance of the "answer" finally suggested by the teacher. When beginning study of a controversial issue, one must first collect all available pertinent data. If the issue is one of sufficient controversy, factual data may be scarce, and the students may be forced to settle for a large measure of "educated" opinion. Nevertheless, the students must aggressively seek all available relevant information, whether fact or opinion or both; for the study of controversy cannot proceed in an academic vacuum.

When teaching about controversial matters, a teacher may not force an answer upon the students. Otherwise the process reduces to an educational charade. If the issue is truly controversial, students must sense the controversy and, based upon all the relevant data and opinion they can gather, must assume

---

[29]Harold Stahmer, "Religion and Moral Values in the Public Schools," *Religious Education* 61 (January-February 1966): 23.

personal responsibility for their own conclusions. If a student is to be responsible for the outcome of the investigation, she must be free to select from a number of potential "answers" or to select no answer. Electing to live with the question for a while without arriving at a conclusion may bespeak the presence of substantial intellectual maturity.

Public schooling must include analysis of significant controversy. Students will not be prepared well for their future if they are exposed only to training in basic academic skills and are asked only to commit a myriad of unrelated facts and processes to memory. If we want our students to be able to think, they must have something to think seriously about. Religion studies, along with the study of other areas of significant controversy, can provide many positive "secular" outcomes if schools remain sufficiently neutral in their educational approach.

The Classroom

If there is any promise for religion studies in public schools, the atmosphere of the classroom will be crucial. One teacher comments on the importance of classroom atmosphere.

> After teaching various types of religion courses for the last fifteen years in public and private schools, I am becoming increasingly conscious of the ways the classroom and the traditional course structure inhibit the learning process, particularly in this subject where so much of the student's self is potentially at stake. A classroom, at least in high school, is for most kids too threatening a situation to permit exposure of their own honest thoughts. It is hard to believe how powerful is the fear of ridicule or how persistent the notion that some thoughts or questions are wrong to have and will have a negative affect on grades.[30]

The rigidly formal, strictly sequential, and intentionally stereotyped schooling experienced by many children in public schools has received its share of criticism from those supporting a more liberal philosophy of education. Whether religion studies are in-

---

[30]Robert S. Wicks, "A Space for Reflection," *Religious Education* 64 (March-April 1969): 105.

tegrated into the curriculum or follow a more ambitious and intensive approach, the success of the study reduces to classroom atmosphere, which reduces largely to the personality and philosophy of the teacher. Will the general philosophy of public school teachers and resulting student attitudes inhibit meaningful religion studies?

Some of the major distinctions between traditional education (represented by the left column) and the approach particularly appropriate for religion studies (the right column) are:

The classroom is teacher-centered.	The classroom is learner-centered.
Communication is largely monologue.	Communication is largely dialogue.
Mistakes tend to be points of judgment of the student by the teacher.	Mistakes are seen as necessary steps in the learning process.
The teacher's ideas and thoughts are the most important.	The student's ideas and thoughts are given major emphasis.
A standard or authoritarian perception is emphasized.	The student's perceptions are of primary importance.
The learning process is planned by the teacher.	The learning process is planned by the teacher and the students together.
Students are expected to follow a standard pre-determined curriculum.	A preplanned curriculum is adjusted to the developmental levels, backgrounds, interests, and needs of students.
The teacher is a director or manager.	The teacher is a helper, a facilitator.
Student performance is undertaken in a lock-step manner.	Student performance is personalized.
Progress of students is judged against norms.	Progress of students is evaluated in terms of the individual.
Evaluation is largely based on test performance.	Evaluation is based on individual performance of many kinds of tasks.
The attempt is made to *make* students learn.	The attempt is made to *help* students learn.
Emphasis is placed on memorizing and retaining subject matter.	Emphasis is placed on insightful and meaningful contact with subject matter.

Stress is placed on knowing, performing.	Stress is placed on meaning, understanding, and feeling.
Learning tends to be extrinsic.	Learning is intended to be intrinsic.
Cognitive growth is the primary concern.	Cognitive and affective development are given equal emphasis.
Gaining knowledge of facts is viewed as an end in itself.	Facts are learned in order to apply them in problems.
Much knowledge is intended for use in adult life.	Knowledge is intended to have relevance for the student's present life.
Class atmosphere is orderly, controlled.	Class atmosphere is open, flexible.
Discipline is based on rules and regulations.	Discipline is based on individual and group responsibility.
Adjustment to the norms of society is a dominant emphasis.	Self-actualization and living responsibly with others is emphasized.
The goal is to help students be better knowers.	The goal is to help students be better persons.
Emphasis is on doing.	Emphasis is on being.

The column on the right represents an approach to teaching that is not common in public schools; some would argue that the approach is impossible there. Most teachers who will be involved in religion studies through curriculum integration will follow, to one degree or another, the procedures outlined in the column to the left, and curriculum integration must be the foundation for a religion studies program. As illustrated repeatedly in this discussion, religion studies cannot be transmissive; religion studies must be an open process of education that encourages critical thought on the part of students. Religion studies must reflect a liberal philosophy of education.[31] Aside, therefore, from the many substantial problems discussed to this point, the philosophical conflict between the nature of religion studies and the predominant educational approach of the public school is, perhaps, the fundamental issue. Considering that re-

---

[31]Richard C. McMillan, "Religion Studies and 'Back to Basics'—Friends or Foes?" *Educational Leadership* 38 (February 1981): 399-401.

ligion studies must follow a liberal educational philosophy and that public education, by and large, follows a conservative philosophy of education, the prospect for religion studies is not good.

This rather gloomy evaluation of the future of religion studies should be qualified. The conflict in philosophy will have its greatest impact in courses in religion or in units of study about religion. Here the goal of understanding religion itself becomes more predominant and the student will, therefore, encounter the controversial nature of religion more frequently. The problem will not be as great in curriculum integration by the classroom teacher. Here the goal is that students understand the relationship of religion to a secular subject in order to fully understand the secular subject and the controversial nature of religion may be less apparent. But, difficulty may arise in curriculum integration. For example, in a study of colonial America, the facts of the colonial religious milieu may be presented rather straightforwardly. But, what if a student should ask why individuals were persecuted in the Massachusetts Bay Colony if they did not affirm the Puritan point of view? The response of the teacher in situations like this (and endless illustrations of such questions could be easily brought to mind) is of crucial significance for religion studies. Will the question be ignored; will it be answered so as to protect a romantic picture of colonial America; will the response degrade religion, employing historic and contemporary illustrations of religious persecution to emphasize the divisiveness of sectarianism; or will the teacher use the question to help students begin to analyze the endless cycle of human suffering caused by fear and prejudice in any area of social life? These possible responses to the student's question illustrate both the promise and the pitfalls of religion studies.

The conclusion of this matter, then, rests precisely with each local community. Each community, nourished by the counsel of its religious and educational leaders, must order its educational priorities, answering a fundamental question: are religion studies in public schools worth the effort? Religion studies will complete the secular education students receive in many subjects, and religion studies may lessen religious tension and bigotry in our society. But, will the religious community ever accept this approach to the study of religion; and can religion studies, as outlined here, be implemented with any success in the educational climate of the public schools?

CHAPTER 7

The Minister's Role

The religion-government relationship in the United States is a delicate and demanding balance between individual commitments and social concerns. As public education is intended to facilitate the intellectual growth and social competence of future citizens, its relationship to religion is particularly sensitive when viewed against the religious pluralism of society and the nation's constitutional dedication to the religious liberty of the individual. A parish minister committed to the preservation of religious liberty and to the maintenance of the American system of public education can exercise substantial influence in the community with respect to the relationship of religion to public education. Because much of the more intense current criticism of public schools is sectarian in nature and origin, continued community support for public education in many localities may finally depend upon the leadership provided by ministers.

Society seems to grow more complex with each passing day. As a result, the historic goals of American public education appear increasingly difficult to attain. Leaders in public education are currently struggling to determine the primary tasks of the public schools in society. It may be terribly difficult, therefore, for laymen to grasp the nature and direction of modern public education. However, in order to facilitate positive, productive leadership, a minister must develop an informed and realistic concept of the goals of public education, of what public education should be expected to contribute to society. The magnitude of the historic goals of American public education and the diversity of clientele to be educated should provide sufficient warning that expectations must be realistic. While one might wish a great deal from a public institution, one must not be naive. Each community must address the fundamental question of just what it can legitimately expect from its public schools. Ministers must also address this issue.

A minister may find some assistance in addressing this issue by reading the literature in education, but the most effective sources are public school administrators and teachers in the community. A minister interested in providing community leadership in the relationship of religion to public education will cultivate relationships with those persons who work daily in the public schools. This rapport will allow a minister to be an advocate of public education without violating one's primary role as minister in the community. Constructive criticism from a friend whose opinion one respects can be of enormous value and, at times, a minister may have to fulfill this role. But a minister dedicated to religious liberty and to public education will avoid that sectarian criticism so common today that is intended to undermine the public schools. The strength of a minister's leadership will be directly related to the way that minister is perceived by public school personnel.

Because the relationship of religion to public education in this nation is basically a legal matter, a minister must keep abreast of the legal issues as they develop. The mass communications media may alert a minister to an emerging issue but should not be relied upon to provide the detail a minister will require. An attorney would be the best source of information; indeed, an attorney with whom a minister could informally discuss these legal issues would be of immense value. Furthermore, a minister should obtain a copy of the major court decisions as soon after their announcement as possible. Public pronouncements on litigation should be avoided until the decision has been read. The cumulative effect of this study will assist in understanding issues before or during litigation.

The educational and legal expertise a minister is able to develop will contribute directly to the quality of a minister's relationship to public schools in the community. A minister, when requested, will be able to render to schools constructive and legal assistance based upon this knowledge. Ministers sympathetic to the legal relationship of religion to public education can help in many ways: as consultants in curriculum planning for religion studies programs, as resource persons for these programs, as speakers to school groups, and so forth. The essential factor in such involvement is that one understand and honor the legal restraints on one's activity and accept only those responsibilities that can be undertaken in good conscience. Of equal importance, this base of legal and educational knowledge will help a minister know what can and cannot be expected of public schools with respect to religion. It is important to avoid advocating illegal practices by requesting more involvement of religion in public schools than is constitutionally permissible.

A minister should be aware of the value of the three sectors of American education: the public, the private, and the parochial. As the three provide essential educational alternatives, a minister should not hesitate to exercise influence on behalf of all three as appropriate for the minister in the community. As two of these sectors are non-public, it would be advisable for a minister to simply withhold comment if a private or parochial school cannot be supported in good conscience. Inefficiency or failure in our public schools, on the other hand, should not be accepted, but positive support, involving a realization of shortcomings and an aggressive search for improvement, is far more valuable than shrill and disruptive criticism. Ministers do not enjoy public anonymity, and their public pronouncements receive attention because of their unique role in the community. Therefore, a minister should take care that criticism of public education be from a public rather than a sectarian viewpoint.

To this point the discussion has focused upon the direct relationship of the minister to public education and has, in a sense,

recommended an extra set of responsibilities for the minister.
Three equally significant suggestions, however, occur which are
more in keeping with the traditional roles and responsibilities of
ministers. The first is a minister's role in generating ecumenical
cooperation. Sectarian strife acted as a catalyst for the development of the secular public school. Current events bear witness to the disruption of community that results from religious
hatred. The dedication of our government to religious freedom
has led to the development of a highly pluralistic society. It
would be unwise for any responsible community leader to jeopardize American society or freedoms by advocating sectarian
divisiveness. It is tragic when the enormous contributions of religion to social life are overshadowed by bigotry.

A parish minister could most effectively assist public education by dedicating one's efforts to strengthening the fundamental social unit, the family. The success of public, private, or
parochial education rests directly on the nature of the homes
from which the students come. This has, of course, always been
the "secret" of the success of private and parochial schools;
there is normally strong support of education in the families of
the students who attend such schools. Sad as it is, many of the
students who attend public schools have must unfortunate, almost nonexistent family lives. The challenge presented to public education by this situation is almost overwhelming. A parish
minister, of course, cannot single-handedly correct such a global
problem, but contributing to the stability of the families in one's
parish is a significant contribution to education *and* to children.

A lasting contribution may also be made by a minister who is
dedicated to developing and maintaining strong programs of religious education in the parish. A religious community should
not request any form of religious instruction in public schools
until it may take pride in the quality of religious education provided by its own religious institutions. For far too long the public schools have been asked to assume many responsibilities for
children and young people that families and other community
agencies should provide. A number of years ago, the comment
was made that one of the primary social roles of public schools

is that of baby sitter.[1] Perhaps we have taken the legal concept of *in loco parentis* too far. The religious community dare not ask its schools to stand *in loco ecclesiasticus.*

Parish ministry is a weighty duty. A minister's duty to assist in the spiritual growth and well-being of God's creatures is a responsibility heavy enough to stagger even the most competent individual. To add to the responsibility the burden of these suggestions may seem ludicrous. Yet, human beings, despite their differing opinions and personal commitments, must resolve to respect other human beings and institute as much freedom as possible for everyone. Disagreement, when honestly expressed, is a constructive force in society; hate and prejudice are debilitating. And can any human being, particularly if dedicated to the Christian faith, have the hubris to try to control the life of another human being? Is not dedication to universal religious freedom a social expression of Christian love?

The Christian church has historically assumed many responsibilities in its social role. The church has preserved the Christian faith and has taken the responsibility to express that faith to the world. But the church has also dedicated itself to the improvement at the human condition. In the United States, efforts directed toward constructing a positive relationship between religion and public education would seem to be part of such a dedication. Is it not possible for the church to make this contribution without undermining or compromising its other missions? In large measure, this is a question that the parish minister must answer.

Surely our children can be given no greater legacy than the witness of Christian love in our society, the preservation of individual freedom, and a meaningful education without restriction. There are no more precious creatures in God's creation than children. Our future is with them. We dare not make their world a battleground for our prejudices and insecurities.

_____

[1]David A. Goslin, *The School in Contemporary Society* (Glenview IL: Scott, Foresman and Co., 1965) 11-13.

APPENDIX A

McGOWAN v. STATE OF MARYLAND.

Mr. Justice Frankfurter.
A separate opinion
366 U.S. 420, 465-67 (1961).

What Virginia had long practiced, and what Madison, Jefferson and others fought to end, was the extension of civil government's support to religion in a manner which made the two in some degree interdependent, and thus threatened the freedom of each. The purpose of the Establishment Clause was to assure that the national legislature would not exert its power in the service of any purely religious end; that it would not, as Virginia and virtually all of the Colonies had done, make of religion, as religion, an object of legislation.

Of course, the immediate object of the First Amendment's prohibition was the established church as it had been known in England and in most of the Colonies. But with foresight those who drafted and adopted the words, "Congress shall make no law respecting an establishment of religion," did not limit the constitutional proscription to any particular, dated form of state-supported theological venture. The Establishment Clause withdrew from the sphere of legitimate legislative concern and competence a specific, but comprehensive, area of human conduct: man's belief or disbelief in the verity of some transcendental idea and man's expression in action of that belief or disbelief. Congress may not make these matters, as such, the subject of legislation, nor, now, may any legislature in this country. Neither the National Government nor, under the Due Process Clause of the Fourteenth Amendment, a State may, by any device, support belief or the expression of belief for its own sake, whether from conviction of the truth of that belief, or from conviction that by the propagation of that belief the civil welfare of the State is served, or because a majority of its citizens, holding that belief, are offended when all do not hold it.

But once it is determined that a challenged statute is supportable as implementing other substantial interests than the promotion of belief, the guarantee prohibiting religious "establishment" is satisfied.

If the primary end achieved by a form of regulation is the affirmation or promotion of religious doctrine—primary, in the sense that all secular ends which it purportedly serves are derivative from, not wholly independent of, the advancement of religion—the regulation is beyond the power of the state. . . . Or if a statute furthers both secular and religious ends by means unnecessary to the effectuation of the secular ends alone—where the same secular ends could equally be attained by means which do not have consequences for promotion of religion—the statute cannot stand. . . .

ENGEL v. VITALE.

Mr. Justice Black.
Opinion of the Court.
370 U.S. 421 at 427-33 (1962).

It is an unfortunate fact of history that when some of the very groups which had most strenuously opposed the established Church of England found themselves sufficiently in control of colonial governments in this country to write their own prayers into law, they passed laws making their own religion the official religion of their respective colonies. Indeed, as late as the time of the Revolutionary War, there were established churches in at least eight of the thirteen former colonies and established religions in at least four of the other five. But the successful Revolution against English political domination was shortly followed by intense opposition to the practice of establishing religion by law. This opposition crystallized rapidly into an effective political force in Virginia where the minority religious groups such as Presbyterians, Lutherans, Quakers and Baptists had gained such strength that the adherents to the established Episcopal Church were actually a minority themselves. In 1785-1786, those opposed to the established Church, led by James Madison and Thomas Jefferson, who, though themselves not members of any of these dissenting religious groups, opposed all religious establishments by law on grounds of principle, obtained the enactment of the famous "Virginia Bill for Religious Liberty" by which all religious groups were placed on an equal footing so far as the State was concerned.

By the time of the adoption of the Constitution, our history shows that there was a widespread awareness among many Americans of the dangers of a union of Church and State. These people knew, some of them from bitter personal experience, that one of the greatest dangers to the freedom of the individual to worship in his own way lay in the Government's placing its official stamp of approval upon one particular kind of prayer or one particular form of religious services. . . . The Constitution was intended to avert a part of this danger by leaving the government of this country in the hands of the people rather than in the hands of any monarch. But this safeguard was not enough. Our Founders were no more willing to let the content of their prayers and their privilege of praying whenever they pleased be influenced by the ballot box than they were to let these vital matters of personal conscience depend upon the succession of monarchs. The First Amendment was added to the Constitution to stand as a guarantee that neither the power nor the prestige of Federal Government would be used to control, support or influence the kinds of prayer the American people can say—that the people's religions must not be subjected to the pressures of government for change each time a new political administration is elected to office. Under that Amendment's prohibition against governmental establishment of religion, as reinforced by the provisions of the Fourteenth Amendment, government in this country, be it state or federal, is without power to prescribe by law any particular form of prayer which is to be used as an official prayer in carrying on any program of governmentally sponsored religious activity.

The Establishment Clause, unlike the Free Exercise Clause, does not depend upon any showing of direct governmental compulsion and is violated by the enactment of laws which establish an official religion whether those laws operate directly to coerce nonobserving individuals or not. . . . When the power, prestige and financial support of government is placed behind a particular religious belief, the indirect coercive pressure upon religious minorities to conform to the prevailing officially approved religion is plain. But the purposes underlying the Establishment Clause go much further than that. Its first and most immediate purpose rested on the belief that a union of government and religion tends to destroy government and to degrade religion. The history of governmentally established religion, both in England and in this country, showed that whenever government had allied itself with one particular form of religion, the inevitable result had been that it had incurred the hatred, disrespect and even contempt of those who held contrary beliefs. That same history showed that many people had lost their respect for any religion that had relied upon the support of government to spread its faith. The Establishment Clause thus stands as an expression of principle on the part of the Founders of our Constitution that religion is too personal, too sacred, too holy, to permit its "unhallowed perversion" by a civil magistrate. Another purpose of the Establishment Clause rested upon an awareness of the historical fact that governmentally established religions and religious persecutions go hand in hand. The Founders knew that only a few years after the Book of Common Prayer became the only accepted form of religious services in the established Church of England, an Act of Uniformity was passed to compel all Englishmen to attend those services and to make it a criminal offense to conduct or attend religious gatherings of any other kind—a law which was consistently flouted by dissenting religious groups . . .

APPENDIX B*

The major decisions of the Supreme Court in the areas of religion-state controversy, excluding religion in public education, announced in the twenty-five years from October Term, 1950, to the October Term, 1975, are listed in this appendix with citation numbers from the *United States Reports*, the *United States Supreme Court Reports, Lawyers' Edition*, and the *Supreme Court Reporter*.

The State and Sectarian Education

Pierce v. Society of the Sisters of the Holy Names of Jesus and Mary
  Pierce v. Hill Military Academy
  268 U.S. 510, 69 L. Ed. 1070, 45 S. Ct. 571, (1925).

Cochran v. Louisiana State Board of Education
  281 U.S. 370, 74 L. Ed. 913, 50 S. Ct. 335, (1930).

Everson v. Board of Education of Ewing TP
  330 U.S. 1, 91 L. Ed. 711, 67 S. Ct. 504, (1947).

Board of Education of Central School District No. 1 v. Allen
  392 U.S. 236, 20 L. Ed. 2d 1060, 88 S. Ct. 1923, (1968).

Flast v. Cohen
  392 U.S. 83, 20 L. Ed. 2d 947, 88 S. Ct. 1942, (1968).

Tilton v. Richardson
  403 U.S. 672, 29 L. Ed. 2d 790, 91 S. Ct. 2091, (1971).

Lemon v. Kurtzman.
  Earley v. DiCenso.
  Robinson v. DiCenso
  403 U.S. 602, 29 L. Ed. 2d 745, 91 S. Ct. 2105, (1971).

*I express my gratitude to the National Association of Baptist Professors of Religion for permission to reproduce this material originally published in Richard C. McMillan, ed., *Education, Religion, and the Supreme Court* (Danville VA: The National Association of Baptist Professors of Religion, 1979).

Lemon v. Kurtzman
  411 U.S. 192, 36 L. Ed. 2d 151, 93 S. Ct. 1463, (1973).

Levitt v. Committee for Public Education and Religious Liberty
  Anderson v. Committee for Public Education and Religious Liberty
  Cathedral Academy v. Committee for Public Education and Religious Liberty
  413 U.S. 472, 37 L. Ed. 2d 736, 93 S. Ct. 2814, (1973).

Hunt v. McNair
  413 U.S. 734, 37 L. Ed. 2d 923, 93 S. Ct. 2868, (1973).

Committee for Public Education and Religious Liberty v. Nyquist
  Anderson v. Committee for Public Education and Religious Liberty
  Nyquist v. Committee for Public Education and Religious Liberty
  Cherry v. Committee for Public Education and Religious Liberty
  413 U.S. 756, 37 L. Ed. 2d 948, 93 S. Ct. 2955, (1973).

Sloan v. Lemon
  Crouter v. Lemon
  413 U.S. 825, 37 L. Ed. 2d 939, 93 S. Ct. 2982, (1973).

Wheeler v. Barrera
  417 U.S. 402, 41 L. Ed. 2d 159, 94 S. Ct. 2274, (1974).

Meek v. Pittinger
  421 U.S. 349, 44 L. Ed. 2d 217, 95 S. Ct. 1753, (1975).

Roemer v. Board of Public Works of Maryland
  426 U.S. 736, 49 L. Ed. 2d 179, 96 S. Ct. 2337, (1976).

Wolman v. Walter
  433 U.S. 229, 53 L. Ed. 2d 714, 97 S. Ct. 2593, (1977).

Religion and Taxation

First Unitarian Church of Los Angeles v. County of Los Angeles, California
  Valley Unitarian-Universalist Church v. County of Los Angeles, California
  357 U.S. 545, 2 L. Ed. 2d 1484, 78 S. Ct. 1350, (1958).

Walz v. Tax Commission of the City of New York
  397 U.S. 664, 25 L. Ed. 2d 697, 90 S. Ct. 1409, (1970).

Diffenderfer v. Central Baptist Church of Miami, Florida, Inc.
  404 U.S. 412, 30 L. Ed. 2d 567, 92 S. Ct. 574, (1972).

United States v. Christian Echoes National Ministry, Inc.
  404 U.S. 561, 30 L. Ed. 2d 716, 92 S. Ct. 663, (1972).

United States v. American Friends Service Committee
  419 U.S. 7, 42 L. Ed. 2d 7, 95 S. Ct. 13, (1974).

Sunday Observance

McGowan v. State of Maryland
  366 U.S. 420, 6 L. Ed. 2d 393, 81 S. Ct. 1101, (1961).

Two Guys from Harrison-Allentown, Inc. v. McGinley
  366 U.S. 582, 6 L. Ed. 2d 551, 81 S. Ct. 1135, (1961).

Braunfeld v. Brown.
  366 U.S. 599, 6 L. Ed. 2d 563, 81 S. Ct. 1144, (1961).

Gallagher v. Crown Kosher Super Market of Massachusetts, Inc.
  366 U.S. 617, 6 L. Ed. 2d 536, 81 S. Ct. 1122, (1961).

Arlan's Department Store of Louisville, Inc. v. Kentucky
  371 U.S. 218, 9 L. Ed. 2d 264, 83 S. Ct. 277, (1962).

Religious Freedom

Niemotko v. State of Maryland
  Kelley v. State of Maryland
  340 U.S. 268, 95 L. Ed. 267, 71 S. Ct. 325, (1951).

Kunz v. People of State of New York
  340 U.S. 290, 95 L. Ed. 280, 71 S. Ct. 312, (1951).

Fowler v. State of Rhode Island
  345 U.S. 67, 97 L. Ed. 828, 73 S. Ct. 526, (1953).

Poulos v. State of New Hampshire
  345 U.S. 395, 97 L. Ed. 1105, 73 S. Ct. 760, (1953).

Torcaso v. Watkins
  367 U.S. 488, 6 L. Ed. 2d 982, 81 S. Ct. 1680, (1961).

Sherbert v. Verner
  374 U.S. 398, 10 L. Ed. 2d 965, 83 S. Ct. 1790, (1963).

Cruz v. Beto
  405 U.S. 319, 31 L. Ed. 2d 263, 92, S. Ct. 1079, (1972).

Church Governance

Kedroff v. St. Nicholas Cathedral of Russian Orthodox Church in North America
  344 U.S. 94, 97 L. Ed. 120, 73 S. Ct. 143, (1952).

Kreshik v. Saint Nicholas Cathedral
363 U.S. 190, 4 L. Ed. 2d 1140, 80 S. Ct. 1037, (1960).

Presbyterian Church in the United States v. Mary Elizabeth Blue Hull Memorial Presbyterian Church
393 U.S. 440, 21 L. Ed. 2d 658, 89 S. Ct. 601, (1969).

Maryland and Virginia Eldership of the Churches of God v. The Church of God at Sharpsburg, Inc.
396 U.S. 367, 24 L. Ed. 2d 582, 90 S. Ct. 499, (1970).

Serbian Eastern Orthodox Diocese for the United States of America and Canada v. Milivojevich
426 U.S. 696, 49 L. Ed. 2d 151, 96 S. Ct. 2372, (1976).

Religion and Military Service

United States v. Nugent
United States v. Packer
346 U.S. 1, 97 L. Ed. 1417, 73 S. Ct. 991, (1953).

Dickinson v. United States
346 U.S. 389, 98 L. Ed. 132, 74 S. Ct. 152, (1953).

Witmer v. United States
384 U.S. 375, 99 L. Ed. 428, 75 S. Ct. 392, (1955).

Sicurella v. United States
348 U.S. 385, 99 L. Ed. 436, 75 S. Ct. 403, (1955).

Simmons v. United States
348 U.S. 397, 99 L. Ed. 453, 75 S. Ct. 397, (1955).

Gonzales v. United States
384 U.S. 407, 99 L. Ed. 407, 75 S. Ct. 409, (1955).

United States v. Seeger
United States v. Jackson
Peter v. United States
380 U.S. 163, 13 L. Ed. 2d 733, 85 S.Ct. 850, (1955).

Oestereich v. Selective Service System Local Board No. 11, Cheyenne, Wyoming
393 U.S. 233, 21 L. Ed. 2d 402, 89 S. Ct. 414, (1968).

Clark v. Gabriel
393 U.S. 256, 21 L. Ed. 2d 418, 89 S. Ct. 424, (1968).

Breen v. Selective Service Local Board No. 16, Bridgeport, Connecticut
396 U.S. 460, 24 L. Ed. 2d 653, 90 S. Ct. 661, (1970).

Welsh v. United States
398 U.S. 333, 26 L. Ed. 2d 308, 90 S. Ct. 1792, (1970).

Mulloy v. United States
398 U.S. 410, 26 L. Ed. 2d 362, 90 S. Ct. 1766, (1970).

Gillette v. United States
Negre v. Larsen
401 U.S. 437, 28 L. Ed. 2d 168, 91 S. Ct. 828, (1971).

Ehlert v. United States
402 U.S. 99, 28 L. Ed. 2d 625, 91 S. Ct. 1319, (1971).

McGee v. United States
402 U.S. 479, 29 L. Ed. 2d 47, 91 S. Ct. 1565, (1971).

Clay v. United States
403 U.S. 698, 29 L. Ed. 2d 810, 91 S. Ct. 2068, (1971).

Johnson v. Robinson
415 U.S. 361, 39 L. Ed. 2d 389, 94 S. Ct. 1160, (1974).

APPENDIX C

*PIERCE v. SOCIETY OF THE SISTERS OF THE HOLY NAMES
OF JESUS AND MARY*
PIERCE v. HILL MILITARY ACADEMY

268 U.S. 510
Decided June 1, 1925.

Mr. Justice McREYNOLDS delivered the opinion of the Court.

The challenged act, effective September 1, 1926, requires every parent, guardian, or other person having control or charge or custody of a child between 8 and 16 years to send him "to a public school for the period of time a public school shall be held during the current year" in the district where the child resides; and failure so to do is declared a misdemeanor. There are exemptions—not specifically important here . . . The manifest purpose is to compel general attendance at public schools by normal children, between 8 and 16, who have not completed the eighth grade. And without doubt enforcement of the statute would seriously impair, perhaps destroy, the profitable features of appellees' business and greatly diminish the value of their property.

Appellee the Society of Sisters is an Oregon corporation, organized in 1880, with power to care for orphans, educate and instruct the youth, establish and maintain academies or schools, and acquire necessary real and personal property. . . . In its primary schools many children between those ages are taught the subjects usually pursued in Oregon public schools during the first eight years. Systematic religious instruction and moral training according to the tenets of the Roman Catholic Church are also regularly provided.

After setting out the above facts, the Society's bill alleges that the enactment conflicts with the right of parents to choose schools where their children will receive appropriate mental and religious training, the right of the child to influence the parents' choice of a school, the right of schools and teachers therein to engage in a useful business or profession, and is accordingly repugnant to the Constitution and void. And, further, that unless enforcement of the measure is enjoined, the corporation's business and property will suffer irreparable injury.

Appellee Hill Military Academy is a private corporation organized in 1908 under the laws of Oregon, engaged in owning, operating, and conducting for profit an elementary, college preparatory, and military training school for boys between the ages of 5 and 21 years. The courses of study conform to the requirements of the state board of education. . . . By reason of the statute and threat of enforcement, appellee's business is being destroyed and its property depreciated; parents and guardians are refusing to make contracts for the future instruction of their sons, and some are being withdrawn.

No question is raised concerning the power of the state reasonably to regulate all schools, to inspect, supervise, and examine them, their teachers and pupils; to require that all children of proper age attend some school, that teachers shall be of good moral character and patriotic disposition, that certain studies plainly essential to good citizenship must be taught, and that nothing be taught which is manifestly inimical to the public welfare.

The inevitable practical result of enforcing the act under consideration would be destruction of appellees' primary schools and perhaps all other private primary schools for normal children within the state of Oregon. Appellees are engaged in a kind of undertaking not inherently harmful, but long regarded as useful and meritorious.

. . . we think it entirely plain that the Act of 1922 unreasonably interferes with the liberty of parents and guardians to direct the upbringing and education of children under their control. As often heretofore pointed out, rights guaranteed by the Constitution may not be abridged by legislation which has no reasonable relation to some purpose within the competency of the state. The fundamental theory of liberty upon which all governments in this Union repose excludes any general power of the state to standardize its children by forcing them to accept instruction from public teachers only. The child is not the mere creature of the state; those who nurture him and direct his destiny have the right, coupled with the high duty, to recognize and prepare him for additional obligations.

Generally, it is entirely true, as urged by counsel, that no person in any business has such an interest in possible customers as to enable him to restrain exercise of proper power of the state upon the ground that he will be deprived of patronage. But the injunctions here sought are not against the exercise of any *proper* power. Appellees asked protection against arbitrary, unreasonable, and unlawful interference with their patrons, and the consequent destruction of their business and property. Their interest is clear and immediate. . .

APPENDIX D

Each term, the Supreme Court of the United States announces many memorandum decisions. These brief statements simply record the decision of the Court not to review the ruling of a lower court. Although an appeal to the Supreme Court is technically obligatory, jurisdiction and substantiality must be established in that limited classification. Most decisions, on the other hand, come to the Court for review through the mechanism of the writ of *certiorari*, invoking the Court's discretionary jurisdiction.

A petition for *certiorari* must demonstrate jurisdiction, but it must also demonstrate that the case is "certworthy"—that it is of sufficient legal and social significance to warrant review by the Court. While the Court must have jurisdiction, a writ of *certiorari* fundamentally contends that litigation is worthy of review by the Court by virtue of its general applicability and significance. Four justices must vote in favor of review on *certiorari*. Although not the controlling factor, the sound judicial discretion of the Court is normally applied to *certiorari* when federal and/or state courts are in conflict as a result of the decision in question, when the decision represents a novel departure from standard legal precedent or interpretation, or when the legal issue is sufficiently significant to warrant attention by the Court.

It is standard procedure that the Court gives no reason for a denial on *certiorari*. Denial simply indicates that fewer than four justices considered the case worthy of review. Unlike denial of appeal, which indicates lack of substance if jurisdiction is established, no view on the merits of the case is to be inferred when *certiorari* is denied.

This appendix contains a representative sample of lower

court rulings on religion in public education which were denied review on *certiorari*. These decisions are provided in edited form, following the same principles as those observed in chapter 5.

The following list describes the major issue of each of these memorandum decisions:

Tudor v. Board of Education (1956)—distribution of the Gideon Bible in the public schools.

Stein v. Oshinsky (1965)—prayer in the public schools.

Despain v. Dekalb County Community School District 428 (1968)—prayer in the public schools.

Commissioner of Education v. School Committee of Leyden (1971)—prayer and Bible reading in the public schools.

Wright v. Houston Independent School District (1973)—teaching evolution in the public schools.

Wiest v. Lebanon School District (1974)—prayer at graduation exercises.

Smith v. Smith (1975)—released-time program.

Flory v. Sioux Falls School District (1980)—Christmas assemblies in the public schools.

Brandon v. Board of Education of the Guilderland Central School District (1980)—prayer meetings in the public schools.*

Karen B. v. Treen (1981)—prayer in the public schools.

---

*This decision is significant in that the Supreme Court denied *certiorari* just prior to its decision in *Widmar v. Vincent*, 102 S. Ct. 269 (1981). In *Widmar*, the Court approved meetings of a religious group on the campus of the University of Missouri at Kansas City. Denial of *certiorari* in *Branden* reinforces the distinction the Court has typically made between religious activity and involvement in colleges and universities and religious activity and involvement in public elementary and secondary schools.

TUDOR v. BOARD OF EDUCATION**
100 A.2d. 857
Supreme Court of New Jersey
Decided December 7, 1953

The Gideons International is a nonprofit corporation organized under the laws of the State of Illinois, whose object is "to win men and women for the Lord Jesus Christ, through . . . (c) placing the Bible—God's Holy Word—or portions thereof in hotels, hospitals, schools, institutions, and also through the distribution of same for personal use." In recent years it began a campaign to make available to pupils in the public schools of this country the so-called "Gideon Bible", which was characterized by the International in its pleadings as "a book containing all of the New Testament, all of the Book of Psalms from the Old Testament, all of the Book of Proverbs from the Old Testament; all without note or comment, conformable to the edition of 1611, commonly known as the Authorized, or King James version of the Holy Bible." In furtherance of this campaign it applied by letter to the Board of Education of the Borough of Rutherford for permission to distribute its Bible to the public schools of that municipality.

The proposal was considered at a meeting of the board of education on November 5, 1951, at which time there was voiced some opposition to the proposal by a Catholic priest and a Jewish rabbi on the grounds that the Gideon's New Testament was sectarian and forbidden to Catholic and Jewish children under the laws of their respective religions. The proposal, however, was passed by the board with one dissenting vote, the resolution adopted providing that "the Gideons International be allowed to furnish copies of the New Testament, Psalms and Proverbs to those pupils who request them."

Prior to the distribution of the books the present action was commenced demanding judgment as to the validity of the distribution under the Federal and New Jersey Constitutions and seeking an injunction against it.

The plaintiff Bernard Tudor is an adherent of the Jewish religion, while plaintiff Ralph Lecoque is a member of the Catholic faith, each being a New Jersey citizen and taxpayer of Rutherford and a parent of a pupil in a Rutherford public school. Each contends that the Gideon Bible is "a sectarian work of peculiar religious value and significance to members of the Protestant faith."

. . . our decision in this case must be based upon the undoubted doctrine of both the Federal Constitution and our New Jersey Constitution, that the state or any instrumentality thereof cannot under any circumstances show a preference for one religion over another. Such favoritism cannot be toler-

---

**The Supreme Court denied *certiorari* under 348 U.S. 816 (1954).

ated and must be disapproved as a clear violation of the Bill of Rights of our Constitutions.

This brings us to the heart of our problem here—namely, whether the resolution of the board of education displays that favoritism that is repugnant to our Constitutions.

A review of the testimony at the trial convinces us that the King James version or Gideon Bible is unacceptable to those of the Jewish faith. . . . Nor is there any doubt that the King James version of the Bible is as unacceptable to Catholics as the Douay version is to Protestants.

The defendant refers us to various statements by legal scholars and others to show that the Bible is not sectarian, but rather is the universal book of the Christian world, but in many of these statements the question of the New Testament was not discussed. . . . Here the issue is the distribution of the New Testament. The uncontradicted evidence presented by the plaintiff reveals that as far as the Jewish faith is concerned, the Gideon Bible is a sectarian book, the teachings of which are in conflict with the doctrines of his religion as well as that of his child, who is a pupil in the Rutherford public school.

We find from the evidence presented in this case that the Gideon Bible is a sectarian book, and that the resolution of the defendant board of education to permit its distribution through the public school system of the Borough of Rutherford was in violation of the First Amendment of the United States Constitution, as incorporated into the Fourteenth Amendment, and of Article I, paragraph 4, of the New Jersey Constitution. It therefore must be set aside.

We cannot accept the argument that here, as in the *Zorach* case . . . the State is merely "accommodating" religion. It matters little whether the teachers themselves will distribute the Bibles or whether that will be done by members of the Gideons International. The same vice exists, that of preference of one religion over another. This is all the more obvious when we realize the motive of the Gideons. Its purpose is "to win men and women for the Lord Jesus Christ, through . . . (c) placing the Bible—God's Holy Word . . .or portions thereof in hotels, hospitals, schools, institutions, and also through distribution of same for personal use." . . . To achieve this end it employs the public school system as the medium of distribution. It is at the school that the pupil receives the request slip to take to his parents for signature. It is at the school that the pupil actually receives his Gideon Bible. In other words, the public school machinery is used to bring about the distribution of these Bibles to the children of Rutherford. In the eyes of the pupils and their parents the board of education has placed its stamp of approval upon this distribution and, in fact, upon the Gideon Bible itself. . . . This is more than mere "accommodation" of religion permitted in the *Zorach* case. The school's part in this distribution is an active one and cannot be sustained on the basis of a mere assistance to religion.

We are here concerned with a vital question involving the very foundation of our civilization. Centuries ago our forefathers fought and died for the principles now contained in the Bill of Rights of the Federal and New Jersey Constitutions. It is our solemn duty to preserve these rights and to prohibit any encroachment upon them. To permit the distribution of the King James version of the Bible in the public schools of this State would be to cast aside all the progress made in the United States and throughout New Jersey in the field of religious toleration and freedom. We would be renewing the ancient struggles among the various religious faiths to the detriment of all. This we must decline to do.

STEIN v. OSHINSKY*

348 F.2d. 999

United States Court of Appeals, Second Circuit

Decided July 7, 1965.

The decision in *Engel v. Vitale* . . . condemning the "Regents' prayer" as violating the Establishment Clause of the First Amendment, held to be applicable to the states by the Fourteenth, was rendered on June 26, 1962, too late to affect the 1961-62 school year. The case now before us reflects a response to that decision by parents who think their children ought have some form of religious observance while in public school.

The fifteen plaintiffs, of varying religious faiths, are parents of twenty-one children, ranging from five to eleven years in age. The children attend Public School 184, at Whitestone, N. Y., in grades ranging from kindergarten to the sixth. The defendants are Elihu Oshinsky, principal of the school; the members of the Board of Education of New York City; and the Board of Regents of the University of the State of New York. On October 5, 1962, Mr. Oshinsky "ordered his teachers who were instructing the kindergarten classes to stop the infant children from reciting the simple and ancient prayer:

'God is Great, God is good and We Thank Him for our Food, Amen!'

before they ate their cookies and milk in the morning session," and "ordered his teachers who were instructing the kindergarten classes for the afternoon session to stop the infant children from reciting the simple and ancient prayer:

---

*The Supreme Court denied *certiorari* under 382 U.S. 957 (1965).

'Thank You for the World so Sweet,
Thank You for the Food We Eat,
Thank You for the Birds that Sing—
Thank You, God, for Everything."

He also "ordered his teachers to stop the saying of any prayer in any class-room in P. S. 184, Whitestone, New York." The Board of Education and the Board of Regents have instituted a policy banning prayers in the public schools even when the opportunity to pray is sought by the students them-selves. . . . The plaintiffs had joined in a written demand to the defendants "that our children be given an opportunity to acknowledge their dependence and love to Almighty God through a prayer each day in their respective classrooms"; defendants had ignored this.

Plaintiffs say that *Engel v. Vitale* . . . and the later decisions in *Abington Tp. School District v. Schempp* and *Murray v. Curlett* . . . held only that under the Establishment Clause of the First Amendment a state may not *direct* the use of public school teachers and facilities for the recitation of a prayer, whether composed by a state official as in *Engel* or not so composed but hav-ing a religious context as in *Abington* and *Curlett*; they argue that these de-cisions did not hold that a state could not *permit* students in public schools to engage in oral prayer on their own initiative. This may be true enough; if the defendants could prevail only by showing that permitting the prayers was prohibited by the Establishment Clause, the question would be whether the use of public property as a *situs* for the prayers, the consumption of some teacher time in preserving order for their duration, and the possible impli-cation of state approval therefrom would attract the condemnation of *People of State of Illinois ex rel. McCollum v. Board of Education* . . . or the bene-diction of *Zorach v. Clauson* . . . and *Sherbert v. Verner*. . . Although we note in this connection defendants' serious contention that in the context of closely organized schooling of young children, "student-initiated" prayers are an illusion and any effective routine requires the active participation of the teachers, we shall assume, *arguendo*, in plaintiffs' favor that the Estab-lishment Clause would not prohibit New York from permitting in its public schools prayers such as those here at issue. Nevertheless New York is not bound to allow them unless the Free Exercise Clause or the guarantee of freedom of speech of the First Amendment compels.

Neither provision requires a state to permit persons to engage in public prayer in state-owned facilities wherever and whenever they desire. . . . We are not here required to consider such cases as that of a Moslem, obliged to prostrate himself five times daily in the direction of Mecca, or of a child whose beliefs forbade his partaking of milk and cookies without saying the blessings of his faith. . . . So far as it appears, the school authorities might well permit students to withdraw momentarily for such necessary obser-vances—or to forego the milk and cookies, just as they excuse children on holidays important to their religions.

Determination of what is to go on in public schools is primarily for the school authorities. Against the desire of these parents that their children "be given an opportunity to acknowledge their dependence and love to Almighty God through a prayer each day in their respective classrooms," the authorities were entitled to weigh the likely desire of other parents not to have their children present at such prayers, either because the prayers were too religious or not religious enough; and the wisdom of having public educational institutions stick to education and keep out of religion, with all the bickering that intrusion into the latter is likely to produce. . . . After all that the states have been told about keeping the "wall between church and state . . . high and impregnable," . . . it would be rather bitter irony to chastise New York for having built the wall too tall and too strong.

The judgment is reversed, with directions to dismiss the complaint.

DeSPAIN v. DeKALB COMMUNITY SCHOOL DISTRICT 428*

384 F.2d. 836

United States Court of Appeals, Seventh Circuit

Decided January 22, 1968.

The plaintiffs, Lyle A. DeSpain and Mary R. DeSpain, are residents of DeKalb, Illinois. They are the parents of Laura I. DeSpain, who at the time the complaint was filed, was five years old and attended kindergarten class at the Ellwood Public School, located in DeKalb County Community School District 428. The plaintiffs brought this action . . . to enjoin the officials of the school district from requiring the plaintiff's child to recite a prayer during regular school hours.

Following a consolidated evidentiary hearing on the request for temporary and permanent injunctive relief, the district court dismissed the plaintiffs' complaint for failure to state a cause of action. . . . The court ruled that a verse which Mrs. Watne, the kindergarten teacher, required the children in her class to recite prior to their morning snack is "not a prayer or religious activity within the meaning of the Constitution. . . . " The verse read:

We thank you for the flowers so sweet;
We thank you for the food we eat;
We thank you for the birds that sing;
We thank you for everything.

*The Supreme Court denied *certiorari* under 390 U.S. 906 (1968).

We are of the view that the verse is a prayer and that its compulsory reci-tation by kindergarten students in a public school comes within the pros-cription of the First Amendment, as interpreted by the Supreme Court in the "school prayer" cases. . . . Accordingly, we reverse.

The evidence showed that for several years prior to the 1965-66 school year Mrs. Watne required the children in her kindergarten class to recite a verse identical to the above-quoted verse except that the last line read, "We thank you, God, for everything." In 1964, Mrs. Watne deleted the word "God," after the plaintiffs complained to Mrs. Watne, the superintendent of schools, the principal, and the Board of Education that the DeSpains' eldest son, then a kindergarten student, was required to recite the verse.

Dr. A. Donald Davies, an Episcopal priest employed at Seabury Western Theological Seminary, Evanston, Illinois, as a professor of Christian Edu-cation and Director of the Master of Arts program in Christian Education, testified that a prayer practically identical to the verse recited in Mrs. Watne's class, with the word "God" included in the last line, is found in a manual entitled "God's Love and Care," published by the National Depart-ment of Christian Education of the Episcopal church for the training of kin-dergarten teachers. Dr. Davies further testified that in his opinion the verse at issue is a prayer regardless of the fact that the word "God" was deleted from the last line, that "the intent is to offer thanks to God."

Dr. John Burkhard, Presbyterian minister and a professor of Systematic Theology at McCormick Theological Seminary in Chicago and Curriculum Consultant for the Presbyterian Board of Christian Education, testified that the verse in question is a prayer in "form and intention." He said that "the you which is the functional word in this prayer would be obviously addressed to someone who is thought to provide everything, and that "this is a common definition of God."

Mrs. Watne testified that she used the verse in question as part of her pro-gram of good citizenship and her "thankfulness" program. . . . She admitted, however, that the use, purpose, and effect of the verse in question and the verse which contained the word "God" in the last line, were the same. She also said that in her mind the word "you" referred to God and that the verse was used by her to give thanks to a divine being for the wonders of nature, thanks which she hoped to impart to her pupils. She added, "Why shouldn't I tell them to thank Him?"

The superintendent of schools testified that he had heard the poem in question recited "hundreds of times" and had "never yet felt that it had any religious connotation to it." . . . He admitted, however, that it would be im-proper if a plain, ordinary nondenominational prayer is said without com-ment in the public school by a teacher, and the children are instructed to recite it.

The district judge decided that "the verse, recited in the setting proved by the testimony in this case, is not a prayer or religious activity within the meaning of the Constitution," because, among other reasons, "[t]he aim of inculcating good manners in the children, the mode of proper serving of a meal, and awaiting eating until all were served, and thanking donors of special treats, were paramount in the teacher's purposes."

It is not to be gainsaid that the verse may have commendable virtues in teaching kindergarten children "good manners" and "gratitude," to use Mrs. Watne's words. The fact, however, that children through the use of required schoolroom prayer are likely to become more grateful for the things they receive or that they may become better citizens does not justify the use of compulsory prayer in our public school systems. As the plaintiffs point out, if prayers which tend to teach and inculcate these virtues are not within the ambit of the bar imposed by the First Amendment against such religious activity, any religious activity of whatever nature could be justified by public officials on the basis that the activity has beneficial secular purposes . . .

The district court characterized this case as *de minimis.* We are tempted to agree. Certainly, this verse was as innocuous as could be insofar as constituting an imposition of religious tenets upon nonbelievers. The plaintiffs have forced the constitutional issue to its outer limits. We are reminded, however, of what the Supreme Court said in *Schempp:*

> [I]t is no defense to urge that the religious practices here may be relatively minor encroachments on the First Amendment. The breach of neutrality that is today a trickling stream may all too soon become a raging torrent.

The judgment of the district court is reversed.

COMMISSIONER OF EDUCATION v.
SCHOOL COMMITTEE OF LEYDEN*
267 N.E.2d. 226
Supreme Judicial Court of Massachusetts
Decided March 2, 1971.

The commissioner's bill seeks to enjoin the school committee from putting into effect a resolution adopted on August 21, 1969, and "from permitting . . . Bible reading or prayer in the . . . [Leyden] public schools."

After reciting the resolution . . . the case stated sets forth that, prior to the opening of school for the academic year 1969-1970, the school committee

---

*The Supreme Court denied *certiorari* under 404 U.S. 849 (1971).

met with several teachers of the Leyden Elementary School and gave them copies of the resolution. They were told that "they could participate or not as they desired; that participation or non-participation was a matter of indifference to the school committee, and that if they participated they would do so in their capacity as private citizens and not in their capacity as teachers." The teachers were instructed to "give similar information to all children."

Each day one school bus arrives about 8:10 A.M. The other two buses arrive between 8:30 and 8:45. At 8:40 a bell indicates that school will start in five minutes. "During the five minutes immediately prior to the 8:45 A.M. bell, some form of prayer or spiritual expression takes place in each of the classrooms. . . . [T]he average duration is two or three minutes. Generally one of the children or one of the teachers . . . read[s] from one of the Bibles, anthologies or other inspirational texts (some are owned by the [t]own, some by the teachers and some by the children). On some occasions prayers, traditional (such as the Lord's Prayer) or innovative, are said. . . . [On some occasions] all . . . who have gathered early join and at other times others just listen. At one time or another all of the children have participated to some extent, and those who do not, on the occasions that they do not, either play outside or remain in the lobby or library areas of the school. The teachers . . . [need not be, but usually] are in their own rooms during the entire five minutes before 8:45 . . . and generally they do participate to a varying extent. . . . The . . . [resolution] has not caused any change in the schedule of the school buses, the time of the opening of and free access to the school building, or the practice of sounding school bells."

Several recent decisions of the Supreme Court of the United States discuss religious exercises and instruction in, or closely related to, the public schools. The most pertinent of these are *Engel v. Vitale* . . . *Abington School Dist. v. Schempp* . . . *Chamberlin v. Dade County Bd. of Public Instruction* . . . *Stein v. Oshinsky* . . . *DeSpain v. DeKalb County Community School Dist.* . . . in which the Court reached a conclusion substantially like the result which we reach.

The Supreme Court thus far has not limited the broad language with which . . . it has held invalid substantially nondenominational and neutral religious observances on public school property. Until and unless such a limitation takes place . . . it would serve no useful purpose to attempt to draw any fine distinction between those observances which have hitherto been proscribed by the Supreme Court and the Leyden practices now presented for our scrutiny. We think that, under the applicable First Amendment decisions, neither students nor teachers may be allowed to participate in the well-intended observances on school property authorized by the Leyden resolution.

The final decree is reversed. A new decree is to be entered consistent with this opinion.

WRIGHT v. HOUSTON INDEPENDENT SCHOOL DISTRICT*
486 F.2D. 137

United States Court of Appeals, Fifth Circuit

Decided November 30, 1973.

In this . . . case, plaintiffs seek to enjoin the Houston Independent School District and the Texas State Board of Education from teaching the theory of evolution, without teaching the other theories regarding human origin. Plaintiffs contend that including the study of evolution in the school's curriculum constitutes the establishment of a sectarian, atheistic religion and inhibits the free exercise of their own religion in violation of the First Amendment to the Constitution of the United States.

Contrary to the sincere, able, and vigorous arguments of plaintiffs, the Federal courts cannot by judicial decree do that which the Supreme Court has declared the state legislatures powerless to do, i.e., prevent teaching the theory of evolution in public school for religious reasons. . . . To require the teaching of every theory of human origin, as alternatively suggested by plaintiffs, would be an unwarranted intrusion into the authority of public school systems to control the academic curriculum.

We find no error in the District Court's denying plaintiff Weber's [Leona Weber, acting as next friend for Rita Wright, a minor] motion for relief from judgment.

WIEST v. MT LEBANON SCHOOL DISTRICT*
Pa. 320 A.2d.362

Supreme Court of Pennsylvania

Decided May 22, 1974.

On April 26, 1973, a complaint in equity was filed by fifty-four plaintiffs seeking to enjoin the Mt. Lebanon School District from including an invo-

---

*The Supreme Court denied *certiorari* under 417 U.S. 969 (1974).

*The Supreme Court denied *certiorari* under 419 U.S. 967 (1974).

cation and benediction at the graduation ceremonies of Mt. Lebanon High School scheduled for June 12, 1973. Ten days earlier at a regular public meeting of the Board of Directors of the School District a commencement program which provided for an audible invocation and benediction had unanimously been adopted.

The commencement exercise is a sixty-year old tradition which is held after all courses of study by the graduating seniors are completed. Attendance at the commencement exercise is voluntary, but usually more than ninety percent of the graduating class attends. Those who do not attend may obtain their diplomas at the high school principal's office any time after the day of commencement.

Appellants premise their claim for relief on the free exercise clause of the First Amendment to the United States Constitution, the establishment clause of the First Amendment, and Article I, section 3, of the Pennsylvania Constitution. We find that the court below properly applied these constitutional provisions to the facts of this case and did not err in dismissing appellants' complaint.

The free exercise clause recognizes the value of religious training, teaching and observance, and in particular, "the right of every person to freely choose his own course with reference thereto, free of any compulsion from the state." This clause acts to withdraw from legislative power, "the exertion of any restraint on the free exercise of religion. . . ."

In a case stated we are confined to the facts presented to the Court by the parties, and we cannot go outside of the case stated for its facts, nor assume them by way of inference. . . . Those facts show that attendance at the graduation ceremonies was purely voluntary. There was no allegation or showing that the inclusion of an invocation and benediction in the commencement program would have any coercive effect upon appellants in the practice of their religion. Accordingly, the court below properly dismissed the free exercise claim.

Although the fact that the observance of a religious exercise is voluntary may serve to free that exercise from the limitations of the free exercise clause, the same is not true with regard to the establishment clause. . . . In determining whether governmental activity, including school board resolutions, runs afoul of the establishment clause, the pertinent inquiry is into the purpose and primary effect of the resolution. If either the purpose or primary effect is the advancement or prohibition of religion, then the resolution or enactment exceeds the scope of legislative power as circumscribed by the First Amendment.

The United States Supreme Court has never been faced with a case in the factual posture of that now before this Court. However, in dictum, that Court has indicated that every technical infringement upon the First Amendment need not be enjoined . . . *Zorach v. Clauson*, 343 U.S. 306, 312-313. . . .

The court below found that the commencement exercises at Mt. Lebanon High School were just such a public ritual or ceremony which Mr. Justice Douglas may have had in mind. We agree that the practice here is a permissible accommodation between church and state. Moreover, the burden of proof in a challenge to the constitutionality of the acts of a school board is upon the challengers. The facts as presented to the court below are, in any event, insufficient to support a finding that either the purpose or primary effect of the resolution providing for an invocation and benediction at the commencement exercises was to advance religion.

SMITH v. SMITH*

523 F.2d 121

United States Court of Appeals, Fourth Circuit

Decided August 26, 1975.

The district court held unconstitutional and enjoined the enforcement of the Harrisonburg, Virginia, release-time program whereby public school students are released during school hours for religious instruction by the Rockingham Council of Week-Day Religious Education (WRE). We think that controlling Supreme Court authority requires the opposite result. We reverse and direct dismissal of the complaint.

WRE is a nonprofit organization supported by the Virginia Council of Churches. It has been providing religious instruction in Harrisonburg since 1923. For forty years, the teaching took place in school classrooms. Since 1963, WRE classes have been held in trailers parked on streets adjacent to the schools or in nearby churches.

The challenged program operates in three elementary schools. WRE obtains the schools' enrollment lists and mails cards to the parents asking if they consent to their children's participation in the program. The children deposit the cards at school; WRE collects them and informs the school which children should be released. Public school officials do not encourage the children to attend WRE classes. WRE officials do not enter the schools to solicit students.

Twenty-seven classes of children receive approximately one hour of WRE instruction a week. The public school principals and WRE officials work together to coordinate their schedules. Each WRE class is drawn from a regular school class; children who do not participate remain in the classroom but

---

*The Supreme Court denied *certiorari* under 423 U.S. 1073 (1976).

the teacher does not provide formal instruction for this small minority of the class.

The Supreme Court's two release-time decisions to which we must look are *Illinois ex rel. McCollum v. Board of Education* . . . and *Zorach v. Clauson* . . . The cases have never been repudiated, although neither the Court nor commentators have wholly succeeded in harmonizing them.

In the instant case, the accommodations of the school program to religious training were generous and thorough-going, but the public school class-rooms, where the students were compelled by state law to be, were not turned over to religious instruction. Therefore, the case is indistinguishable from and controlled by *Zorach*. Under it, the Harrisonburg release-time program must be constitutional.

With respect to the effect of the program's advancing or inhibiting religion, the district court found that the necessary effect of the cooperation between the public school officials and the WRE is to "create an impression of an indorsement of the program and in so doing obscure any distinction between the religious and secular classes and teachers." Moreover, the program is directed toward elementary school children, and they are more likely to be susceptible to this "impression of . . . indorsement." Therefore, the district court reasoned, the principal or primary effect of the cooperation which it enjoined is to advance WRE's program. Under the second part of the modern test, it concluded, the program is unconstitutional.

Although the district court's reasoning is persuasive, its opinion was filed before *Meek* was decided. In *Meek*, the Court expressly cited *Zorach* as viable authority. . . . Although *Zorach* was decided many years before the Court fashioned the tripartite test, the *Meek* citation indicates that *Zorach* is not inconsistent with the tripartite test.

Since *Zorach* is still good law, it must be that this effect is indirect or incidental rather than principal or primary. As the Court has recently reasserted, with a citation to *Zorach*, "not all . . . programs that provide indirect or incidental benefit to a religious institution are prohibited by the Constitution." *Meek v. Pittinger*, 421 U.S. 349, at 359.

We take this language to mean that the primary effect of the public school's release-time program in *Zorach* must be seen as simply the innocuous diminishing of the number of children in school at a certain time of day. According to this view, public school cooperation with the religious authorities in *Zorach* and the instant case is a largely passive and administratively wise response to a plenitude of parental assertions of the right to "direct the upbringing and education of children under their control." *Pierce v. Society of Sisters*, 268 U.S. 510, 534-35. . . . With these premises, our conclusion must be that the Harrisonburg public school's cooperation with the WRE program by itself does not necessarily advance or inhibit religion. Therefore, the Harrisonburg release-time program is not unconstitutional, under the modern test, as understood in the light of *Zorach*'s apparent continuing validity.

FLOREY v. SIOUX FALLS SCHOOL DISTRICT*

619 F.2D 1311

United States Court of Appeals, Eighth Circuit

Decided April 22, 1980

In response to complaints that public school Christmas assemblies in 1977 and prior years constituted religious exercises, the School Board of Sioux Falls, South Dakota, set up a citizens' committee to study the relationship between church and state as applied to school functions. The committee's deliberations, which lasted for several months, culminated in the formulation of a policy statement and set of rules outlining the bonds of permissable school activity. After a public hearing, the School Board adopted the policy statement and rules recommended by the committee.

The appellants brought suit for declaratory and injunctive relief, alleging that the policy statement and the rules adopted by the School Board violate the Establishment and Free Exercise Clauses of the First Amendment to the United States Constitution. The district court reviewed the practices of the Sioux Falls School District and found that the 1977 Christmas program that was the subject of the initial complaints "exceeded the boundaries of what is constitutionally permissible under the Establishment Clause." The court also found, however, that programs similar to the 1977 Christmas program would not be permitted under the new School Board guidelines and concluded that the new rules, if properly administered and narrowly construed, would not run afoul of the First Amendment.

The appellants' claim is that the School Board policy and rules are unconstitutional both on their face and as applied. At the time of the district court proceeding, however, no holiday season had passed with the rules in effect.Consequently, little evidence was presented on the actual implementation of the rules, and the district court made no findings in that regard.

The close relationship between religion and American history and culture has frequently been recognized by the Supreme Court of the United States. . . . As the Supreme Court has noted, "total separation [between church and state] is not possible in an absolute sense." . . . As a result, the Court has de-

---

*The Supreme Court denied *certiorari* under 499 U.S. 987 (1980).

veloped a three-part test for determining when certain governmental activity falls within the constitutional boundaries:

> First, the [activity] must have a secular . . . purpose; second, its principal or primary effect must be one that neither advances nor inhibits religion . . . finally, the [activity] must not foster "an excessive governmental entanglement with religion."

The appellants' contention that the School Board's adoption of the policy and rules was motivated by religious considerations is unsupportable. The record shows that the citizens' committee was formed and the rules drawn up in response to complaints that Christmas observances in some of the schools in the district contained religious exercises. The motivation behind the rules, therefore, was simply to ensure that no religious exercise was a part of officially sanctioned school activities. This conclusion is supported by the opening words of the policy statement: "It is accepted that no religious belief or non-belief should be promoted by the school district or its employees, and none should be disparaged."

The express language of the rules also leads to the conclusion that they were not promulgated with the intent to serve a religious purpose. Rule 1 limits observation of holidays to those that have both a religious *and* a secular basis. Solely religious holidays may not be observed. Rule 3 provides that music, art, literature and drama having a religious theme or basis may be included in the school curriculum only if "presented in a prudent and objective manner and as a traditional part of the cultural and religious heritage of the particular holiday." Similarly, Rule 4 permits the use of religious symbols only as "a teaching aid or resource" and only if "such symbols are displayed as an example of the cultural and religious heritage of the holiday and are temporary in nature." We view the thrust of these rules to be the advancement of the students' knowledge of society's cultural and religious heritage, as well as the provision of an opportunity for students to perform a full range of music, poetry and drama that is likely to be of interest to the students and their audience.

This purpose is quite different from the express and implied intent of the states of New York, Pennsylvania and Maryland in the Supreme Court "School Prayer Cases." . . . Since prayer, by its very nature, is undeniably a religious exercise, the conclusion is inescapable that the advancement of religious goals was the purpose sought by the school officials in *Engel*.

Moreover, in the Supreme Court prayer cases, compulsory religious exercises were imposed on all schools by state law. The Sioux Falls rules, by contrast, do not require the individual schools to have holiday activities; they merely permit the inclusion of certain programs in the curriculum in the event that classroom teachers feel that such programs would enhance their overall instructional plan. The rules are an attempt to delineate the scope of permissable activity within the district, not to mandate a statewide program of religious inculcation.

The appellants contend that, notwithstanding the actual intent of the School Board, the "principal or primary effect" of the rules is to either advance or inhibit religion. . . . We cannot agree. The First Amendment does not forbid all mention of religion in public schools; it is the *advancement* or *inhibition* of religion that is prohibited. . . . Hence, the *study* of religion is not forbidden "when presented objectively as part of a secular program of education." . . . We view the term "study" to include more than mere classroom instruction; public performance may be a legitimate part of secular study. . . . When the primary purpose served by a given school activity is secular, that activity is not made unconstitutional by the inclusion of some religious content.

The appellants assert, however, that something more than secular study is authorized by the Sioux Falls rules. They point to Rule 1, which states that holidays that have a religious and secular basis may be "observed" in the public schools. "Observation," they maintain, necessarily connotes religious ceremony or exercise and the rule thus has the impermissible effect of advancing religion.

A review of the policy statement and rules as a whole leads us to conclude that the appellants' emphasis of the word "observe" is misplaced and their interpretation of it incorrect. First . . . the rules must be read together with the policy statement of the School Board. That statement makes it clear that religion is to be neither promoted nor disparaged in the Sioux Falls schools. Consequently, any ambiguity in the meaning of the word "observe" must be resolved in favor of promoting that policy. Moreover, the only evidence presented on the definition of the word "observed" was the testimony of the School Superintendent, Dr. John Harris. Dr. Harris explained that "observed" means "that programs with content relating to both the secular and religious basis of [the holiday] could be performed, could be presented in the school." . . . Thus, the use of the word "observe" does not mean that the rules have the effect of advancing religion so long as the religious content of the programs is "presented objectively as part of a secular program of education."

It is unquestioned that public school students may be taught about the customs and cultural heritage of the United States and other countries. This is the principal effect of the rules. They allow the presentation of material that, although of religious origin, has taken on an independent meaning.

Since all programs and materials authorized by the rules must deal with the secular or cultural basis or heritage of the holidays and since the materials must be presented in a prudent and objective manner and symbols used as a teaching aid, the advancement of a "secular program of education," and not of religion, is the primary effect of the rules. It would be literally impossible to develop a public school curriculum that did not in some way affect the religious or nonreligious sensibilities of some of the students or their parents. School administrators should, of course, be sensitive to the religious beliefs or disbeliefs of their constituents and should attempt to avoid conflict, but they need not and should not sacrifice the quality of the students' education. They need only ensure that the primary effect of the school's policy is secular.

The appellants contend that the new guidelines in Sioux Falls unconstitutionally "foster 'an excessive government entanglement with religion.' " . . . The rules are guidelines designed to aid in the decisionmaking process. Rather than entangling the schools in religion, the rules provide the means to ensure that the district steers clear of religious exercises. We think the district court was correct in finding that the new rules do not unconstitutionally entangle the Sioux Falls school district in religion or religious institutions.

The appellants also contend that implementation of the policy and rules of the Sioux Falls School Board should be enjoined because the rules violate the Free Exercise Clause of the First Amendment. This contention does not withstand scrutiny.

The public schools are not required to delete from the curriculum all materials that may offend any religious sensibility. . . . These inevitable conflicts with the individual beliefs of some students or their parents, in the absence of an Establishment Clause violation, do not necessarily require the prohibition of a school activity. On the other hand, forcing any person to participate in an activity that offends his religious or nonreligious beliefs will generally contravene the Free Exercise Clause, even without an Establishment Clause violation.

We recognize that this opinion affirming the district court will not resolve for all times, places or circumstances the question of when Christmas carols, or other music or drama having religious themes, can be sung or performed by students in elementary and secondary public schools without offending the First Amendment. The constitutionality of any particular school activity conducted pursuant to the rules, in association with any particular holiday, cannot be determined unless and until there is a specific challenge, supported by evidence, to the school district's implementation of the rules. We simply hold, on the basis of the record before us, that the policy and rules adopted by the Sioux Falls Board of Education, when read in the light of the district court's holding that segments of the 1977 Christmas program at one of the elementary schools were impermissible, are not violative of the First Amendment.

For the foregoing reasons, the judgment of the district court is affirmed.

BRANDON v. BOARD OF EDUCATION
OF THE GUILDERLAND CENTRAL SCHOOL DISTRICT*
635 F.2d 971
United States Court of Appeals, Second Circuit
Decided November 17, 1980

To many Americans, the state's noblest function is the education of our nation's youth. We entrust this responsibility largely to the public schools, and hope our children grow into responsible citizens by learning the enduring values of Western Civilization we all share—an appreciation of critical reasoning, a commitment to democratic institutions, and a dedication to principles of fairness. In this immigrant nation of dreamers and dissidents, however, no broad consensus regarding the spiritual side of the human condition exists. Our Founding Fathers recognized the disharmony and drafted the Bill of Rights to require the separation of church and state. Accordingly, religious activity under the aegis of the government is strongly discouraged, and in some circumstances—for example, the classroom—is barred. The sacred practices of religious instruction and prayer, the Framers foresaw, are best left to private institutions—the family and houses of worship. In short, logic, tradition, and law create in our nation a "wall between church and state." . . . In this case, brought by students seeking to force a public school to allow joint prayer sessions in the school before classes begin, we are asked to dismantle that wall. Because the First Amendment does not require—or even allow—such permission, we affirm the dismissal below of the students' complaint.

In 1978, several students at Guilderland High School organized a group called "Students for Voluntary Prayer." They sought permission in September 1978 from the school's principal, Charles Ciaccio, to conduct communal prayer meetings in a classroom immediately before the school day commenced. The group noted that it was not seeking supervision or faculty involvement, and stated that its activities were voluntary and would not conflict with other school functions.

The principal denied the request by letter dated September 23, 1978. Shortly thereafter, the Superintendent of the Guilderland School District refused permission. The Guilderland Board of Education voted on December 19, 1978, and again on March 6, 1979, to deny the group's request. Six students filed suit in June 1979 individually and on behalf of those students similarly situated. They stated in the complaint that the defendants—the Board of Education and its individual members, the Superintendent of the school district, and Ciaccio, the principal—violated their First and Four-

---

*The Supreme Court denied *certiorari* under 102 S. Ct. 970 (1981).

teenth Amendment rights to the free exercise of religion, freedom of speech, freedom of association, and equal protection.

On April 16, 1980, Judge McCurn granted summary judgment for the defendants, holding that the students were not entitled to relief as a matter of law and dismissing the complaint. . . . Judge McCurn found that while a school's decision involving the use of school premises might have a secular purpose, the granting of the group's request would have had the impermissible effect of advancing religion. In addition, if the prayer meetings were conducted, an excessive entanglement between a supposedly secular school and clearly religious activities would result because faculty surveillance would be needed to assure that the meetings were voluntary.

The Supreme Court has consolidated these historical antecedents to articulate three major policies underlying religious freedom: voluntarism of religious thought and conduct, government neutrality towards religion, and the separation of church and state. Voluntarism recognizes that private choice, not official coercion, should form the basis for religious conduct and belief. . . . Government neutrality reinforces voluntarism, for it assures its citizens, on the other hand, that no official imprimatur lies behind any set of religious beliefs or practices and, on the other, that no particular dogma is officially condemned. . . . Separation is meant to foster voluntarism and neutrality, and also to preserve the integrity of both religion and government.

The suit was brought by advocates of religious activity, who seek to compel the granting of permission. Our focus, therefore, is to determine whether the school's refusal violated the Free Exercise rights of the "Students for Voluntary Prayer," and exhibited a degree of hostility towards a particular religious organization sufficient to transgress the principle of government neutrality, thereby violating the Free Exercise Clause.

A limitation on religious exercise is justified only if the state can demonstrate that its compelling interest in public health, welfare, morality, or other secular values justifies the restriction, and that less restrictive means to achieve the state's secular ends are not available.

We find that the Free Exercise rights of the "Students for Voluntary Prayer" were not limited by the Guilderland School District's refusal to permit communal prayer meetings to occur on school premises. . . . We do not challenge the students' claim that group prayer is essential to their religious beliefs. The effect of the school's actions, however—denying the students the opportunity to pray together in a classroom at the commencement of a school day—is hardly analogous to the coercive restraints on religious observation imposed by state action in *Sherbert* or *Yoder*.

The dilemma presented to individuals in *Sherbert* and *Yoder* was absolute. Individuals were forced to choose between neglecting their religious obligations and rendering themselves liable for criminal sanctions or ineligible for state benefits. The choice for the students in this case is much less difficult because the school's rule does not place an absolute ban on communal prayer, nor are sanctions faced or benefits forfeited. While school attendance is compelled for several hours per day, five days per week, the students, presumably living at home, are free to worship together as they please before and after the school day and on weekends in a church or any other suitable place. . . . We do not have before us the case of a Moslem who must prostrate himself five times daily in the direction of Mecca, or children whose beliefs require prayer before lunch, sports or other school activities.

Authorization for prayer at public universities, for example, has been required because students both study and reside there. Frequently they are unable to hold prayer meetings off campus. . . . Similarly, because the isolated member of the armed forces or the prison inmate may have no access to the regular religious facilities of the community, Free Exercise freedoms would be jeopardized if religious activity on a military base or in a prison were not authorized. . . . Here, however, the students have made no showing that they lack other facilities for communal prayer.

Our nation's elementary and secondary schools play a unique role in transmitting basic and fundamental values to our youth. To an impressionable student, even the mere appearance of secular involvement in religious activities might indicate that the state has placed its imprimatur on a particular religious creed. This symbolic inference is too dangerous to permit.

The record indicates that school buses discharge students at the Guilderland High School between 7:20 A.M. and 7:40 A.M., and that the official school day "begins" at this point. Any voluntary student prayer meetings conducted after the arrival of the school buses and before the formal "homeroom" period at 7:50 A.M., therefore, would occur during school hours. The prayer meetings would create an improper appearance of official support, and the prohibition against impermissably advancing religion would be violated.

School officials in this case would be forced to monitor the activities of the "Students for Voluntary Prayer." The School Board has a duty under New York law to provide adequate supervision of all students in its "care and charge" during school hours. . . . Since the voluntary prayer meetings, to be conducted after the arrival of school buses, would, as we have said, occur during school hours, official supervision is required by law to ensure the smooth functioning of the school's secular schedule and the maintenance of the school's safety and order. More importantly, surveillance will be required to guarantee that participation in the prayer meetings would always remain voluntary.

Finally, we note that the state's compelling Establishment Clause interest in removing from the school any indication of sponsoring religious activity leads to the inescapable conclusion that no alternative accommodations were possible.

The student's argument, in short, is that they merely seek to exercise their rights to free speech in a public forum, unencumbered by governmental regulation of the context of their "speech." They state that, in general, students retain their fundamental constitutional right to free speech while attending school . . . and that restraints on religious speech in a public forum are impermissible. . . . Moreover, they argue that the School Board's denial of their request, in light of the ability of other student organizations to use school facilities, infringes their Fourteenth Amendment right to equal protection.

Two significant factors, however, defeat the claims. First, a high school is not a "public forum" where religious views can be freely aired. The expression of religious points of view, and even the performance of religious rituals, is permissible in parks and streets when subject to reasonable time, place, and manner regulations. . . . The facilities of a university have also been identified as a "public forum," where religious speech and association cannot be prohibited. . . . While students have First Amendment rights to political speech in public schools . . . sensitive Establishment Clause considerations limit their right to air religious doctrines. Equally compelling, the students in this case propose to conduct *prayer* meetings in the high school, not merely discussions about religious matters. When the explicit Establishment Clause proscription against prayer in the public schools is considered . . . the protections of political and religious speech . . . are inapposite. . . . In short, these two vital distinctions indicate that the student's free speech and associational rights, cognizable in a "public forum," are severely circumscribed by the Establishment Clause in the public school setting. Because of the symbolic effect that prayer in the schools would produce, we find that Establishment Clause considerations must prevail in this context.

Also, the students' equal protection argument is not persuasive. Other organizations are permitted to utilize school facilities, but their use does not raise serious problems of the establishment of religion. Moreover, since all religious groups are equally denied access to school facilites, any equal protection argument lacks merit.

We must be careful that our public schools, where fundamental values are imparted to our children, are not perceived as institutions that encourage the adoption of any sect or religious ideology.

KAREN B. v TREEN*

653 F.2d. 897

United States Court of Appeals, Fifth Circuit

Decided August 5, 1981

Parents of students were denied declaratory and injunctive relief from the Louisiana statute and derivative Jefferson Parish School Board regulations

---

*The Supreme Court denied *certiorari* under 102 S. Ct. 1267 (1982).

which establish guidelines for student participation in prayer at school. They contend that the statute and regulations offend the First Amendment proscription against enactment of laws respecting the establishment of religion. We agree and reverse the district court.

Louisiana Revised Statutes § 17:2115 (1981) has two components. Subsection A provides that each parish and city school board shall permit the appropriate local school authorities to allow those students and teachers who so desire to observe a brief period of silent meditation at the beginning of each school day. The statute expressly declares that this observance can neither be intended nor identified as a religious exercise. The plaintiffs have no quarrel with the silent meditation provision of the statute, and it is not involved in this litigation.

The challenged provision, subsection B, is essentially enabling legislation. It provides that a school board may authorize the appropriate school officials to allow each classroom teacher to ask whether any student wishes to offer a prayer and, if no student volunteers, to permit the teacher to pray. The statute limits any prayer offered to no longer than five minutes and provides that no student or teacher may be compelled to pray. In the event a student in the classroom objects or the student's parents or legal guardian objects in writing to the school authority, subsection B provides that the student may not be required to participate or to be present during the time prayer is being offered.

The Jefferson Parish School Board has adopted a resolution establishing guidelines to implement section 17:2115(B) in parish schools. These guidelines provide that each school day will begin at the regular time with a minute of prayer followed by a minute for silent meditation. Under the school board guidelines, each teacher must ask if any student wishes to volunteer a prayer, and, if no student wishes to do so, the teacher may offer a prayer of his own. If the teacher elects not to pray, then the period of silent meditation would be observed immediately. The school board guidelines provide that no prayer may be longer than one minute in duration.

Jefferson Parish has also made elaborate provisions for excusing students who do not want to participate in the prayer portion of the morning exercises. According to a school board letter explaining the program to parents, any student who desires to participate in the minute of prayer must submit the express written permission of his parents and make a verbal request to join in the exercise. Students without this permission may either report to class, where they must remain seated and quiet throughout the morning exercises, or remain outside the classroom under other supervision. The school board guidelines also establish two alternative methods for dealing with the supervision of non-participating students. After the minute of prayer has been completed, all students must report to the classroom for a minute of silent meditation.

First, the district court found that section 17:2115(B) and the implementing regulations had a secular legislative purpose. It reached this conclusion relying upon the testimony of two state legislators who were primarily responsible for enactment of the statute and the school board member who had sponsored the implementing resolution in Jefferson Parish. These witnesses stated that the purpose of the school prayer program was to increase religious tolerance by exposing school children to beliefs different from their own and to develop in students a greater esteem for themselves and others by enhancing their awareness of the spiritual dimensions of human nature.

Under the decisions of the Supreme Court, however, this testimonial avowal of secular legislative purpose is not sufficient to avoid conflict with the Establishment Clause.

. . . the plain language of section 17:2115(B) and of the Jefferson Parish guidelines makes apparent their predominantly religious purpose. Prayer is perhaps the quintessential religious practice for many of the world's faiths, and it plays a significant role in the devotional lives of most religious people. Indeed, since prayer is a primary religious activity in itself, its observance in public school classrooms has, if anything, a more obviously religious purpose than merely displaying a copy of a religious text in the classroom. Even if the avowed objective of the legislature and school board is not itself strictly religious, it is sought to be achieved through the observance of an intrinsically religious practice. The unmistakable message of the Supreme Court's teachings is that the state cannot employ a religious means to serve otherwise legitimate secular interests. . . . Furthermore, the legislature's provision for excusing students who do not desire to participate in the daily prayer session betrays its recognition of the fundamentally religious character of the exercise.

Second, the district court held that section 17:2115(B) and the Jefferson Parish program do not inhibit or promote religion. This conclusion was predicated upon the judge's conviction that the prayer offered by a student or by a teacher could very well comprehend some secular objective.

This analysis is disingenuous. Prayer is an address of entreaty, supplication, praise, or thanksgiving directed to some sacred or divine spirit, being, or object. That it may contemplate some wholly secular objective cannot alter the inherently religious character of the exercise. Section 17:2115(B) and the parish implementing guidelines promote religion by encouraging observance of a religious ritual in the classroom.

That the challenged provisions do not prescribe any particular form of prayer and do not promote some sectarian religious practice is without constitutional significance. The Supreme Court consistently has expressed the view that the First Amendment demands absolute governmental neutrality with respect to religion, neither advancing nor inhibiting any particular religious belief or practice and neither encouraging nor discouraging religious belief or unbelief.

State and school officials point out that student participation in the daily prayer session is allowed to be wholly voluntary. This fact is not relevant to the Establishment Clause inquiry. As the Supreme Court said in *Engel*, "Neither the fact that the prayer may be denominationally neutral nor the fact that its observance on the part of students is voluntary can serve to free it from the limitations of the Establishment Clause...." The Court then reiterated this principle in *Schempp* ... Because section 17:2115(B) and the parish regulations promote an inherently religious practice, it violates the second prong of the test.

Third, the district court found that the statute, as implemented in the Jefferson Parish regulations, would not result in excessive governmental entanglement with religion. This finding was based on the provision for affirmative voluntary participation. As we have shown, this feature of the plan does not cure the constitutional infirmity.

The Jefferson Parish program has yet to be put into effect. Thus, the nature and extent of state involvement in religious activity is in some measure speculative at this time. What is certain is that the statue itself makes inappropriate governmental involvement in religious affairs inevitable. Louisiana makes school attendance compulsory for children seven to sixteen years of age.... The morning exercises take place on school property during regular school hours. The statute authorizes the classroom teacher to conduct the prayer observance ... Moreover, school authorities have a statutory duty to supervise the implementation of the prayer program in order to guarantee that all participation would remain purely voluntary. It is clear that "the very restrictions and surveillance necessary to ensure that teachers play a strictly nonideological role give rise to entanglements between church and state." ... Because section 17:2115(B) and the Jefferson Parish procedures necessarily entail excessive governmental entanglements with religious activity, they violate the third prong of the test.

For the foregoing reasons, the judgment of the district court is reversed and the case remanded for proceedings not inconsistent with this opinion.

BIBLIOGRAPHY

Religion-Government Relationships

I am deeply indebted to Dr. Waldo Beach, Professor of Ethics, Department of Religion, Duke University for selecting the following books on the religion-government relationship for this bibliography.

Arnold, O. Carroll. *Religious Freedom on Trial*. Valley Forge PA: Judson Press, 1978.

Fellman, David. *Religion in American Public Law*. New York: Holmes and Meier, 1965.

Harmon, Francis. *Religious Freedom in America*. 2d ed. New York: Interchurch Center, 1975.

Howe, Mark D. *Garden and the Wilderness: Religion and Government in American Constitutional History*. Chicago: University of Chicago Press, 1965.

Kauper, Paul G. *Religion and the Constitution*. Baton Rouge: Louisiana State University Press, 1964.

Kurland, Philip B. *Church and State: The Supreme Court and the First Amendment*. Chicago: University of Chicago Press, 1975.

Littell, Frank, ed. *Religious Liberty in the Crossfire of Creeds.* Philadelphia: Ecumenical Press, 1978.

Menendez, Albert, ed. *The Best of Church and State, 1948-1975.* Silver Spring MD: Americans United for Separation of Church and State, 1975.

Miller, Glenn. *Religious Liberty in America: History and Prospects.* Philadelphia: Westminster Press, 1976.

Morgan, Richard E. *The Supreme Court and Religion.* New York: Free Press, 1972.

Pfeffer, Leo. *Church, State, and Freedom.* Boston: Beacon Press, 1967.

Sanders, Thomas. *Protestant Concepts for Church and State: Historical Backgrounds and Approaches for the Future.* New York: Holt, Rinehart and Winston, 1964.

Smith, Elwyn A. *Religious Liberty in America.* Philadelphia: Fortress Press, 1972.

_____, ed. *Church-State Relations in Ecumenical Perspective.* Atlantic Highlands NJ: Humanities Press, 1966.

Sorauf, Frank J. *The Wall of Separation: The Constitutional Politics of Church and State.* Princeton: Princeton University Press, 1976.

Stokes, Anson, and Leo Pfeffer. *Church and State in the United States.* rev. ed. Westport CT: Greenwood Press, 1975.

Tussman, Joseph. *Obligation and the Body Politic.* New York: Oxford University Press, 1968.

_____, ed. *Supreme Court on Church and State.* New York: Oxford University Press, 1962.

Wilson, John F. *Public Religion in American Culture.* Philadelphia: Temple University Press, 1981.

Wolf, Donald J. *Toward Consensus: Catholic-Protestant Interpretations of Church and State.* Magnolia MA: Peter Smith, 1968.

Religion and Public Education

ARTICLES

Abernathy, William. "The Bennington Religious Education Foundation: A Contemporary Model of Quality Religious Education." *Religious Education* 65 (January 1970): 36-43.

Alcorn, Wallace. "Who Should Teach Religion in the Public Schools?" *Religious Education* 69 (November 1974): 654-64.

Alexander, Chanon. "Schools Without Faith." *Religious Education* 76 (May-June 1982): 307-21.

American Jewish Committee. "Dual Enrollment." *Religious Education* 67 (March 1972): 117.

————."Religion and Public Education." In *Education in the World Today*. Edited by J. D. Grams et al. 160-65. Reading MA: Addison-Wesley Publishing Co., 1972.

Austin, J. S. "Religion in Elementary School Social Studies: A Vehicle for Attitudinal Change." *Religious Education* 71 (September 1976): 474-87.

Baker, John H., "Religion in Public Education: Some Problems in Political Sociology." *Religious Education* 62 (May 1967): 245-50.

Bennett, W. F. "Religion and the Public Schools." *Religious Education* 65 (July 1970): 340-43.

Bird, Wendall R. "Creationism and Evolution." *Educational Leadership* 38 (November 1980): 157.

Bischoff, G. G., "The Search for Common Definitions of Religion Studies and Public Education." *Religious Education* 71 (January 1976): 68-81.

Brickman, William W. "A New Birth of Freedom for Education." *Religious Education* 60 (May-June 1965): 215-23.

————. "Symposium: Religion in Public Schools." *Religious Education* 59 (November 1964): 443-80.

D'Alessio, E. R. "Public Policy Implications of Public Assistance to Nonpublic Schools." *Religious Education* 70 (March 1975): 174-84.

Darst, David. "Some Personal Reflections in Teaching High School Religion." *Religious Education* 63 (March 1968): 97-105.

Dierenfield, R. B. "The Impact of the Supreme Court Decisions on Religion in Public Schools." *Religious Education* 62 (September 1967): 445-52.

————. "The Extent of Religious Influence in American Public Schools." *Religious Education* 56 (May 1961): 173-80.

————. "Religion in the American Secondary School Curriculum." *Religious Education* 74 (July-August 1979): 373-80.

————. "Religion in Public Schools: Its Current Status." *Religious Education* 68 (January 1973): 96-114.

————. "Teaching About Religion: Attitudes and Backgrounds of Beginning Teachers." *Religious Education* 66 (March 1971): 137-44.

Dillion, J. D., "Introducing Religion to Public School Curriculum?" *Religious Education* 64 (March 1969): 83. [This is the first of nine articles in this issue related to religion in public school curriculum. The articles appear on pages 83-128.]

Dow, Peter B. "MACOS: Social Studies in Crisis." *Educational Leadership* 34 (October 1976): 35-39.

Duker, Sam. "The Issue of Shared Time." *Educational Forum* 29 (January 1965): 235-41.

Engel, David E. "A New Perspective in Religion and Education." *Religious Education* 67 (November 1972): 457-60.

————. "Objectivity in the Teaching of Religious Studies in Public Schools." *Religious Education* 71 (January 1976): 81-90.

————. "Toward A Theory of Religion in General Education." *Religious Education* 65 (July 1970): 344-51.

Erickson, D. A. "Public School Alternatives: How Sweeping a Reform." *Religious Education* 70 (March 1974): 163-69.

Finucan, J. R. "Is Shared Time a Practical Possibility?" *Religious Education* 60 (November 1965): 451-56.

Fischer, Louis. "Teaching-Style and Religion in the Classroom." *Educational Forum* 32 (January 1968): 211-15.

Fishman, Ethan M. "School Prayer: Principle and Circumstance in American Politics." *Religious Education* 77 (May-June 1982): 269-78.

Flygare, T. J. "State Aid to Parochial Schools: Diminished Alternatives." *Phi Delta Kappan* 57 (November 1975): 204-205.

Gerard, Bert S. "Teaching About Religion: When and Where to Begin." *Religious Education* 63 (May 1968): 215-18.

Gleason, Philip. "Blurring the Line of Separation: Education, Civil Religion, and Teaching About Religion." *Journal of Church and State* 19 (Autumn 1977): 517-38.

Gloger, Sheldon. "The Bible in the Science Program." *Religious Education* 68 (January 1973): 126-32.

Hahn, Harlan. "Public School Support and Shared Time Programs." *Religious Education* 60 (November 1965): 456-59.

Hall, R. T. "Morality and Religion in Public Education: A Dialogue." *Religious Education* 72 (May-June 1977): 273-92.

Haney, Eleanor H. "The Mortal Life and Public Education." *Religious Education* 60 (November 1965): 467-72.

Hardie, C. D. "Religion and Education." *Educational Theory* 18 (Summer 1968): 199-223.

Healey, R. M. "An Interim Report on the Study of Religion in Public Schools." *Journal of Church and State* 20 (Autumn 1978): 469-89.

Hepburn, L. R. "Religion in the Social Studies: The Question of Religious Attitudes." *Religious Education* 66 (May 1971): 172-79.

Hill, Brian. "Teacher Commitment and the Ethics of Teaching for Commitment." *Religious Education* 76 (May-June 1981): 322-36.

Hume, Bonnie. "Education and Parents' Rights." *Religious Education* 60 (November 1965): 460-66.

Jacobson, Philip. "Religion and Public Education: Issues and Concerns." *Religious Education* 68 (March 1973): 204-11.

Kamhi, Michelle M. "Censorship vs. Selection—Choosing the Books Our Children Shall Read." *Educational Leadership* 39 (December 1981): 211-15.

Kelly, Dean M. "Religion, Education and the Constitution." *Religious Education* 75 (November-December 1980): 619-30.

Kniker, Charles R. "Changing Perceptions: Religion in the Public Schools, 1848-1981." *Religious Education* 77 (May-June 1982): 251-68.

Kraus, J. E. "The Religious Education Foundation Plan." *Religious Education* 62 (January 1967): 46-70.

Landon, Elliott. "NEA and the Church-State Issue, 1961-68." *Educational Forum* 35 (November 1970): 25-34.

Lannie, Vincent. "The Teaching of Values in Public, Sunday, and Catholic Schools: An Historical Perspective." *Religious Education* 70 (March 1975): 115-37.

LaNove, George R. "Public Funds for 'Private' Schools." *Educational Forum* 35 (November 1970): 7-13.

LaPota, Marguerite. "Religion: Not 'Teaching' but 'Teaching About.' " *Educational Leadership* 31 (October 1973): 30-33.

Layton, Donald H. "Scientists Versus Fundamentalists: The California Compromise." *Phi Delta Kappan* 54 (June 1973): 696-97.

Locigno, Joseph P. "Jefferson on Church and State in Education." *Religious Education* 64 (May 1969): 172-75.

McMillan, Richard C. "Religion Studies and 'Back to Basics'—Friends or Foes?" *Educational Leadership* 38 (February 1981): 399-401.

————. "The Ten Commandments and the Curriculum: Some Questions." *Educational Forum* 46 (Winter 1982): 239-43.

McNearney, C. L. "The Kanawha County Textbook Controversy." *Religious Education* 70 (September 1975): 519-40.

Marshner, Connaught. "The Pro-Family Movement: A Response to Charles Park." *Educational Leadership* 38 (November 1980): 152-53.

Martin, D. L. "Strip the Halls of Boughs of Holly." *Learning* 5 (December 1976): 29-30.

Mayer, William V. "The Incompatability of Science and the Supernatural." *Educational Leadership* 38 (November 1980): 158-59.

Michaelson, Robert. "Beyond the Ground Rules: Next Steps in the Study of Religion in the Public Schools." *Religious Education* 68 (March 1973): 212-17.

————. "Moral and Spiritual Values Revisited." *Religious Education* 62 (July-August 1967): 344-51.

Miller, Donald. "Religious Education and Cultural Pluralism." *Religious Education* 74 (July-August 1979): 339-49.

Mol, J. J. "Religion and Education in Sociological Perspective." *Religious Education* 60 (May 1965): 238-43.

Morris, Barbara M. "The Real Issues in Education as Seen by a Journalist on the Far Right." *Phi Delta Kappan* 61 (May 1980): 613-15.

Myers, Bill. "Suburbia's High School and the Church." *Religious Education* 72 (May-June 1977): 306-11.

Neuhaus, Richard J. "Educational Diversity in Post-Secular America." *Religious Education* 77 (May-June 1982): 309-20.

————. "No More Bootleg Religion." In *Controversies in Education*. Edited by D. W. Allen and J. C. Hecht, 72-82. Philadelphia: W. B. Saunders Co., 1974.

O'Connor, Daniel W. "Should Religion Be Taught in the Public School?" *Educational Leadership* 30 (April 1973): 649-51.

Oppewal, Donald. "Religion and Public Education: An Emerging Quandry." *Educational Forum* 31 (March 1967): 323-31.

Park, J. C. "Preachers, Politics, and Public Education: A Review of Right-Wing Pressures Against Public Schooling in America." *Phil Delta Kappan* 61 (May 1980): 608-12.

_____. "The New Right: Threat to Democracy in Education?" *Educational Leadership* 38 (November 1980): 146-49.

Parker, Franklin. "National Policy and Curriculum Controversy." *Educational Leadership* 34 (November 1976): 112-17.

Peri, Paul F. "Education and Religion: The Question of Human Potential." *Religious Education* 77 (May-June 1982): 300-308.

Phenix, P. H. "Religion in American Public Education." *Teachers College Record* 57 (1955): 26-31.

_____. "The Role of Religion." In *Foundations of Education*. Edited by G. F. Kneller, 153-74. 3d ed. New York: John Wiley and Sons, 1971.

Piediscalzi, Nicholas. "The Separation of Church and State: Public Education Religion Studies." *Religious Education* 75 (November-December 1980): 631-39.

Piel, Gerard. " 'Congress Shall Make No Law. . . . ' " *Educational Leadership* 34 (November 1976): 105-11.

Powers, E. A. "Education and the Church's Agenda." *Religious Education* 91 (January 1966): 13-20.

Purpel, David, and Kevin Ryan. "Moral Education: Where Sages Fear to Tread." *Phi Delta Kappan* 56 (June 1975): 659-62.

Riordan, Timothy. "William James: A Foundation for Religion in Public Schools." *Religious Education* 72 (May-June 1977): 312-22.

Schiff, Alvin I. "Religion in Education: A Jewish Perspective." *Religious Education* 64 (November 1969): 485-90.

Seckinger, R. K. "School Prayers and Bible Reading by Constitutional Amendment: An Analysis of 152 Congressional Proposals." *Religious Education* 60 (September 1965): 362-67.

Siegel, Harvey. "Creationism, Evolution, and Education: The California Fiasco." *Phi Delta Kappan* 63 (October 1981): 95-101.

Singer, Sholom A. "Church and School: The Problem Revisited." *Religious Education* 65 (July 1970): 352-58.

Skoog, Gerald. "Legal Issues Involved in Evolution vs. Creationism." *Educational Leadership* 38 (November 1980): 154-56.

Smith, C. B. "Keeping Public Schools Secular." *Educational Forum* 29 (November 1964): 71-77.

Smith, Richard U. "Public School Authorities and Religious Leaders Meet." *Religious Education* 61 (January 1966): 26-29.

————. "Now is the Time for Dual Enrollment." *Religious Education* 68 (March 1972): 112-16.

Spivey, R. A. "A New Shape for Religion and Public Education in Changing Times." *Journal of Church and State* 14 (Autumn 1972): 441-56.

Stahmer, Harold. "Religion and Moral Values in the Public Schools." *Religious Education* 61 (January 1966): 20-26.

Stanley, W. O. "Freedom of Conscience, Religion, and the Public Schools." *Educational Forum* 29 (May 1965): 407-15.

Stoff, S. P. "How Can the Public Schools Manage Religion Issues?" *Clearing House* 38 (January 1964): 271-74.

Stravinskas, Peter M. J. "Education, Religion and the Old Left." *Educational Leadership* 39 (April 1982): 540-41.

Swyhart, Barbara A. "The Academic Teaching About Religion: A Teacher Education Program at San Diego State University (in progress)." *Religious Education* 71 (March 1976): 202-13.

————. "Paradigms-of-Reality-in-Process: A Methodology for Interdisciplinary Religion-Studies." *Religious Education* 72 (July-August 1977): 414-26.

Tietjen, Mary L. "Missing Ingredient: CCD Options in Junior and Senior High School Religious Education." *Religious Education* 61 (May 1972): 199-201.

Tobin, W. J. "Religion and Public Education: A Roman Catholic Perspective." *Religious Education* 67 (March 1972): 117-32.

Ulich, Robert. "The Schools and Religion, the Historical Present." *Harvard Graduate School of Education Association Bulletin* 10 (Summer 1965): 2-6.

Uphoff, James K. "Religious Minorities: In or Out of the Culturally Pluralistic Curriculum?" *Educational Leadership* 32 (December 1974): 199-202.

Wakin, Edwin. "Experiment in Educational Sharing." *Religious Education* 60 (January-February 1965): 43-48.

Warshaw, Thayer S. "The Bible as Textbook in Public Schools." *Religious Education* 77 (May-June 1982): 279-99.

Watras, Joseph. "The Textbook Dispute in West Virginia: A New Form of Oppression." *Educational Leadership* 33 (October 1975): 21-33.

Welch, E. H. "Textbook Crisis in West Virginia." *Educational Forum* 41 (November 1976): 26, 30-32.

Welch, I. David et al. "Education, Religion, and the New Right." *Educational Leadership* 39 (December 1981): 203-208.

Whitney, John R. "Introducing Religious Literature in Pennsylvania Secondary Schools." *Religious Education* 63 (March 1968): 89-96.

_____. "Religious Studies in Post Exchaton America's Public Schools." *Religious Education* 71 (March 1976): 154-64.

Will, Paul J. "An Approach to Teaching About Religion in Public Schools." *Religious Education* 66 (March 1971): 145-48.

_____. "Implementing the Study of Religion in High Schools: One State's Experience." *Religious Education* 71 (January 1976): 90-95.

BOOKS

Boles, Donald. *The Bible, Religion, and the Public Schools*. Ames: Iowa State University Press, 1965.

_____. *The Two Swords*. Ames: Iowa State University Press, 1967.

Bower, William C. *Church and State in Education*. Chicago: University of Chicago Press, 1944.

Byrnes, Lawrence. *Religion and Public Education*. New York: Harper and Row, 1975.

Clayton, A. Stafford. *Religion and Schooling*. Waltham MA: Blaisdell Publishing Co., 1969.

Cole, W. O. *World Faiths in Education*. Winchester MA: Allen and Unwin, 1978.

Commission on Religion in the Public Schools. *Religion in the Public Schools*. American Council on Education Studies, Series 1, *Reports of Committees and Conferences*, no. 26, vol. 11, Washington DC, 1947.

Committee on Religion and Education. *The Relation of Religion to Public Education*. American Council on Education Studies, Series 1, *Reports of Committees and Conferences*, no. 26, vol. 11, Washington DC, 1947.

Cox, Claire. *The Fourth R: What Can Be Taught About Religion in the Public Schools*. New York: Hawthorne Books, 1969.

Ducker, Sam. *The Public Schools and Religion, The Legal Context*. New York: Harper and Row, 1966.

Engel, D. E., ed. *Religion in Public Education*. Ramsey NJ: Paulist Press, 1974.

Friedlander, A. F. *The Shared Time Strategy*. St. Louis MO: Concordia, 1966.

Jacobson, Philip. *Religion in Public Education*. New York: American Jewish Committee, 1969.

Katz, W. G. *Religion and American Constitutions*. Evanston IL: Northwestern University Press, 1964.

Lannie, Vincent P. *Public Money and Parochial Education*. Cleveland: Press of Case Western University, 1968.

Locigno, J. P. *Education: To Whom Does It Belong?* New York: Desclee Co., 1968.

Lynn, Robert W. *Protestant Strategies in Education*. New York: Association Press, 1964.

McLaughlin, M. R. *Religious Education and the State: Democracy Finds A Way*. Washington DC: Catholic University of America Press, 1967.

McMillan, R. C., ed. *Education, Religion, and the Supreme Court*. Danville VA: Association of Baptist Professors of Religion, 1979.

Michaelson, Robert. *Piety in the Public School: Trends and Issues in the Relationship Between Religion and the Public School in the United States*. New York: Macmillan, 1970.

Moehlman, Conrad H. *School and Church: The American Way*. New York: Harper and Row, 1944.

Muir, William K., Jr. *Prayer in the Public Schools—Law and Attitude Change*. Chicago: University of Chicago Press, 1967.

Nielsen, Niels C. *God in Education: A New Opportunity for American Schools*. New York: Sheed and Ward, 1966.

Panoch, James V., and D. L. Barr. *Religion Goes to School*. New York: Harper and Row, 1968.

Piediscalzi, Nicholas, and W. E. Collie. *Teaching About Religion in Public Schools*. Allen TX: Argus Communications, 1977.

Phenix, Philip H. *Education and the Worship of God*. Philadelphia: Westminster Press, 1966.

_____. *Religious Concerns in Contemporary Education*. New York: Columbia University, Bureau of Publications, Teachers College, 1959.

Sizer, Theodore M., ed. *Religion and Public Education*. Boston MA: Houghton Mifflin Co., 1967.

Smith, J. W. D. *Religion and Secular Education.* Laurinburg NC: St. Andrew Press, 1975.

Smith, Richard U. *Religion and the Schools: From Prayer to Public Aid.* Washington DC: National School Public Relations Association, 1970.

_____, ed. *Religion and the Public School Curriculum.* New York: Religious Education Association, 1972.

Stoops, John A. *Religious Values in Education.* Danville IL: Interstate Publishers, 1967.

Taylor, Lynn. *Religion and Culture in Education: Open Door for the Fourth R.* Lawrence: University of Kansas: University of Kansas Publications, 1977.

Thayer, V. T. *Religion in Public Education.* New York: Viking Press, 1947.

_____. *The Attack Upon the American Secular School.* Boston MA: Beacon Press, 1951.

Van Dusen, Henry P. *God in Education.* New York: Charles Scribner's Sons, 1952.

Warshaw, T. S. *Religion, Education, and the Supreme Court.* Nashville TN: Abingdon, 1979.

ORGANIZATION

National Council on Religion and Public Education, University of Kansas, 1300 Oread, Lawrence KS 66045.

Bibliography in Education

ARTICLES

Allen, Dwight W. "The Seven Deadly Myths of Education." *Psychology Today* 4 (March 1971): 71-72, 100.

The author calls for legislation providing for alternate forms of schools as a means of educational reform. The author laments the hold on education of several "powerful fantasies," such as "original stupidity, "pure rationality," "one best way," "stable knowledge," "isolated learning," "the educational machine," and "the teacher as an interchangeable part."

Banks, J. A. "Cultural Pluralism and the Schools." *Educational Leadership* 32 (December 1974): 163-66.

The lead article in an entire issue of *Educational Leadership* devoted to discussion of cultural diversity in the schools.

Berman, Louise M. "More than Choice." *Educational Leadership* 35 (March 1978): 424-29.

 The first article in a special section devoted to a new approach to values and moral education—judgment education. According to this approach, schooling should help children learn how to make personal judgments.

Brodinsky, Ben. "Back to the Basics: The Movement and its Meaning." *Phi Delta Kappan* 58 (March 1977): 522-27.

 An excellent analysis of this strong force in contemporary education. Basic philosophical and practical reasons for the movement are clearly presented as are the general characteristics of schooling adhering to movement goals.

Broudy, Harry S. "Educational Alternatives—Why Not?" *Phi Delta Kappan* 54 (March 1973): 438-40.

 The author takes issue with some of the basic assumptions of those who advocate alternatives to schooling.

Brumstead, R. A. "Educating Your Child at Home: The *Perchemlides* Case." *Phi Delta Kappan* 61 (October 1979): 97-100.

 One of the newest issues in education is the right of parents to educate their children at home. Discussed is the ruling of a Massachusetts state lower court in which parents were allowed to withdraw their child from the public school in order to teach him at home.

Bruner, Jerome S. "The Act of Discovery." *The Nature of Teaching*. Edited by L. N. Nelson. 198-209. Waltham MA: Blaisdell Publishing Co., 1969. Also printed in *Harvard Educational Review* 21 (Winter 1961): 21-32.

 The author urges the use of discovery techniques as a means of encouraging problem solving and information processing—abilities that are of real value both in the present and the future.

Clinchy, Evans, and E. A. Cody. "If Not Public Choice, then Private Escape." *Phi Delta Kappan* 60 (December 1979): 270-73.

 The authors assert that the very success of public education in this country is now causing its great distress—its type of organization, a necessity in the historical attempt to provide education for all, is now alienating many parents who opt for some form of private education that in their judgment, is more open to their opinions as to how their children should be educated. The message to the public schools is clear—move away from rigid uniformity to diversification.

Coleman, James S. "The Children Have Outgrown the Schools." *Psychology Today* 5 (February 1972): 72-75, 82.

 The author believes that today's schools are still modeled after institutions created to serve an "information-poor society." That model will not serve contemporary society; the schools of today must focus on those activities that, in the past, were undertaken outside the school.

Combs, Arthur W. "Seeing is Behaving." *Teaching in the American Secondary School.* Edited by F. R. Cyphert et al., 64-71. Washington DC: McGraw-Hill Book Co., 1964. Also printed in *Educational Leadership* 16 (October 1958): 21-26.

An excellent article on the effect of perception on behavior.

_____. "The Personal Approach to Good Teaching." *American Education: Foundations and Superstructure.* Edited by W. Beckner and W. Dumas. 510-21.Scranton PA: International Textbook Co., 1970. Also printed in *Educational Leadership* 21 (March 1964): 369-77.

A discussion of the problems in defining the qualities that make a good teacher. The author believes that the effective teacher is "a unique human being who has learned to use his self effectively and efficiently for carrying out his own and society's purposes."

Cox, C. B. "Responsibility, Culpability, and the Cult of Accountability in Education." *Phi Delta Kappan* 58 (June 1977): 761-66.

Supporting the premise that teachers cannot control some of the more important inputs and outcomes of the schooling process, the author takes the welcome approach of calling for a clear statement of teacher responsibilities and an end to unrealistic calls for accountability.

Crawford, A. B. and W. R. Brown. "Missing: A Viable Aim for American Education." *Educational Theory* 21 (Fall 1971): 407-17.

Education must deal with students' personal problems in actualization and in solving social problems.

Divoky, Diane. "Opting for an Old-Fangled Alternative." *Learning* 2 (February 1974): 13-17.

The author sees a growing disenchantment with the new open approaches to education leading to a return to more traditional forms.

Doyle, Walter. "Educational Opportunity—A National Commitment." *Educational Leadership* 33 (January 1976): 252-56.

Historically, according to the author, the purpose of American education has been based upon the "social-benefit theory." Early in this century, and especially in the last two decades, the "personal-benefit theory" has arisen to compete with the other as the major purpose of schooling. The author raises some serious doubts concerning the probable future of the newcomer.

Drucker, Peter F. "School Around the Bend." *Psychology Today* 6 (June 1972): 49-51, 86, 89.

The author lists eight ways in which schools must change if they are to be of value to contemporary society.

Dunn, Rita and Kenneth. "Learning Styles/Teaching Styles: Should They . . . Can They . . . Be Matched?" *Educational Leadership* 36 (January 1979): 238-44.

The first in an issue devoted to differences in learning and teaching styles.

Ebel, Robert L. "The Declining Scores: A Conservative Explanation"; and V. R. Rogers and Joan Baron. " Declining Scores: A Humanistic Explanation." *Phi Delta Kappan* 58 (December 1976): 306-13.

An interesting point/counterpoint discussion about "declining scores" on national standardized tests. Philosophical issues are evident in both articles, extending their value beyond the specific problem discussed.

————. "What are Schools For?" *Phi Delta Kappan* 54 (September 1972): 3-7.

The schools have overextended themselves. Schools are for learning: they must stress cognitive growth and development rather than all the other emphases set forth today.

Eder, Alan H. "In Praise of Public Schooling." *Educational Forum* 42 (March 1978): 285-97.

In a positive defense of the ideal of public education, the writer points out some serious flaws in the major criticisms of current schooling. A refreshing change in a day characterized by harsh criticism of public education.

Fatini, Mario D. "Alternative Educational Programs: Promote or Problems?" *Educational Leadership* 32 (November 1974) 83-87.

Introduces a journal issue devoted to assessing alternative approaches to education. An important subject and some very good articles.

————. "From School System to Educational System." *Phi Delta Kappan* 57 (September 1975): 10-12.

Looking into the future, the author calls for a movement from the present system of schools to a system of education that will have this effect on twenty-first-century people: "The educated man of the twenty-first century will not only be literate and talented, but will have a disciplined sense of caring for others and be an active participant in the restructuring of environments that truncate the values of dignity, equality, and human growth."

Fischer, J. H. "Public Education Reconsidered." *Today's Education* 61 (May 1972): 23-31.

A general discussion of some of the problems and issues facing public education. The author ends on a positive note—public education is here to stay.

Goodlad, John I. "Can Our Schools Get Better?" *Phi Delta Kappan* 5 (January 1979): 342-47.

The author states and discusses seven propositions concerning problem areas that must be addressed if the schools are to be changed for the better. An excellent critique of contemporary schooling.

_____. "On the Cultivation and Corruption of Education." *Educational Forum* 42 (March 1978): 267-78.

An excellent critique of the historic and current goals and purposes of American education. A solid and thoughtful affirmation of the humanistic approach.

_____. "Schools Can Make a Difference." *Educational Leadership* 33 (November 1975): 108-17.

"What I am asking for is that we suspend for a time as a matter of policy our pathological preoccupation with pupil effects, as defined in statements of objectives or norm-based achievement tests. What I am asking for is that we concentrate, as an alternative, on the quality of life in schools—not just for pupils but for all who live there each day."

Gorden, G. G. "Must Schools be Custodial Institutions." *Educational Leadership* 33 (December 1975): 209-12.

A truly disturbing article representing the school as a kind of prison that, by its structure, encourages "crime" in its midst. Recommendations are made for correction of the situation.

Grannis, Joseph C. "The School as a Model of Society." *Kaleidoscope: Readings in Education.* Edited by Kevin Ryan and J. M. Cooper, 224-38. Boston: Houghton Mifflin Co., 1972. Also printed in *Harvard Graduate School of Education Bulletin* 21 (Fall 1967): 15-27.

Using different social structures as models for looking at public education, the author discusses the place and function of schools in society.

Hamachek, D. E. "Personality Styles and Teacher Behavior." *Educational Forum* 36 (March 1972): 313-22.

A statement of importance: the kind of teacher a person will be is determined largely by the kind of person he is.

Jarrett, J. L. "I'm for Basics, But Let Me Define Them." *Phi Delta Kappan* 59 (December 1977): 235-39.

An evenhanded, thoughtful position on basic education stressing the basic academic skills, but in terms of developing humanity and its stress on thinking, creating, and feeling.

Jennings, Wayne, and Joe Nathan. "Startling/Disturbing Research on School Program Effectiveness." *Phi Delta Kappan* 58 (March 1977): 568-72.

A valuable article reviewing the often ignored research on the effectiveness of alternative schooling. Research presented shows some striking advantages for alternative schooling as opposed to traditional schooling. Such evidence should weigh heavily in any decision to return to the basics via the route of traditional education.

Johnson, Howard M. "Are Compulsory Attendance Laws Outdated?" *Phi Delta Kappan* 55 (December 1973): 226-32.

The lead article of a section devoted to discussion of compulsory school attendance.

Kaplan-Sanoff, Margot. "In Search of Self: Teaching and Practice." *Educational Forum* 44 (March 1980): 339-47.

Places the behavioristic, developmental, and romantic learning theories on a continuum and shows how an understanding of this continuum will affect the choice of teaching strategies.

Levin, Henry M. et al. "School Achievement and Post-School Success; A Review." *The Changing High School Curriculum: Readings*. Edited by W. M. Alexander, 8-23. 2d ed. New York: Holt, Rinehart and Winston, Inc., 1972. Also printed in *Review of Educational Research* 41 (February 1971): 1-16.

The authors conclude that there are positive corollaries between educational attainment and opportunity. Excellent bibliography.

Longo, Paul. "America's Schools: A Perspective." *Educational Forum* 44 (January 1980): 211-24.

Raises a multitude of excellent questions respecting the nature of public education. Among the problems discussed are compulsory school attendance and the predominantly elitist model of schooling.

Miller, W. C. "What Will the Future Bring for Education?" *Phi Delta Kappan* 60 (September 1978): 287-89.

An interesting, thoughtful, and concise description of the implications of current social change for future schooling.

Mohl, R. A. "Cultural Assimilation versus Cultural Pluralism." *Educational Forum* 45 (March 1981): 323-30.

"Cultural pluralism should point the way toward a less destructive, a more humanistic, and a more democratic schooling. A truly democratic society is one which accepts those who are different, which respects and encourages individuality, and which accords dignity to all."

Mosher, Edith K. "Politics and Pedagogy: A New Mix." *Educational Leadership* 38 (November 1980): 110-11.

The first article in an issue devoted to discussing governance of public schools.

Pine, G. J. and P. J. Horne. "Principles and Conditions for Learning in Adult Education." *Adult Leadership* (October 1969): 108-10, 126, 133-34.

Although human cognitive ability is a difficult topic to discuss in article form, this article is a most meaningful brief analysis.

Robinson, Donald W. "Is This the Right Approach to Student Rights?" *Phi Delta Kappan* 61 (December 1974): 234-35.

Introduces several articles dealing with the problem of students' rights in the schools.

Rogers, Carl R. "Significant Learning: In Therapy and Education." *Teaching: Vantage Points for Study*. Edited by R. T. Hyman, 152-65. New York: J. B. Lippincott, 1968. Also printed in *Educational Leadership* 16 (January 1959): 232-42.

An excellent discussion of some of the elements of learning from the perceptual point of view.

————. "The Interpersonal Relationship: The Core of Guidance." *Nature of Teaching*. Edited by L. N. Nelson, 297-311. Waltham MA: Blaisdell Publishing Co., 1969. Also printed in *Harvard Educational Review* 32 (Fall 1962): 416-29.

The author discusses the major characteristics necessary for one intending to work in one of the helping professions—including teaching. Such elements as congruence, empathy, and positive regard are discussed. Good bibliography.

Rubin, Louis. "Educational Achievement and Public Satisfaction." *Educational Leadership* 36 (May 1979): 537-40.

The first of a number of articles in the issue concerning minimum competency testing, basic education, and more.

Ruff, Thomas P. "Strategies for a School Critic: Villain or Benefactor." *Journal of Teacher Education* 23 (Fall 1972): 371-73.

For those who wish to change education, the author offers some very good, systematic advice on how to do so.

Saylor, Galen. "What Is Relevant for Today's Students?" *Educational Leadership* 31 (October 1973): 41-44.

In discussing relevancy, the author defines several major functions of schools and concludes that a less than total attainment of these functions does not call for the radical change some critics seem to want.

Scanlon, Robert G. "A Curriculum for Personalized Education." *Journal of Teacher Education* 25 (Summer 1974): 119-23.

Moving beyond the idea of individualized instruction, the author calls for a personalized education that will "emphasize students becoming effective thinkers and learners with inquiry and problem-solving skills, affective and social skills, and emotional awareness and self-identity."

Shane, Harold G. "The Academic Score Decline: Are Facts the Enemy or Truth?" *Phi Delta Kappan* 59 (October 1977): 83-86, 145-46.

Reported here is an interview with W. W. Wirtz, chairman of the panel commissioned by CEEB to study the decline on SAT performance during the past fifteen years.

Wellington, J. K. "American Education: Its Failure and its Future." *Phi Delta Kappan* 58 (March 1977): 527-30.

It is difficult to tell if Wellington is a more moderate advocate of "basic education" or a proverbial wolf at the door, but this article does present a more moderate suggestion for "basic education" as an alternative in public schools.

BOOKS

Bigge, Morris L., and Maurice P. Hunt. *Psychological Foundations of Education*. 3d ed. New York: Harper and Row, 1980.

Brameld, Theodore. *Patterns of Educational Philosophy*. New York: Holt, Rinehart and Winston, 1971.

Brembeck, Cole S. *Social Foundations of Education*. 2d ed. New York: John Wiley and Sons, 1971.

Broudy, Harry S. *The Real World of the Public Schools*. New York: Harcourt Brace Jovanovich, 1972.

Bruner, Jerome S. *The Process of Education*. Cambridge: Harvard University Press, 1960.

Butts, R. Freeman. *Public Education in the United States*. New York: Holt, Rinehart and Winston, 1978.

Combs, Arthur W., ed. *Perceiving, Behaving, Becoming*. Washington DC: Association for Supervision and Curriculum Development, 1962.

Dewey, John. *Democracy and Education*. New York: Macmillan Co., 1916.

Goslin, David A. *The School in Contemporary Society*. Glenview IL: Scott, Foresman and Co., 1965.

Lucas, Christopher J. *Our Western Educational Heritage*. New York: Macmillan Co., 1972.

Meyer, Adolphe E. *An Educational History of the American People*. 2d ed. Washington DC: McGraw-Hill Book Co., 1967.

Morris, Van Cleve, and Young Pai. *Philosophy and the American School*. 2d ed. Boston: Houghton Mifflin Co., 1976.

Pounds, Ralph L. *The Development of Education in Western Culture*. New York: Appleton-Century-Crofts, 1968.

Power, Edward J. *The Transit of Learning*. Sherman Oaks CA: Alfred Publishing Co., 1979.

Purkey, William W. *Inviting School Success*. Belmont CA: Wadsworth Publishing Co., 1978.

Rogers, Carl A. *Freedom to Learn*. Columbus OH: Charles E. Merrill Publishing Co., 1969.

Saylor, J. Galen, and William M. Alexander. *Planning Curriculum for Schools*. New York: Holt, Rinehart and Winston, 1974.

Silberman, Charles A. *Crisis in the Classroom*. New York: Random House, 1970.

Tanner, Daniel, and Laurel N. Tanner. *Curriculum Development*. New York: Macmillan Publishing Co., 1975.

Tesconi, Charles A., Jr. *Schooling in America*. Boston: Houghton Mifflin Co., 1975.

Whitehead, Alfred North. *The Aims of Education*. New York: New American Library, 1929.

Wingo, G. Max. *Philosophies of Education: An Introduction*. Lexington MA: D. C. Heath and Co., 1974.

INDEX